"Andrew Spencer's wise book
creation and of God's glory. Sp
a theology that takes some cu
logical warrants to rationalize it. Rather, he begins with orthodox readings
of the Bible and shows how our doctrinal confessions should lead us to
love and care for God's good creation. Spencer's posture toward complex
questions about theology and science and policy is exemplary: he is never
fearful or reactionary, he is faithful to theological convictions, and he is
eager to learn from and build bridges to those who may disagree. There
is no fear-mongering or doom in this book. Instead, Spencer offers a
Christ-rooted hope for all of creation and the practical wisdom that helps
us imagine how to practice this hope today."

—**Jeffrey Bilbro**, associate professor of English, Grove City College

"Andrew Spencer has written what will surely become the go-to book
for Christians seeking to rightly understand, enjoy, and cultivate God's
good creation."

—**Dustin Messer**, vicar of All Saints Dallas,
and adjunct professor at The King's College
and Reformed Theological Seminary

"Academically rigorous and biblically faithful, *Hope for God's Creation* is
a gift for the church. Spencer has written an approachable and thorough
account of creation care that should be taught and read widely."

—**Alan Noble**, associate professor of English, Oklahoma Baptist
University

"Many Christians are unconvinced about the need for environmental
ethics, either because they associate this project with partisan ideologies
or because they view them as a distraction to the life and mission of the
church. But *Hope for God's Creation* illustrates that faithful followers of
Jesus who prioritize the Great Commission and the Great Commandments can and should pursue the well-being of our Father's world. As
both an evangelical ethicist and a science educator, Spencer is uniquely
qualified to provide a clear and accessible introduction to these topics
for Christian readers."

—**Rhyne R. Putman**, associate vice president of academic affairs,
Williams Baptist University, and associate professor of theology,
New Orleans Baptist Theological Seminary

"Andrew Spencer's *Hope for Creation* is an example of the 'dual apologetic' we find ourselves needing at the intersection of Christian practice and environmentalism. The book gives faithful, orthodox Christians a reason to care for creation while also giving others passionate about the environment confidence the Christianity can be good for the environment. Readers of various persuasions will find something important in this work."

—**Noah Toly**, provost, Calvin University

"*Hope for God's Creation* is an accessible guide for Christian creation care. Andrew Spencer's goal is to encourage Christians to construct a pattern of life toward creation consistent with the hope we have in the gospel. In that sense, this book is very much about discipleship. Aware of the dangers in taking up this topic, to accomplish his task, Spencer invites the reader into a wide-ranging exploration in which he translates important ideas for the non-specialist and introduces the reader to significant thinkers, helping them to assess their ideas based on the authority of Scripture. It covers an impressive amount of ground, and it will help the reader reconsider how they think about their existence on God's creation and how they are stewarding it in light of the ultimate hope found in the gospel."

—**Keith S. Whitfield**, associate professor of theology,
Southeastern Baptist Theological Seminary

"Is humanity responsible for the well-being of the world? Andrew Spencer's compelling answer to this critical question is hopeful yet realistic, dignified yet responsible, firmly grounded in Scripture, and directed toward bringing glory to the Creator. While Spencer argues from a conservative evangelical perspective, his solutions will appeal to anyone concerned with the environment. I highly recommend this positive and practical essay in theological ethics."

—**Malcolm B. Yarnell III**, research professor of theology,
Southwestern Baptist Theological Seminary

HOPE

FOR GOD'S
CREATION

Stewardship in an Age of Futility

HOPE
FOR GOD'S CREATION

Andrew J. Spencer

B&H
ACADEMIC
BRENTWOOD, TENNESSEE

Contents

Acknowledgments

This book would not have been possible without a large number of people. My wife, Jennifer, read the entire manuscript at least twice. She has been a faithful editor of all my printed works. Additionally, a number of other people read portions of the manuscript along the way, providing invaluable feedback. The group of early readers includes Donny Mathis, Jay Anderson, James Wagner, Jay Williamson, David Jones, and Alan Noble. My publisher also found a helpful external reader whose comments were both encouraging and challenging. Everyone's input on this volume has made it a better book; the weaknesses and errors that remain are, of course, my own fault. I am also thankful for Dennis Greeson, who reached out to me and gave me an opportunity to pitch this project.

My family has made the deepest sacrifice to get this project completed. I have spent many hours in my office tapping away at another chapter instead of other activities. Much of my vacation time from work has been invested in writing and editing instead of doing more fun activities. I am grateful for their patience, convinced that I could have balanced the demands more effectively, but hopeful that the outcome will be a blessing that will help redeem the sacrifices.

Introduction

Most books on ecology, environmental ethics, and creation care begin with a personal anecdote of a moment of revelation when the importance of treating God's creation properly became a priority.[1] I never really experienced such a moment. If I were to attempt to nail down some point where I was overawed by God's wonder, it might be the halcyon days of my youth in rural western New York or some of my kayaking adventures in college. Or, perhaps, it might be sitting topside on the bridge of a submarine driving out beyond the continental shelf off the coast of Virginia, with the dolphins jumping in the bow wake as the sun rose before me. Those were wonderful times in my life surrounded by God's handiwork. No doubt some of those adventures shaped my appreciation of creation, but I would venture a guess that like many people, an interest in creation care has been something encouraged by the prevailing themes of culture rather than something to which I was dynamically converted.

Nevertheless, my perspective on creation care has changed over the years, not because I suddenly saw that it was important, but because I came to a deeper understanding of *why* caring for creation is important. This book is less an argument for the need for some sort of Christianized environmentalism and more an explanation of the orthodox, evangelical theology that leads to an ethics of creation care. This is a book that is heavy on doctrinal reasoning and light on statistics designed to frighten readers into action. As it turns out, fear and guilt are terrible motivators for sustained environmental action.[2] Also, knowing the facts does not lead to an immediate response. Sometimes overwhelming knowledge leads to a sense of futility, and at other times it can lead to seeking a way

---

[1.] Lawrence B. Slobodkin, *A Citizen's Guide to Ecology* (New York: Oxford University Press, 2006), 15.

[2.] Katharine Hayhoe, *Saving Us: A Climate Scientist's Case for Hope and Healing in a Divided World* (New York: One Signal), 63–83.

1

to reinterpret reality to arrive at some alternate picture of the universe.[3] For an ethics of creation care to result in real and lasting change, it has to begin with values that establish a reason *why*. That *why* can translate into long-term actions that will benefit the created order.

Christian ethics is in some ways simpler and in some ways more complex than many other approaches to morality. Many approaches to environmental ethics rely on a utilitarian approach, where decisions are made through some sort of calculus weighing various goods but always focused on the goal of reducing environmental impact. Utilitarianism is a dangerous ethical approach for Christians.[4] If the primary goal is to preserve an ecosystem, and research shows that human population has an impact on that ecosystem, then that leads to the conclusion it would be morally good to eliminate some or all humans. That basic argument has been made many times (it will be discussed in greater detail in chapter 6), and it can lead to a dark place. The problem is not the goal of maintaining a healthy environment; it is in the ethical theory that moves so quickly from a shared good into evil. Christians must find a better way to frame their moral reasoning as they seek to do good works in the world.

A CHRISTIAN ETHICS

According to the Heidelberg Catechism question 91, good works are "only those [works] which are done out of true faith, conform to God's law, and are done for God's glory; and not those based on our own opinion or human tradition."[5] The last part rules out some more subjective ways of making moral decisions. The first portion of the answer breaks ethics into three parts: conduct, character, and goals.[6] All three aspects are essential to doing good works.

Our conduct is best determined by conformity to God's law. The norms of God's law are most clearly seen in Scripture, which is a gift of God's self-revelation to humanity. God's character is also revealed

---

[3.] Hayhoe, *Saving Us*, 49–61.

[4.] David W. Jones, *Introduction to Biblical Ethics* (Nashville: B&H Academic, 2013), 7–11.

[5.] "The Heidelberg Catechism," Q91, in Van Dixhoorn, *Creeds, Confessions, & Catechisms*, 319.

[6.] Jones, *Introduction to Biblical Ethics*, 20–26.

in the order of creation (Rom 1:20), so we should not be surprised to learn particulars about caring for creation through the study of order in nature. Nevertheless, the conclusions drawn from the created order should never cause us to violate the clearer standards of Scripture.

Character is derived first from the status of having faith in Christ, a God-initiated transaction that grants an individual the status of new creation (2 Cor 5:17). Character is also determined by one's position in life; it determines whether someone is the right sort of person to perform a particular action that conforms to God's law. So, it might be lawful to eat fruit to the glory of God, but if that fruit did not belong to the hungry man, eating it would not be a good work.

Goals are the basic reasons that someone has in mind when they perform a particular action. For someone of the right character, a lawful act done for selfish gain would be sin. A pastor can preach a sermon with perfect content on a Sunday morning and sin the entire time he is proclaiming God's inerrant Word because his focus is on his own standing rather than on God's glory. On the other hand, Paul made clear that every type of action can be done for the glory of God (1 Cor 10:31; Col 3:17). This includes the way we treat God's creation. We should treat it well for God's glory. Since God's glory is the goal of an ethics of creation care, it makes a Christian approach to the environment *theocentric*—centered on God. A focus on anything other than the glory of God will quickly deform any environmental ethics.

FUTILITY

Some environmentalists believe a Christian approach to environmental ethics is futile because they believe that Christianity is fundamentally *anthropocentric*—that is, focused on the good of humanity to the exclusion of other concerns. For example, the environmentalist Naomi Klein writes, "You don't get much more human-centered than the persistent Judeo-Christian interpretation that God created the entire world specifically to serve Adam's every need."[7] She sees this as a reason

---

[7.] Naomi Klein, *On Fire: The (Burning) Case for a Green New Deal* (New York: Simon & Schuster, 2013), 141.

to discard the Christian tradition. Even some critics within the Christian tradition agree with Klein's critique, arguing that the Bible must be approached with suspicion to reject unhelpful passages of Scripture and emphasize helpful ones.[8]

Other environmentalists argue the belief that the present creation will end in a fiery judgment is sufficient reason to discount the possibility of a Christian environmental ethics. I once had a New Testament professor read a paper on environmental ethics to give me feedback. He summed up his opinion with the note "It's like shuffling deck chairs on the *Titanic.*" In other words, he did not see creation care as a useful topic for study. He was not alone among Christians. Many non-Christians have noticed that dismissive attitude, coming to assume that it is the logical conclusion of orthodox Christianity. As a result, some environmentalists argue that a Christian eschatology is a sort of escapism that prevents caring for creation.[9]

Even with a high view of Scripture, there are legitimate grounds for questioning the possibility of a Christian environmental ethics. After all, Paul wrote that "creation was subjected to futility." Moreover, that subjection to futility was "not willingly, but because of him who subjected it" (Rom 8:20). Given that creation's groaning is the result of God's specific action against it, that might seem to be a nail in the coffin against a distinct Christian approach to creation care.[10]

Christian environmental ethics would have been in a bad place if Paul hadn't finished the thought. But he did. The natural world has hope because creation was "subjected to futility . . . in the hope that the creation itself will also be set free from the bondage to decay into the glorious freedom of God's children" (Rom 8:20–21). It is that hope by creation and for creation that changes everything.

[8.] E.g., Norman C. Habel, "Introducing Ecological Hermeneutics," in Norman C. Habel and Peter Trudinger, eds., *Exploring Ecological Hermeneutics* (Atlanta: Society of Biblical Literature, 2008), 1–8.

[9.] E.g., Bill Moyers, "Welcome to Doomsday," March 24, 2005, https://billmoyers.com/2005/02/25/welcome-to-doomsday-march-24-2005/.

[10.] Or it leads to attempts to significantly revise traditional readings of this passage. See Brendan Byrne, "Creation Groaning: An Earth Bible Reading of Romans 8.18–22," in *Readings from the Perspective of Earth*, ed. Norman Habel (Cleveland: Pilgrim, 2000), 193–203.

HOPE CHANGES EVERYTHING

One of the dominant themes of much environmental discourse has been despair that any real improvement in the environment can come without a massive shift in nearly every area of human life. Dale Jamieson writes, "The dusk has started to fall with respect to climate change and so the owl of Minerva can spread her wings. We can now begin the process of understanding why the global attempt to prevent serious anthropogenic climate change failed and begin to chart a course for living in a world that has been remade by human action."[11] Jeremy Rifkin claims that we have only twelve years to stop the worst effects of global warming. He writes, "This will require a transformation of our global economy, our society, and our very way of life without precedent in human history."[12] Such a transformation seems unlikely in a big hurry, even if the shape of the proposed new society is deemed beneficial. This has led some, like activist Greta Thunburg, to depression and outright despair.[13] Hopelessness lends itself toward the sentiment "Let us eat and drink, for tomorrow we die" (1 Cor 15:32). Despair leads to apathy. At the same time, there are some environmental advocates writing with an element of hope.

Common themes among hopeful environmentalists include real evidence of improvement, even on a small scale, and engagement of young people. Katharine Hayhoe's book *Saving Us: A Climate Scientist's Case for Hope and Healing in a Divided World* finds hope "based on the idea of a future . . . [where] the next generation embodies the future."[14] Jane Goodall finds hope in the successes that she has witnessed in restoring prairie land, cleaning up industrial sites, and installing wildlife corridors. She also finds hope in the engagement of the children in her Roots and Shoots clubs, whose members demonstrate enthusiasm for improving the environment and take specific action to make local changes.[15] Such hopefulness is more likely to result in continued action,

[11] Dale Jamieson, *Reason in a Dark Time: Why the Struggle Against Climate Change Failed—and What It Means for Our Future* (New York: Oxford University Press, 2014), ix.

[12] Jeremy Rifkin, *The Green New Deal: Why the Fossil Fuel Civilization Will Collapse by 2028, and the Bold Economic Plan to Save Life on Earth* (New York: St. Martin's, 2019), 2.

[13] Klein, *On Fire*, 7–16.

[14] Hayhoe, *Saving Us*, 241.

[15] Jane Goodall, *Seeds of Hope: Wisdom and Wonder from the World of Plants* (New York: Grand

but it falls short of the glorious hope of cosmic renewal that Christians hope for because of God's promise.

Hope that real improvement is possible leads to action. In contrast, pessimism leads to inaction because any effort would be futile, frustrated by other people and the curse that is upon the earth. Hopelessness can result in hating the creation or its inhabitants, but a Christian hope encourages us to love the creation for the sake of the one who made it. Christians should have hope, unless we are to join in a pact that will end in our own demise and the termination of the species.[16] Our hope comes because of the anticipation of the coming renewal of creation, because we are a part of the creation for which we long to flourish. Creation is our home and our neighbor all wrapped into one. As G. K. Chesterton argues, "When you do love a thing, its gladness is a reason for loving it, and its sadness a reason for loving it more."[17] Love gives a reason for attempts to make creation better today.

Real improvement is only possible by someone who loves the thing being improved. Again, Chesterton notes, "Before any cosmic act of reform, we must have a cosmic oath of allegiance."[18] Some environmentalists want to reform humanity, but they do not care for humans. Some Christians who ignore their duty toward creation think themselves totally distinct from creation, so they can ignore its fate while waiting for their release from the physical world. Hope comes from loving both humanity as an abstract category and loving particular humans individually, which is a much harder thing. Hope arises from the knowledge that creation and new creation exist on a continuum, and humans are part of both. Hope remains because of the knowledge that though our efforts may fail to make things better, they are worth trying because God is going to renew everything one day.

Romans 8 is helpful in defining Christian hope. The creation hopes to be set free from its futility by the sovereign work of God (vv. 20–21). We humans, also, like creation, are waiting for the redemption of our physical bodies (v. 23). Paul made it clear that hope is something

---

Central, 2014), 307–22.

[16.] For example, Patricia MacCormack, *The Ahuman Manifesto: Activism for the End of Anthropocene* (London: Bloomsbury Academic, 2020), 14–16.

[17.] Gilbert Keith Chesterton, *Orthodoxy* (New York: John Lane Co., 1908), 121.

[18.] Chesterton, *Orthodoxy*, 129.

beyond the horizon that we should not expect to catch sight of (v. 24). And yet, we are called to wait on the final redemption of all creation with patience (v. 25). There is a sense of anticipation that God is going to set things right someday.[19]

The hope of Christians for creation is not that we will be able to make things entirely correct through our efforts. Rather, we work with the knowledge that we have been given a ministry of reconciliation, which includes all of creation (cf. Col 1:20; 2 Cor 5:16–18). We work toward reconciliation in hope but recognize that hope will not be fulfilled until Christ comes again. Creation exists in futility in the present age because of God's curse on creation (Gen 3:17–19). Our task is to till the ground in hope, making our living (Gen 3:20), looking forward to the moment when God supernaturally sets everything right.

Christian hope is unique because it is not based on human action but on divine power. It anticipates human action but recognizes that human efforts are insufficient without God's intervention. Hope does not falter when human efforts fail, but continues to inspire perseverance when the outcome seems least sure. It does not require visible success in this life, but it encourages persistence because it is by our faithfulness that our works will be judged (Heb 11:6). So Christian hope is distinct and more powerful than the counterfeits of this world. That is the hope that should inspire us to care for creation.

TARGET AUDIENCE

This is a book written with the church in mind. Although this volume comes from an academic publisher, this is a book that is intended to be useful to the educated church member who, after spending some time in discipleship to pick up the basics of the Christian faith, has come to wonder what the Bible has to say about how creation should be treated by humanity. This book is an attempt to answer that question.

As such, I have made every effort to carefully explain technical theological language and avoid it when possible. Theology is often not as

---

[19.] Francis Schaeffer, *The Finished Work of Christ* (Wheaton: Crossway, 1998), 207–20. Also, Richard Bauckham, "Ecological Hope in Crisis?", in *The Bible in the Contemporary World* (Grand Rapids: Eerdmans, 2015), 104–6.

hard as it seems. Sometimes theology seems harder than it ought to be because authors use jargon to obscure their arguments. As Jane Jacobs observes, "Jargon often hides what 'experts' are actually advocating, but worse than that, it conceals illogical thought from the readers of the jargon—and even the writers of it. It's hard for muddled thoughts to hide in plain English sentences."[20] No doubt there are places where I could have been clearer, but my goal is to provide enough clarity for every reader to benefit.

There are two main groups that I have had in mind as I have written this volume. First, faithful, orthodox Christians who have seen little reason to practice creation care. My prayer is that some from this group will be inspired to be more careful stewards of creation. Second, readers who are passionate about environmentalism and are questioning whether Christianity can be good for the environment. I am hopeful that some from the second group will grow in their knowledge of the faith as they see the ways that faithful Christianity calls us to care for creation.

LIMITS OF THE VOLUME

Since this volume is an effort to build an evangelical ethics of creation care, there are many alternative approaches that are not covered in detail here. This is not a critical volume; it is a constructive volume. For those looking for something closer to a survey of Christian approaches to environmental ethics, my volume *Doctrine in Shades of Green: Theological Perspective for Environmental Ethics* may be of some interest.[21]

This present book begins with the fundamental belief that orthodox theology need not change to be applied to contemporary issues.[22] In contrast, Walter Rauschenbusch argues, "If theology stops growing or is unable to adjust itself to its modern environment and to meet its present

---

[20.] Leticia Kent, "More Babies Needed, Not Fewer: An Interview with Jane Jacobs," *Vogue*, August 15, 1970, 86.

[21.] Andrew J. Spencer, *Doctrine in Shades of Green: Theological Perspective for Environmental Ethics* (Eugene, OR: Wipf & Stock, 2022).

[22.] For example, Paul Santmire describes his environmental project as explicitly intending to revise Christianity. H. Paul Santmire, *Nature Reborn: The Ecological and Cosmic Promise of Christian Theology* (Minneapolis: Fortress, 2000), 6–15.

tasks, it will die."[23] He claims that his theology for the Social Gospel "is just as orthodox as the Gospel would allow."[24] For Rauschenbusch, theology follows after ethics, conforming to the desired ethics of the present age.[25] The approach I take is exactly the opposite of this. This volume begins with the belief that the Word of God is inerrant and sufficient, that theology flows from the Word of God, and that ethics is derived from theology. Thus, there should be nothing theologically novel or innovative in this book. I am simply attempting to apply the orthodox faith to a prevalent issue of our day.

This book is an attempt to build an ethics of creation care from an orthodox, evangelical theology. I am confessionally and convictionally Baptist, with all the blessings and limitations that entails. As such, this is not an argument for reforming the doctrines of Christianity for the sake of the environment. Instead, it is an effort to build an approach to creation care consistent with "the faith that was delivered to the saints once and for all" (Jude 3). If adherence to traditional theological formulations seems stodgy and uninteresting to some readers, I must point them to Dorothy L. Sayers, who argues, "It is the dogma that is the drama."[26] As a novelist and playwright, she finds Christian doctrine to be among the most exciting ideas. Furthermore, as Sayers writes, "It is worse than useless for Christians to talk about the importance of Christian morality unless they are prepared to take their stand upon the fundamentals of Christian theology."[27] So, this volume is decidedly theological, and hopefully it is interesting as well.

OUTLINE OF CHAPTERS

This book is divided into three parts. Part 1 provides a background for the discussion of creation care beginning with a chapter discussing the need for and the dangers of taking up creation care as a topic of interest.

[23.] Walter Rauschenbusch, *A Theology for the Social Gospel* (1917; repr., Louisville: Westminster John Knox, 1997), 1.

[24.] Rauschenbusch, foreword, n.p.

[25.] Rauschenbusch, 14–15.

[26.] Dorothy L. Sayers, "The Dogma Is the Drama," in *The Whimsical Christian* (Springfield, OH: Collier Books), 27.

[27.] Sayers, "Creed or Chaos?", 34.

The first chapter explains why, for Christians, treating creation properly is an important part of our witness to the world and suggests ways that an incautious focus on the environment can lead Christians astray. Chapter 2 offers an abbreviated survey of the history of environmentalism, including connections with religion and evangelical engagement in creation care.

Part 2 contains the main substance of a theological perspective for creation care in five chapters. Chapter 3 introduces a theology for creation care, with an emphasis on the four key doctrines that will be highlighted in this volume. The fourth chapter explores sources of moral authority for creation care, emphasizing the supreme place of Scripture while encouraging an appropriate appreciation of information available only through scientific study. Chapter 5 describes the types of value creation has, emphasizing the inherent value of the created order, despite the fall. The sixth chapter considers the role of humanity within creation, noting that men and women were uniquely created in the image of God. This entails, among other things, the duty to exercise well the role of steward of all creation within the limits ascribed by God as we seek to imitate Christ. The seventh chapter looks forward to the new creation, where the creation's curse of futility is lifted and everything is renewed. The chapter points toward the need for Christians to pursue substantial healing while we wait for Christ's return.

Part 3 takes a more practical turn. In chapter 8 the central question is how the church, gathered and scattered, will live out our calling to be ambassadors of Christ's cosmic reconciliation without allowing concern for activism to drown out the message of the gospel. The ninth chapter explores the question of climate change, including consideration of conspiracy thinking, political conflict, and the possibility of cooperation without compromise. Chapter 10 lays out a few hopeful suggestions for specific actions Christians should take individually, as a church community, and as participants in a democratic society to care for creation well.

The book closes with a prayerful epilogue, some words of exhortation, a reminder of the primacy of the gospel message, and a hopeful conclusion. Some in the world may have lost hope for the future of creation, but Christians have every reason to look forward to the work that God will do when he makes everything new. Creation care is one way that Christians can demonstrate in a practical fashion the hope that lives within us (1 Pet 3:15).

PART ONE
THE BACKGROUND OF CREATION CARE

CHAPTER 1

The Need for and Dangers of Environmental Ethics

Within my lifetime there have been several significant advances in environmental quality as a result of cooperative efforts and individual concern. One has been the recovery of the bald eagle, our nation's symbol. When I was a child, I never saw an eagle outside of the television screen or the zoo in a nearby city. Now, my father watches multiple groups of eagles at different nesting sites near our long-time family home. I have seen many bald eagles while on walks in my neighborhood park in Michigan, and there are many that live by Lake Erie, which is only a few miles away. The bald eagle has gone from a prominent member of the endangered species list to being designated a "species of least concern" by the International Union for Conservation of Nature.[1] That population recovered because of special efforts by many people who believed the bald eagle is a valuable member of the ecosystem.

Another major advance in my lifetime has been the curbing of acid rain, especially in the Adirondack region of New York. Acid rain is the phenomenon where sulfur dioxide and nitrogen dioxide are released from burning fossil fuels. These chemicals tend to concentrate within lakes and rivers, resulting in changes to the pH, which can kill fish and plants, causing great harm to the complex web of natural dependencies.[2] This is an example where there was awareness of the problem for more than a century, but it took decades of focused research and efforts to raise public awareness to lead to policy changes that began to curb the sources of acid rain. There has been significant improvement in the health of the Adirondack ecosystems, made possible by

---

[1.] Alfredo Begazo, "From Endangered to Recovered: A Timeline of the Bald Eagle's Journey," Avian Report, accessed July 26, 2022, https://avianreport.com/endangered-bald-eagle/#1800s-beginning-of-the-bald-eagle-population-decline.

[2.] Jerry Jenkins et al., *Acid Rain in the Adirondacks* (Ithaca, NY: Comstock, 2007), 5–15.

cooperative stewardship. However, it will take another generation or more to recover, and the sources of acid rain have yet to be fully abated.[3] This represents a modest advance, but it demonstrates what is possible when values are aligned with practices.

This book is written with realistic hope that some readers will be convinced to make creation care a part of their individual decision-making, their efforts within their communities, and their political concerns. Sometimes the environmental problems we face can seem to make any effort futile, but this book relies on the expectation that there is hope for improvement and that by properly caring for God's creation, we are acting out of an anticipation of the coming renewal of all things.

CARE FOR CREATION

Care for the creation does not always register high on the list of concerns for Christians. After all, there are billions of people in this world who have never heard a credible expression of the gospel.[4] There is a Great Commission to fulfill (Matt 28:18–20). Additionally, there are crystal-clear calls in Scripture for caring for the poor (Prov 19:17).[5] In contrast, the case for the environment is more difficult to reduce to a chapter and verse. Given the need for the advance of the gospel message and the greater clarity of other ethical duties, isn't it justifiable that Christians should prioritize other matters over the environment?

As Christians, we recognize that the transmission of the gospel is a central calling of our lives. However, obedience to the gospel requires more of us than simply evangelizing. It includes honoring God in every aspect of our lives (Col 3:17). There are strong biblical and theological justifications for caring for God's creation. At the same time there are real dangers in allowing concerns about ecology to overwhelm other issues. In this chapter I will provide a defense of creation care as well as a warning of some of the dangers of an excessive focus on

---

[3.] Jenkins et al., 215–25.

[4.] "Global Statistics," Joshua Project, accessed July 26, 2022, https://joshuaproject.net/people_groups/statistics.

[5.] See Abraham Kuyper, *The Problem of Poverty*, ed. James W. Skillen (Grand Rapids: Baker, 1991).

environmental well-being. We must engage in creation care from a robustly orthodox theological perspective while avoiding the dangers that have shipwrecked the faith of others.

IN DEFENSE OF ENVIRONMENTAL ENGAGEMENT

From the very beginning of our existence, God has given humanity a unique role within creation as stewards (Gen 2:5). We are certainly part of creation, having been formed from the same dust that makes up the rest of the cosmos (v. 7). Yet humans were made in the image of God (Gen 1:26) and have been charged to "fill the earth, and subdue it" (v. 28). The dominion God gave humans over creation must not be turned to domination. Creation care seeks the good of the whole cosmos for the glory of God.

The Common Good

One of the most basic reasons for engaging in creation care is that it is part of seeking the good of the city in which we live. Jeremiah 29:11 has frequently been embroidered on samplers hung on living room walls. After all, when God tells his people good things, we want to have a part of it: "'For I know the plans I have for you'—this is the LORD's declaration—'plans for your well-being, not for disaster, to give you a future and a hope'" (Jer 29:11). Taken by itself, this is a very comforting verse that sounds like God is going to take care of all the details and make sure that everything goes well for us materially. This verse seems to support a version of the prosperity gospel—God's got a plan to make you healthy, wealthy, and wise.[6]

In context Jer 29:11 communicates something quite different. The verse is from a letter written to a people who were being ripped from their homes by an oppressive conqueror and taken off to live in a foreign land, away from the temple, away from their ancestral homes, and among people who lived and worshipped radically differently.

[6.] For more on the prosperity gospel, see David W. Jones and Russell S. Woodbridge, *Health, Wealth & Happiness: How the Prosperity Gospel Overshadows the Gospel of Christ* (Grand Rapids: Kregel, 2011).

Considering that Jeremiah was commanded to buy land with the expectation of a descendant getting to use it (Jer 32), the message here is of near-term futility with a promise of future hope.

With that framework, God commands his people to pursue the common good. Jeremiah wrote, "Build houses and live in them. Plant gardens and eat their produce. . . . Pursue the well-being of the city I have deported you to. Pray to the LORD on its behalf, for when it thrives, you will thrive" (Jer 29:5, 7). God's message to his people in that time and place was clear: *Go out and live as healthy, engaged citizens of this alien city I will place you in, because I will work things out for good.* There are parallels here between Jeremiah's prophecy and the language Paul used in Romans 8.

In many ways we too are people in exile. By some estimates, there are 2.4 billion Christians in the world, which is little less than a third of the global population.[7] And Christianity is on the rise in the Global South. But in the United States and Europe, the percentage of faithful Christians is shrinking, and for various reasons, the influence of Christian ideas on contemporary culture is dwindling. We may be ideological exiles while living in the same house our parents built on land owned by our family for generations.[8] But even if we feel at home in our neighborhood, that is only more reason to pursue the well-being of the city, because those closest to us should be the people whose well-being we are most interested in. In other words, though the exact application of God's command to the Israelites may be different, we should understand it as a general command to all God's people at all times.[9] It is a specific application of the broader stewardship mandate.

Clean air, fresh water, and a stable climate are common good concerns. Everyone wants a healthy environment. However, the thresholds of concern for environmental problems typically vary with proximity to the problem. Many reading this book are far removed from any real environmental dangers. Unfortunately, the poorest citizens are often the most significantly impacted by pollution because they have the

[7] "The Future of World Religions: Population Growth Projections, 2010–2050," Pew Research Center, April 2, 2015, https://www.pewforum.org/2015/04/02/religious-projections-2010-2050/.

[8] See Lee Beach, *The Church in Exile: Living in Hope after Christendom* (Downers Grove: IVP Academic, 2015), 15–27.

[9] Jones, *Introduction to Biblical Ethics*, 58–63 (see introduction, n. 4).

greatest need for economic benefits brought by polluting businesses, the least political clout to resist bad policies, and a lack of resources to relocate away from the problem.[10] If this were simply a case of individuals choosing higher risk for themselves in exchange for a lower cost of living, then we might be inclined to argue that the market should do its work. However, some pollutants can have generational impacts, which can sometimes take many years to accumulate and rise to our attention. In a real sense, making wise choices about the environment is a way for caring for the poor. Creation care is one way we can love our neighbors as we seek the good of the city.

Gospel Friendships

A secondary, but not unimportant, benefit of engaging in creation care is that it puts us in common cause with neighbors that have vastly different understandings of the moral fabric of the universe. This gives us a chance to become friends with and share the gospel with those around us while we work alongside them. Developing such evangelistic friendships is not a reason to become interested in creation care, but it is a positive opportunity provided by joining in common cause with neighbors with a different worldview.

Friendship is a rare gift in our lonely time. In a 2019 survey, 22% of millennials reported they had no friends.[11] C. S. Lewis in his 1960 book, *The Four Loves*, notes that by his observation, many people never experience true friendship.[12] He argues, "Friendship arises out of mere Companionship when two or more of the companions discover that they have in common some insight or interest or even taste which the others do not share and which, till that moment, each believed to be his own unique treasure (or burden)."[13] It is in such friendships over a common concern—like the well-being of the environment—that opportunities may arise for discussing other interests. However, it is also true that as society fragments, Christians tend to have fewer social

---

[10.] Kathryn D. Blanchard and Kevin J. O'Brien, *An Introduction to Christian Environmentalism: Ecology, Virtue, and Ethics* (Waco: Baylor University Press, 2014), 91–98.

[11.] Brian Resnick, "22 Percent of Millennials Say They Have 'No Friends,'" Vox, August 1, 2019, https://www.vox.com/science-and-health/2019/8/1/20750047/millennials-poll-loneliness.

[12.] C. S. Lewis, *The Four Loves* (San Francisco: HarperOne, 1960), 74.

[13.] Lewis, 83.

relationships outside of their local church unless they intentionally cultivate them.

Friendships among dissimilar individuals can certainly form around common interests. These can be fruitful for the gospel, especially when the agreement is not total. There is little that makes evangelism more difficult for the church than the social, political, and ideological homogenization of our congregations.[14] Agreement on core doctrinal issues is important for unity within a local congregation, but when a local church begins to demand unanimity on non-doctrinal issues, even if the "demand" simply comes through the dominance of certain opinionated voices, then it becomes more difficult for that church to reach outsiders and bring them in to the gospel. Whether it is an official position or not, a church that is nearly entirely Republican or Democrat (for example), will show non-Christians that you have to convert politically to convert religiously.[15]

Active participation in creation care activities by doctrinally orthodox Christians is a way to ensure we are reaching outside of our bubble into the world around us. The local environmental initiatives I have participated in have included a remarkable diversity of participants, with people from every ethnicity, the pierced, tattooed, dreadlocked, the recreational-marijuana proponent, and at least one family of socially and doctrinally conservative Baptists all picking up trash and making the world a better place. It is perfectly natural in those situations to talk about why you decided to show up on a chilly morning to wade in the river or clear a trail. If we have our minds in gear, that is the perfect opportunity to put 1 Pet 3:15 into practice and give a reason for the hope we have within us. While we face in the same direction with our non-believing neighbor picking trash, we can explain the gospel with our words. As social isolation increases, local environmental initiatives provide one of many outstanding ways to break down social barriers to offer gospel hope to our neighbors as we demonstrate our love for the community.

Caring for God's creation is the right thing to do because it

---

[14.] See Francis Schaeffer, "Two Contents, Two Realities," in *The Complete Works of Francis A. Schaeffer* (Wheaton: Crossway, 1982), 3:410.

[15.] See Scott Sauls, *Jesus Outside the Lines: A Way Forward for Those Who Are Tired of Taking Sides* (Carol Stream, IL: Tyndale, 2018), 12–19.

demonstrates an appropriate valuation of creation. It is also a way to show neighbor love, especially for our poor neighbors. Furthermore, it is a way to engage non-Christians in a common cause, which can provide opportunities to talk about the thing most important to us—the gospel.[16] And yet, even as we seek to properly steward the environment, we should be aware that activism without caution can lead to spiritual danger.

DANGERS OF ENVIRONMENTAL ENTANGLEMENT

No Christian who gets deeply involved in any cultural activity should forget the dangers for a moment (2 Tim 2:4). The dangers are real, are subtle, and bear significant consequences. That is true whether the activity is participating in sports, fighting for the end of abortion, or working to eradicate abject poverty. There are obvious goods associated with any of these issues. There are strong, biblical arguments that permit or encourage engagement in such activities. However, if those activities begin to define the Christian more than the pursuit of holiness in the image of Jesus Christ, then the wheels will begin to wobble and may eventually fall off.

In Mark's gospel, Peter tried to focus Jesus on his earthly, messianic role. He looked for Jesus to become an earthly liberator and king for the Jewish people. Jesus used this as a teaching moment for Peter, for his disciples, and for a crowd that was following them. He presented this paradox: "Whoever wants to save his life will lose it, but whoever loses his life because of me and the gospel will save it. For what does it benefit someone to gain the whole world and yet lose his life?" (Mark 8:35–36). As Jesus made clear at the end of his life, "My kingdom is not of this world" (John 18:36).

If we lose sight of the doctrinal core of our motivation for creation care, we can fall prey to ideologies that will lead us into unholy places. If we lose sight of our theological convictions for the sake of cooperation, we can find ourselves drifting into soul-sapping heterodoxy or

---

16. Mark D. Liederbach and Evan Lenow, *Ethics as Worship: The Pursuit of Moral Discipleship* (Phillipsburg, NJ: P&R, 2021), 409–11.

worse. If we allow issues like the environment to become the center of our lives, we can lose focus on our explicit calling to take the gospel to the ends of the earth. These are all dangers that can befall those who engage in environmental activism without proper caution.

A Big Idea

One of the most important tidbits of observational wisdom I've gleaned over the years is that it is a good thing to carefully sift the words of people who are captured by a big idea or an ideology.[17] The big idea may even be true and important, but big idea reasoning emphasizes the centrality of that one thing over all other things and allows the justification of evil in the name of good. For example, the movement to stop abortion has been used to justify killing abortionists, bombing clinics, and other similar acts of violence.[18] Ending elective abortion is an excellent goal, but the big idea fallacy has, in some cases, enabled its supporters to justify otherwise unacceptable actions on utilitarian grounds.

The problem with a big idea is not necessarily that it is wrong. In fact, many times the big idea is well-grounded in justifiable data. The problem with the big idea is that it can become an ideology, which then enables a great number of bad things along with the good. As Aleksandr Solzhenitsyn writes, "To do evil a human being must first of all believe that what he's doing is good, or else that it's a well-considered act in conformity with natural law. Fortunately, it is in the nature of the human being to seek a *justification* for his actions."[19] Solzhenitsyn goes on to identify one of the more significant sources of self-justification of evil as ideology: "Ideology—that is what gives evildoing the necessary steadfastness and determination. That is the social theory which helps to make his acts seem good instead of bad in his own and others' eyes, so that he won't hear reproaches and curses but will receive praise and honors."[20]

[17.] This falls somewhere behind never getting in a land war in East Asia and not going up against a Sicilian when death is on the line.

[18.] Sarah Frostenson, "40 Years of Attacks on Abortion Clinics, Mapped," Vox, December 1, 2015, https://www.vox.com/2015/12/1/9827886/abortion-clinic-attacks-mapped.

[19.] Aleksandr Solzhenitsyn, *The Gulag Archipelago* (New York: Harper & Row, 1973), 1:173.

[20.] Solzhenitsyn, 1:174.

Within environmental ethics, the big idea of climate change has recently been used by some environmentalists to minimize the problem of ecoterrorism,[21] support human extinction,[22] and advocate for techno-surveillance programs.[23] In an earlier generation, the big idea of overpopulation was the basis for one former Southern Baptist professor to lobby for compulsory birth control, despite writing in the shadow of the nightmare eugenics programs of the early twentieth century.[24] When something like climate change is described as an "existential threat," as some politicians and scientists have claimed, then there are many things that would otherwise not be justifiable that may become justified.

The purpose here is not to argue that climate change or other environmental problems are not significant. Indeed, as Katharine Hayhoe argues, climate change is a threat to civilization *as we know it* rather than the planet. She writes, "The planet is going to survive—it has, after all, been warmer before on geological timescales. It is our human systems that are at risk, our cities and economies and buildings and food systems and, at the end of it all, our civilization."[25] There is still potential for a big idea in this approach, as we have seen in the way some defenders of Western Civilization approach challenges to that tradition, but there is more room for nuance and debate. If the goal is to preserve the good aspects of the systems and culture that we have, then we need to debate which of those we ought to save and then consider working together toward doing it. If the goal is to "save the planet," which is on the verge of meltdown, then any and all actions can be considered within bounds.

But the danger of a big idea does not belong to the environmentalists alone. An unswerving commitment to libertarian economics may be a big idea that defeats all ethical objections. Or it might come in the form of preserving American representative democracy, or Western Civilization, or the rejection of the designated hitter in baseball. History has revealed some fairly minor concepts that have served as big ideas to justify evil

---

[21.] Blanchard and O'Brien, *An Introduction to Christian Environmentalism*, 159–61.

[22.] MacCormack, *The Ahuman Manifesto* (see introduction, n. 16).

[23.] Rifkin, *The Green New Deal*, 22–23 (see introduction, n. 12).

[24.] Edgar R. Chasteen, *The Case for Compulsory Birth Control* (Englewood Cliffs, NJ: Prentice-Hall, 1971).

[25.] Hayhoe, *Saving Us*, 95 (see introduction, n. 2).

in the world. Those skeptical of environmentalism, and particularly of anthropogenic climate change theories, need to be careful that their opposition is not as much an ideology as those they are resisting.

Christianity has room for one big idea: the gospel. Any approach to issues like environmental ethics that treat this penultimate thing as an ultimate thing will lead to radicalism, sin, and unhealthy distrust of other humans.[26] Because of the cultural energy being invested in environmental ethics, it has the potential to become an ultimate thing in our minds in our support or opposition to it; we must be careful not to let that be. We must also be careful not to let the important issue of caring for creation lead to compromise on Christian doctrine.

Theological Drift

Those who have followed debates on any socially contentious topic for very long will have observed theological drift, as some previously professedly orthodox slide away from the "faith that was delivered to the saints once for all" (Jude 3). When advocates on a particular issue drift toward a more "conservative" position, the result is often not a denial of specific doctrines but an overwhelming focus on a particular social or political issue to the extent that Christian demeanor—being kind, loving neighbor in word and deed—is neglected. The problem for theological conservatives tends to be in the practice of Christian ethics in the public square. For theological liberals, the problem is often a reshaping of doctrines to fit a perceived cultural need, with a desire to make Christianity more acceptable in the public square.

One of the basic tenets of liberal Protestant theology is that doctrines should be interpreted through a practical or moral lens.[27] As Roger Olson argues, "Under the influence of Kant, liberal Protestant thinkers insisted on reinterpreting all doctrines and dogmas of Christianity in ethical and moral terms, and those that could not be so reinterpreted were neglected if not discarded entirely."[28] This concern is readily identifiable in modern academic theologies that tend toward

26. Dietrich Bonhoeffer, *Ethics* (1955; repr., New York: Touchstone, 1995), 128–29.

27. Rauschenbusch, *Theology for the Social Gospel*, 12–13 (see introduction, n. 23).

28. Roger E. Olson, *The Story of Christian Theology: Twenty Centuries of History and Reform* (Downers Grove: IVP Academic, 1999), 550.

deconstruction of the faith. To have a righteous outcome, theology must be done for the glory of God and not to score rhetorical points or to encourage a particular cultural behavior. Christian theology can answer all of life's most important questions, but it must do so on its own terms and with its own character, without being deformed for the sake of social cause.

When leftward drift happens on an issue, it tends to result in denial or modification of aspects of Christian orthodoxy.[29] There are numerous examples in the history of environmental ethics of leaders in the movement who grew up in a Christian context, but who abandoned the faith as adults.[30] It is a troubling truth that seems to be repeated frequently as once-orthodox Christians begin advocating for a valid social concern. When these concerns overlap with cultural and theological progressives, it can sometimes cause believers to slowly drift away from orthodox theology as their engagement on the issue increases.

American environmentalism has its roots in liberal Protestantism.[31] It is woven into the language of much of the environmental movement. The historian Evan Berry argues, "Theological vocabularies, especially those related to salvation and the goodness of creation, provided the basis for an emergent environmental imagination."[32] If Berry's conclusions are true, then it may be possible to find places where theological language that overlaps with Christian doctrine may have alternative meanings in environmental conversations.[33] This can create confusion and enable theological and ethical drift among well-meaning Christians seeking to engage in creation care. The solution, of course, is not to withdraw from just action, but to affirm proper terminology by holding to Scripture as the ultimate authority for life and practice.

[29.] Liberal Catholic Michael Langford argues this is an essential part of liberal theology. *The Tradition of Liberal Theology* (Grand Rapids: Eerdmans, 2014), 52.

[30.] Mark Stoll, *Inherit the Holy Mountain: Religion and the Rise of American Environmentalism* (New York: Oxford University Press, 2015), 2.

[31.] Evan Berry, *Devoted to Nature: The Religious Roots of American Environmentalism* (Oakland: University of California Press, 2015), 181–82.

[32.] Berry, 13.

[33.] See, for example, Ernst Conradie, "The Salvation of the Earth from Anthropogenic Destruction," *Worldview* 14 (2010): 111–40. In this article, Conradie surveys ways that *salvation* has been used in various theologies for the environment that are much different than what is encountered in most traditionally orthodox theologies.

This will prevent a drift away from orthodox doctrine and distraction from the core concerns of Christianity.

Distractions from Other Initiatives

In his extended criticism of the first Earth Day, Richard Neuhaus comments, "What emerged as the ecology movement in the early 1970s is in some important respects a needed corrective. In other ways it is both frivolous and harmless. In more important respects it is a diversion from, and a distortion of, the political questions that will reshape life on Spaceship Earth during the latter part of the century."[34] He worried that the all-encompassing focus on ecology would distract from efforts to end poverty, end the war in Vietnam, and pursue real justice in society.

Environmentalism has the ability to consume all of the oxygen in the room. It is the sort of movement that can become "The Movement," as Neuhaus calls it. The Movement is a thing intended to accomplish everything it deems good, but in reality, it accomplishes little. He writes, "When something claims to mean everything, it almost inevitably comes to mean nothing."[35] The vision of some very vocal environmental activists is not a humane society. It is a society that mirrors the progressive worldview at every turn. The intent is to build a coalition centered on environmentalism that consumes all other possible causes. As it was in the 1970s, so it continues today.

Contemporary activist Naomi Klein writes, "To change everything, it takes everyone. And to build that kind of coalition, it's got to be about justice: economic justice, racial justice, gender justice, migrant justice, historical justice. Not as afterthoughts but as animating principles."[36] Klein's goal is to create a wall of propaganda from "many different kinds of storytellers: artists, psychologists, faith leaders, historians, and more" to focus everyone's hope in the so-called Green New Deal.[37] Engaging in environmentalism in this manner will necessarily distract from

---

[34] Richard Neuhaus, *In Defense of People: Ecology and the Seduction of Radicalism* (New York: Macmillan, 1971), 9.

[35] Neuhaus, 62.

[36] Klein, *On Fire*, 202 (see introduction, n. 7).

[37] Klein, 271.

other important initiatives. There can only be one central, animating idea in an ideological movement.

There is danger, therefore, in engaging in environmentalism as a Christian. The danger is that holiness, the Great Commission, and the glory of God will become secondary to the pragmatic concerns of the environment. We have already seen this with the Social Gospel movement, which intentionally sidelined historical Christian doctrines for the pursuit of a specific vision of economic justice.[38] We can see this with Christian environmentalists like Willis Jenkins, who argues for redefining the church as a social justice movement. He writes, "The fundamental moral community for Christian ethics, this suggests, may not be a group explicitly shaped for the maintenance of a Christian identity or worldview, but might rather be an association of shared practice formed by attempts to respond to the world's wounds, as before God."[39] This may sound delightfully practical and tenderly loving to the uninitiated, but what Jenkins is presenting is a sort of Social Gospel 2.0, where attempts to redesign Christianity for some perceived social good have tended to result in a loss of both the good and the central ideas of Christianity that both motivated the pro-social desires and animated the activism.

Any engagement in environmental ethics by a Christian must rightly see creation care as an implication of the gospel, not the central idea that replaces the gospel. Gospel centrality must be guarded in practice, not simply in word, lest the church lose its zeal for the lost and zeal for the otherworldly glory of God, and lest believers be drawn into attempts to reconcile incompatible ideas with the truths of Scripture. Creation care is an important part of a holistic Christian ethics, but it should complement other concerns, not overwhelm them.

Summary

There are clear dangers in engaging in environmental ethics as a Christian. However, these dangers are present in nearly every arena of ethics. For example, Christians invented hospitals and universities, and

---

[38.] See Rauschenbusch, *Theology for the Social Gospel*, 10–22.

[39.] Willis Jenkins, *The Future of Ethics: Sustainability, Social Justice, and Religious Creativity* (Washington, DC: Georgetown University Press, 2013), 84–85.

they were the originators of social programs for the poor in the West.[40] These are good and proper exercises in gospel stewardship of resources. They can also become distractions from proclaiming the good news of Jesus's perfect life, substitutionary death, and subsequent resurrection. Desires to build coalitions and engage cooperatively can lead to theological drift if we are not careful and precise in our language. Furthermore, any secondary concern can become a primary focus that drowns out ultimate concerns. These are pitfalls that are possible for creation care. That does not excuse inaction in this area, but it should lead us to engage carefully, with a robustly theological approach that is deeply rooted in the authority of Scripture and applies an ethical methodology consistent with the Christian tradition.

CONCLUSION

If Christianity is true, it has the answers to life's most difficult questions. That includes questions related to creation care as well as the salvation of the soul. As this book unfolds, it will become abundantly clear this is not a book primarily about climate change or any other specific environmental issue. Though specific issues will be part of this discussion, my goal is to get above the debates that drive our politics to ask more basic questions from a theological perspective. When we frame those questions more clearly, it will be easier to get beyond debates about specific policies and numbers and seek a pattern of life that is consistent with the hope that we, as Christians, have been given in Christ. That is, after all, what Christian ethics ought to be primarily about.

More specifically, this is a book about the way we ought to live as Christians in a God-created world, where through misuse of our God-given power, humans have harmed the created order and may continue to harm our civilization's prospects if we do not begin to live more carefully. The planet will survive, and God's purposes will not be thwarted by our action or inaction toward better environmental

---

[40.] See Carter Lindberg, *Beyond Charity: Reformation Initiatives for the Poor* (Minneapolis: Fortress, 1993), 22–33.

stewardship. However, God has also made it abundantly clear through Scripture that people have a responsibility to treat the creation well. Humanity has been given a special place within the created order, which brings both privileges and responsibilities.

In the next chapter we will survey the history of environmental ethics to consider how we got to this moment. That overview will help lay the groundwork for the need for a theological perspective rooted in the orthodox Christian tradition, which will form the foundation for a robust environmental ethics. There are signs of hope in the recovery of bald eagle populations and the diminution of the effects of acid rain. As we continue to seek the good of the city and long for the city that is to come, we can continue to work as Christ-followers to minimize our negative impact on the environment and encourage others to do the same for the glory of God.

KEY TERMS

Ideology
Social Gospel
Theological Drift

STUDY QUESTIONS

1. What are the dangers of a big idea (i.e., ideology)?
2. How have orthodox Christians been negatively influenced by excessive concern for the environment?
3. How can Christians remain faithful in their own context, especially with regard to the environment?
4. Why is it important to be faithful to the tradition of Christian orthodoxy as we wrestle with contemporary ethical questions?

CHAPTER 2

Environmental Ethics and the Church

One common accusation that some Christians make against environmentalism is that it is a religion in and of itself. Even the non-Christian Michael Shellenberger writes, "Environmentalism today is the dominant secular religion of the educated, upper-middle-class elite in most developed and many developing nations. It provides a new story about our collective and individual purpose. It designates good guys and bad guys, heroes and villains. And it does so in the language of science, which provides it with legitimacy."[1] Shellenberger is something of a provocateur, but his accusation is not without merit; in some cases, environmentalism does function as a dominant worldview in the West, displacing the Judeo-Christian tradition as the narrative that is understood to best explain the world. However, that should be seen as an opportunity rather than a cause for alarm for faithful Christians. The history of environmentalism in the United States since the Industrial Revolution reveals both the engagement in environmental causes by Christians and the dangers of that engagement.

This chapter begins by highlighting environmental concern as deeply connected to religion though much of history. Then it engages with the Lynn White thesis that Christianity is at fault for contemporary ecological problems. It then briefly surveys the history of environmentalism in the West since the Industrial Revolution. The chapter concludes with a brief discussion of the relationship of evangelical Christians to the environmental movement.

[1.] Michael Shellenberger, *Apocalypse Never: Why Environmental Alarmism Hurt Us All* (New York: Harper Collins, 2020), 263.

ENVIRONMENTALISM AND RELIGION

Humans are an inherently religious species. In the beginning, God made humanity in his own image, and ever since then we have been trying to return the favor. There are no cultures without gods of some sort. Often these gods are made of wood or stone (Isa 44:9–20), though they may be understood to exist in the form of animals or in the spirit of ancestors. Despite attempts by modern philosophers to uproot metanarratives as central to human experience,[2] the hunger for meaning and purpose that religion provides drives humans to be mythmakers.[3]

Ancient Humanity and Nature

In his seminal work *Traces on the Rhodian Shore*, Clarence Glacken writes,

> In ancient and modern times alike, theology and geography have often been closely related studies because they meet at crucial points of human curiosity. If we seek after the nature of God, we must consider the nature of man and the earth, and if we look at the earth, questions of divine purpose in its creation and of the role of mankind on it inevitably arise.[4]

Glacken's thesis and analysis seem fairly obvious once pointed out. After all, creation narratives that focus on the place of humanity within the created order are a nearly universal phenomenon across human cultures.[5]

For example, Glacken highlights the theme of humanity's place in nature in the story of Prometheus. He argues, "This may represent an early attempt to explain how man, a part of nature, has a position with relation to it far different from that of other forms of life."[6] Similarly,

---

[2.] See Jean-Francois Lyotard, *The Postmodern Condition: A Report on Knowledge* (Minneapolis: University of Minnesota Press, 1984), 14–23.

[3.] Joseph Campbell, *The Hero with a Thousand Faces*, 2nd ed. (Princeton: Princeton University Press, 1968), 3–25.

[4.] Clarence Glacken, *Traces on the Rhodian Shore: Nature and Culture in Western Thought from Ancient Times to the End of the Eighteenth Century* (Berkeley: University of California Press, 1967), 35.

[5.] Campbell, *The Hero with a Thousand Faces*, 255–95.

[6.] Glacken, *Traces on the Rhodian Shore*, 41.

Aristotle was wrestling with purpose within nature, and Cicero was wrestling with human impact on the planet.[7] Thus, according to Glacken, "Man becomes a kind of caretaker of the earth; his cultivation combats disease, and his struggles with the wild animals exercise a control over excesses which might occur without his superintendence."[8] Some of the questions that are central to environmental ethics have been at the core of human thought since the beginning of recorded history. Glacken's hefty volume, which surveys a massive span of culture, undermines much of the recency bias of environmentalism and obliterates accusations that humanity's special place in creation is a unique feature of the Judeo-Christian tradition.

The common thread of a special role for humans in creation across religions is exactly what a thoughtful Christian should expect because general revelation provides real, but limited, access to true information about the world (Rom 1:19–23). There is, therefore, some truth embedded in all religions as they try to make sense of cosmic reality.[9] Given that for much of human history, mere existence has been a battle for survival against an environment that can kill quickly or slowly through storm or through drought, it should not surprise us that the human relationship with creation has been deeply religious and that it has often been antagonistic.

Modern Humanity and Nature

The modern human in the developed world is a highly unusual figure, historically speaking. When I was working at a summer camp in college, we received a busload of high schoolers from New York City who were still giggling about seeing cows for the first time as they stepped off the bus. They were aghast that the cabins were not air-conditioned and surprised at how little of the camp's surface was paved. There are many adults I work with now who have never eaten anything they have killed or experienced the delight of gathering vegetables from the garden. There is an awe toward creation that comes from being aware

---

[7.] Glacken, 46–49.

[8.] Glacken, 59–60.

[9.] C. S. Lewis, "Religion without Dogma?", in *Essay Collection and Other Short Pieces* (London: HarperCollins, 2000), 165–66.

of the processes in nature that threaten and provide. For the Christian, awe is shaped by understanding this is God's creation. For the pagan, fear and hope lead to attempts to worship and placate nature's gods. In both cases, the result is fundamentally religious.

Among orthodox Christians, there has been some backlash against "the environmentalist Litany [that] provides the foundation of an alternate religion or worldview for those who reject Western civilization."[10] Christians should not be surprised when big ideas like the preservation of the environment become dominant concerns such that "a religion with a vision of sin and repentance, heaven and hell," develops.[11] As we are reminded in Eccl 3:11, the basic truths of the universe are written on the human heart. This results in distortions apart from the special revelation of Scripture, but paganized attempts at self-salvation sometimes improve receptivity to the gospel.

Indeed, I agree with C. S. Lewis that if our culture actually returned to a form of paganism, it would be easier to evangelize.[12] This is because the chief problem Lewis encountered in evangelism is comfortable apathy toward concepts like salvation and sin.[13] The same seems true today. When someone is deeply interested in an environmentalist worldview—pagan, materialistic, or deistic—there are clear cultural points of contact that can provide a beachhead for the gospel. Honor of creation presents opportunities, as Paul found in Acts 17, to point beyond nature to the reality of the Creator.

Therefore, while we may recognize that for some environmentalism is a sort of religion that competes with Christianity, we may also find that the truth of Christianity can outcompete that religion by virtue of its internal coherence and correspondence with reality.[14] The challenge is for us to communicate and embody that truth in such a way that people struggling with futility are willing to ask us about our

---

[10.] James Wanliss, *Resisting the Green Dragon: Dominion, Not Death* (Burke, VA: Cornwall Alliance for the Stewardship of Creation, 2010), 38.

[11.] Wanliss, 38.

[12.] C. S. Lewis, "Is Theism Important?", in *Essay Collection and Other Short Pieces* (London: HarperCollins, 2000), 54.

[13.] C. S. Lewis, "Christian Apologetics," in *Essay Collection and Other Short Pieces* (London: HarperCollins, 2000), 152–53.

[14.] Francis Schaeffer, *Escape from Reason*, in *The Complete Works of Francis A. Schaeffer* (Wheaton: Crossway, 1983), 1:218–19.

hope (1 Pet 3:15). Unfortunately, too often Christians have found themselves the subject of blame for environmental woes.

IS CHRISTIANITY TO BLAME?

Lynn Townsend White Jr. gave a talk at the 1966 meeting of the American Association for the Advancement of Science that has had an outsized influence on the last half century of dialogue about environmentalism and Christianity. A historian of science, White set the narrative for many histories of environmentalism in the West with his 1967 essay, "The Historical Roots of Our Ecological Crisis," where he puts the blame squarely on Christianity and Christendom.

According to White, the Christian missionary Boniface cutting down the sacred grove and building a church was a statement of humanity's dominance over nature, not of the supremacy of YHWH over the Norse gods.[15] This attitude of dominance led to development of the metal plowshare, and thereby Christianity has literally ruined the world. The solution White proposes is for Christianity to become less Christian by adopting elements of the pagan religions that it displaced.

The impact of the White thesis on the attitudes about the environment remains an unfortunate case of too much weight being placed in a faulty vessel.[16] As we have already observed, Glacken's efforts in *Traces on the Rhodian Shore* undermine the idea that Christianity is uniquely at fault because he shows that all Western religions (at least) are anthropocentric to some degree.[17] Moreover, John Gatta argues, "It remains unclear what practical ecological consequences can be traced

---

[15.] Lynn White Jr., "The Historical Roots of Our Ecological Crisis," in *Ecology and Life* (Waco: Word, 1988), 125–37.

[16.] The weakness in White's approach is recognized by some who celebrate his "environmentalist critique of the Judeo-Christian world view." J. Baird Callicott, *In Defense of the Land Ethic: Essays in Environmental Philosophy* (Albany, NY: State University of New York Press, 1989), 137. At the same time, Callicott recognized that White misses how the transcendence of God enables what he calls *intrinsic* value in creation, which more closely approximates what I refer to as *inherent* value. Callicott, *In Defense of the Land Ethic*, 136–37.

[17.] Glacken, *Traces on the Rhodian Shore*, vii–xii. J. Douma argues the debate over Christianity as an anthropocentric religion is unhelpful because it generally presumes the options are a focus on the good of humanity or the good of creation, rather than a *theocentric* position that focuses on the good of God. J. Douma, *Environmental Stewardship*, ed. Nelson D. Kloosterman, trans. Albert H. Oosterhoff (Eugene, OR: Wipf & Stock, 2015), 33–35.

to any society's religious beliefs."[18] Thus, there are strong counterexamples, like deforestation caused by Buddhist cultic practices despite their pantheistic leanings. It may be that the link between professed doctrine and practice is a universal weakness of all religions. Nevertheless, Lynn White's critique of Christian theology is often the focal point for discussions of Christianity and the environment.

White's Continued Influence

White's thesis became the idea that launched a thousand ships, though in this case they went in different directions. There have been basically four responses to White's thesis. Some Christians—those who see modernity as a source for Christian theology—tend to see White's thesis as correct and try to modify Christianity to improve its environmental impact, often by making Christianity more pantheistic.[19] Some readers have rejected White's thesis, arguing that his understanding of historic Christianity is flawed.[20] Others have ignored his thesis entirely as simply another attempt to justify turning from orthodoxy. Still others have accepted there is a kernel of truth in what White wrote and tried to show that real Christianity is better for the environment than what he presented.[21] As Sabrina Danielsen notes, the White thesis has choked out more helpful responses to environmental ethics because White's accusations, rather than the issues themselves, have become the focus of the debate.[22]

White's basic argument is that Western Christianity devalues creation, promoting a dualistic framework that treats the physical world as *merely* existing for human benefit. White puts the blame on Christianity for de-paganizing the world because, he argues, Christian missionaries chopped down the sacred groves and taught the barbarians that there

---

[18.] John Gatta, *Making Nature Sacred: Literature, Religion, and Environment in America from the Puritans to the Present* (New York: Oxford University Press, 2004), 22.

[19.] See Richard Means, "Why Worry about Nature?", in *The Complete Works of Francis A. Schaeffer* (Wheaton: Crossway, 1982), 5:71–76.

[20.] See Francis Schaeffer, *Pollution and the Death of Man*, in *The Complete Works of Francis A. Schaeffer* (Wheaton: Crossway, 1982), 5:3–55.

[21.] For example, H. Paul Santmire, *The Travail of Nature: The Ambiguous Promise of Christian Theology* (Minneapolis: Fortress, 1985).

[22.] Sabrina Danielsen, "Fracturing over Creation Care? Shifting Environmental Beliefs among Evangelicals, 1984–2010," in *Journal for the Scientific Study of Religion* 52, no. 1 (2013): 201–2.

was one true God in spirit form and that the nyads and dryads of their mythologies were false gods. The solution, according to White, is to adopt a more pagan conception of reality, viewing the world as sacred and adapting Christianity to a more nature-centric worship.

White is generally correct about his diagnosis of the problem: a great deal of environmental damage has been done because of a devaluation of creation. A lack of concern for the created order is endemic in Western society, which can be seen in the sort of economy that prioritizes convenience, expedience, and comfort over nearly any other attribute. Consumers—humans with purchasing power—are at the center of the economy and the structure of society. There is no question that the status quo is disenchanted and that evaluating decisions from an ecological perspective is a secondary concern. White asserts that the source of the problem is Christianity, specifically the dualistic view of creation held by Christians.

Like many attempts to find the one thing that is the root cause of a large cultural trend, White's explanation falls short. White tried to claim that Christianity is at the root of everything that is wrong with the environment. However, particularly in the United States, environmentalism has been enabled by a distinctly Christian ethos. As environmental historian Evan Berry argues, "American environmentalism is related to religion, not out of serendipitous resemblance but by way of historically demonstrable genealogical affinity with Christian theological tradition."[23] His extended discussion proves there is not only a terminological, but also a conceptual connection between strains of Christian theology and American environmentalism. He notes, "American environmentalism is premised on an ethic of salvation, grounded in efforts to transcend human depravity."[24] There is a deep affinity between many environmental arguments and modernistic theological concepts of the early twentieth century.[25] This affinity is so apparent that one environmentalist has described the movement as "Calvinism without God."[26] Therefore, it is not Christianity per se

---

[23.] Berry, *Devoted to Nature*, 2 (see chap. 1, n. 31).

[24.] Berry, 187.

[25.] Berry, 82.

[26.] Robert H. Nelson, "Calvinism without God: American Environmentalism as Implicit Calvinism," *Implicit Religion* 17, no. 3 (2014): 249–73.

that presents a problem to White, but certain Christian doctrines he does not like.

Dualism and Creation

Whatever White got wrong, he was correct that a major issue that leads to abuse of creation is a low view of nature. He is correct that a form of dualism that sees creation as evil or, at best, not truly good has contributed to that low view, especially as materialism evolved from dualism through Deism.[27] The problem, therefore, is not that Christianity is bad for the environment, but that bad Christian theology is bad for the environment.

Though Christianity has been frequently blamed for the environmental problems of the world, that blame properly rests on modernity.[28] When Christians influenced by modernity abuse creation, it is because they are not properly living out the basic principles of their faith. Simply put, White's critique of Christianity as the source of the problems of the environment falls short because he does not critique an orthodox Christianity. White seems to be engaging with a version of Christianity more inspired by a sociological construction, like that of Max Weber, than engaging with central theological sources in the Christian tradition.

Max Weber's work has encouraged the development of a common caricature of Protestants, particularly the Calvinistic American Puritans.[29] Building on Ernst Troeltsch's evolutionary understanding of religion, Weber proposed a largely utilitarian and self-serving origin to the capitalist economic system that was heavily influenced on a Calvinist conception of the created order.[30] According to J. Douma, "Many [environmentalists] use the connection [Weber] laid between Calvinism and capitalism to link pollution in a capitalist society with

---

[27.] Olson, *Story of Christian Theology*, 530 (see chap. 1, n. 28).

[28.] Andrew Spencer, "The Modernistic Roots of Our Ecological Crisis: The Lynn White Thesis at Fifty," in *Journal of Markets & Morality* 22, no. 2 (Fall 2019): 355–71.

[29.] Weber's approach can be seen in the influence over basic readings, like that in Jeffrey Bilbro, *Loving God's Wilderness: The Christian Roots of Ecological Ethics in American Literature* (Tuscaloosa: The University of Alabama Press, 2015), 1, 183.

[30.] Peter Ghosh, *Max Weber and the Protestant Ethic: Twin Histories* (New York: Oxford University Press, 2014), 85–101.

those who cause it [i.e., the capitalist society]."[31] This link, he argues, is not very strong. Instead, abuse of the environment is a human problem rooted in sin because of the fall of humanity.

Environmental abuse has existed among Christians, yet so have intentionally positive approaches to caring for creation. In his discussion on the religious roots of the environmental movement in America, Mark Stoll argues that the Calvinism that dominated New England taught early settlers to respect the created order.[32] The Puritans valued creation and desired order because the world belonged to God.[33] Thus, they set aside land for natural areas, regulated sound farming practices, and encouraged wise use of God's created order.[34] As early as 1626, the Plymouth Colony created ordinances to regulate the cutting and sale of timbers. In 1634, Plymouth settlers prohibited the setting of forest fires.[35] The early American settlers took these steps *because* they were Christian. Unfortunately, intentional care for creation was not a consistent feature of the cultural Christianity that dominated the West before, during, and after the Industrial Revolution.[36]

ENVIRONMENTALISM IN THE WEST

The Industrial Revolution often serves as the landmark for environmental deterioration. When that seismic change in technology began, the human population was much smaller, and the ability for humans to negatively impact the environment was, relatively speaking, limited.[37] Population densities tended to be much lower because a much higher portion of the population was engaged in farming on a small scale. But even prior to the Industrial Revolution, despite the limited population of humans, there is evidence of extinction of animal species

---

[31.] Douma, *Environmental Stewardship*, 14.

[32.] Stoll, *Inherit the Holy Mountain*, 2 (see chap. 1, n. 30).

[33.] Leland Ryken, *Worldly Saints: The Puritans as They Really Were* (Grand Rapids: Zondervan, 1986), 15.

[34.] Stoll, *Inherit the Holy Mountain*, 54–111.

[35.] Roderick Nash, *American Environmentalism: Readings in Conservation History* (New York: McGraw-Hill, 1990), xi.

[36.] Gatta, *Making Nature Sacred*, 15–33.

[37.] Joshtrom Isaac Kureethadam, *Creation in Crisis: Science, Ethics, Theology* (Maryknoll, NY: Orbis, 2014), 45.

due to human interaction, desertification of previously rich lands, and dangerous pollution due to human activity.[38] Although human impact existed, it was limited because the global population was kept small and had shorter lifespans due to a relative lack of resources and medical technology. The Industrial Revolution led to technological advancements, which served to lengthen life expectancies and thus caused the global population to increase dramatically. At the beginning of the nineteenth century, there were about 1 billion humans on the planet. Earth's population is estimated to have exceeded 8 billion at the end of 2022.[39] Even by the mid-nineteenth century, the impact of humans on the ecosystem was evident to careful observers.

George Perkins Marsh wrote a volume that was influential in creating the conservation movement.[40] In his 1864 book, *Man and Nature*, his purpose was

> to indicate the character and, approximately, the extent of the changes produced by human action in the physical conditions of the globe we inhabit; to point out the dangers of imprudence and the necessity of caution in the operation which, on a large scale, interfere with the spontaneous arrangements of the organic or the inorganic world; to suggest the possibility and the importance of the restoration of disturbed harmonies and the material improvement of waste and exhausted regions; and, incidentally, to illustrate the doctrine that man is, in both kind and degree, a power of a higher order than any of the other forms of animated life, which, like him are nourished at the table of bounteous nature.[41]

Marsh was one of the first to treat concern for human disruption of the created order in a systematic fashion, recognizing the

---

38. Douma, *Environmental Stewardship*, 8.

39. See "World Population Prospects 2022," United Nations Department of Economic and Social Affairs, accessed November 14, 2022, https://www.un.org/development/desa/pd/sites/www .un.org.development.desa.pd/files/wpp2022_summary_of_results.pdf.

40. Benjamin Kline, *First Along the River: A Brief History of the U.S. Environmental Movement* (New York: Rowman and Littlefield, 2011), 53.

41. George Marsh, *Man and Nature: Or, Physical Geography as Modified by Human Nature* (Cambridge, MA: Harvard University Press, 1967), 3.

potential of that disruption at a macroscopic level. Marsh saw that human action necessarily changed the balance of the created order and caused ecosystems to change, often in ways that were never desired or anticipated.

Conservation and Preservation

In the early twentieth century, as the effects of the Industrial Revolution were becoming more apparent, both through the cumulative effects of pollution and the increasing population, the three distinct camps on the spectrum of environmentalism emerged: consumption, preservation, and conservation. Consumption is "the attitude of using up a resource without regard to the foreseeable future."[42] This is what Douma calls having a "'cowboy economy' that follows the principle 'use something once and then pitch it.'"[43] Preservation is the opposite pole of an attitude of consumption and argues, "Nature [has] objective value, value in her own right. Humans [are] part and parcel of nature and to harm her [is] not only evil in itself, but also [has] long-term repercussions for posterity."[44] Proponents of preservation, like John Muir, argued human development runs contrary to God's design for the world, and thus, pristine wilderness must be preserved.[45] Conservation sits somewhere between these two poles. According to Pojman, in the early days of the discussion, "the conservationists argued that while nature and its accompanying wilderness had significant aesthetic value, their greatest use was as a *resource* for the human good."[46] Conservationists, like Gifford Pinchot, argued for a utilitarian approach to the created order in which nature is valued for its beauty but natural resources are used for the benefit of humans in the most efficient manner.[47] Attitudes of consumption have been popularly applied, but there are very few advocates for the position in principle. The most significant debate

---

[42.] Louis P. Pojman, *Global Environmental Ethics: Readings and Application* (Mountain View, CA: Mayfield, 2000), 155.

[43.] Douma, *Environmental Stewardship*, 53. It is not clear whether Douma is quoting someone or simply using scare quotes.

[44.] Pojman, *Global Environmental Ethics*, 155.

[45.] Bilbro, *Loving God's Wilderness*, 97.

[46.] Pojman, *Global Environmental Ethics*, 154–55.

[47.] See Pojman, *Global Environmental Ethics*, 154–57.

has occurred between advocates of conservation and preservation, with Pinchot and Muir as key spokesmen.

One of Muir's primary concerns in his evangelistic crusade for wilderness was for general revelation to function as the primary source for environmental ethics.[48] A literalistic approach to Scripture, which reflects a sort of Baconian scientific method of inductive study, was appropriated by Muir and applied to nature.[49] Thus, Muir presented observation of nature and reading of nature writing as an essential part of becoming a disciple of the wilderness.[50] The rationalist idea that true knowledge of ultimate truth can be obtained through the observation of nature deeply shaped Muir's concepts of the value of creation and the impact of humans on the created order.

Muir's perception of the intrinsic value of the created order stands in contrast to the largely instrumental understanding held by Gifford Pinchot. Pinchot is hated by some in the preservationist movement for his utilitarian approach to environmentalism. His idea of conservation proposed to maximize the benefit of natural resources for humans. He wrote, "The first great fact about conservation is that it stands for development. . . . Conservation does mean provision for the future, but it means also and first of all the recognition of the right of the present generation to the fullest necessary use of all the resources with which this country is so abundantly blessed."[51] This perspective was opposed to Muir's quest for preservation of as much land as possible.

Pinchot's conservationism calls for the elimination of waste of natural resources. In particular, Pinchot provides the example of fighting forest fires, which were previously "considered simply and solely as acts of God, against which any opposition was hopeless and any attempt to control them not merely hopeless but childish."[52] This desire for waste prevention leads Pinchot to argue, "The first duty of the human race is to control the earth it lives upon."[53] Such a bold proclamation stands

---

[48.] John Pierce, "'Christianity and Mountainanity': The Restoration Movement's Influence on John Muir," in *Religion and the Arts* 17 (2013): 122.

[49.] Pierce, "'Christianity and Mountainanity,'" 118.

[50.] Gatta, *Making Nature Sacred*, 148–57.

[51.] Gifford Pinchot, "The Birth of 'Conservation,'" in *American Environmentalism: Readings in Conservation History*, ed. Roderick Nash (New York: McGraw-Hill, 1990), 76.

[52.] Pinchot, 77.

[53.] Pinchot, 77.

in stark contrast to some theological understandings of the human role in the created order, but it also serves to illustrate the significance of the question for a theology of creation care.

Despite the popularity of Muir's approach in our time, in the late nineteenth to early twentieth centuries, such arguments were less likely to compel a change of heart among people who still assumed the uniqueness of humanity. Pinchot's arguments were based on economics and appealed to prosperity. They were opposed by individuals in the coal and timber industries who would be regulated by the federal appropriation of land; however, the idea of wise stewardship and efficient use was more readily accepted by the American population. As a result, Pinchot's argumentation succeeded over Muir's.[54] Though Muir and his supporters were unsuccessful in achieving their ultimate ends, their arguments have influenced later environmental discussions as Muir's reverential language about nature is reflected in the deep ecology movement and in writers like Aldo Leopold.

Another Wave of Environmentalism

In the United States after WWII, the environmental movement began to shift away from arguments about the use of national parks and toward a more holistic view of ecology.[55] In 1949, Aldo Leopold published his classic work, *A Sand County Almanac*, arguing for an approach to environmentalism that rejects an "Abrahamic concept of land," which allows for humans to "abuse land because we regard it as a commodity belonging to us."[56] Instead of valuing earth instrumentally, he argued for the ecosystem to be viewed as a community in which humans live. Leopold's land ethic contained a subtle rejection of Judeo-Christian sources for environmental ethics; he correlated a biblical approach to nature with environmental destruction.[57] Leopold, who was raised a Lutheran, created an entire approach to environmental ethics in his

---

[54.] For an engaging discussion of the manner of argumentation of both men in their debates, see Michael B. Smith, "The Value of a Tree: Public Debates of John Muir and Gifford Pinchot," *Historian* 60, no. 4 (Summer 1998): 757–78.

[55.] Kline, *First Along the River*, 79–93.

[56.] Aldo Leopold, *A Sand County Almanac: And Sketches Here and There* (New York: Ballentine, 1968), xviii.

[57.] Leopold does argue that prophets like Isaiah and Ezekiel opposed environmental destruction but

writing that relied on a non-instrumental view of creation's value.[58] He had been a forester committed to a managed conservationist approach, such as was championed by Pinchot, but became disenchanted with the practice of exterminating predators.[59] He began to see the value native within the created order, though he did not revere nature as Muir did. Leopold did not fully embrace an independent, intrinsic value in nature but appears to have valued the integrity of nature inherently. Leopold's land ethic was a reasonable step forward toward a more appropriate environmental ethics.

Often cited as the beginning point of contemporary environmentalism, Rachel Carson published her landmark book, *Silent Spring*, in 1962. Carson was a naturalist who wrote lyrical pleas for the environment and created images of a dystopia with the environment denuded by widespread pesticide spraying and the population riddled with cancer from a buildup of carcinogens.[60] During the writing, Carson was herself dying of breast cancer, which may have increased her concern for carcinogens.[61] *Silent Spring* pointed to environmental despoliation but did not explicitly implicate a Judeo-Christian worldview as the root problem. However, her volume accelerated the growth of what is now the deep ecology movement. Carson was also a significant figure in the popularizing of environmental writing; she was able to inspire a reevaluation of the human relationship with nature through her writing.[62] As the issue of environmentalism came into focus, her contribution of a romanticized description of pristine nature and the devastating effects of humans on it inspired a genre of nonfiction. This attitude was evident in the shift in content of popular writing, especially among writings that concerned the pursuit of scientific knowledge and tied that to environmentalism.

As we will discuss in more detail in chapter 5, for many in the

---

notes that society did not accept their view. Leopold, *A Sand County Almanac,* 239. Leopold's overall attitude is a casual dismissal of Christianity rather than overt hostility like other, later, commentators.

[58.] Nelson, "Calvinism without God," 260.

[59.] Frank Stewart, *A Natural History of Nature Writing* (Washington, DC: Island Press, 1995), 143–52.

[60.] See Rachel Carson, *Silent Spring* (Boston: Houghton Mifflin, 2002).

[61.] William Souder, *On a Farther Shore: The Life and Legacy of Rachel Carson* (New York: Crown Publishers, 2012), 306–9.

[62.] Charles T. Rubin, *The Green Crusade: Rethinking the Roots of Environmentalism* (Lanham, MD: Rowman & Littlefield, 1998), 35.

environmental movement, contemporary scientific data is often presented as the final authority for environmental ethics. For example, Paul and Anne Ehrlich explicitly pit religious ideas against science, which has become an increasing and unhelpful aspect of environmentalism.[63] This has led some environmental activists, like Naomi Klein, to cheer any sign of change of religious doctrines to being more "green."[64] More dangerously, a concern for open and honest engagement has been replaced by calls for an overwhelming level of propagandistic capture of media, religion, and history to lobby for particular policy outcomes.[65] In the United States, environmentalism has been a uniquely para-Christian movement. As the movement has gained cultural dominance, it has sometimes threatened to detach itself from the worldview and values that have supplied its moral force. Given this trend in some very vocal segments of the environmental movement, it is apparent why theologically conservative Christians have often resisted the ideologies of environmentalism.

EVANGELICALS AND THE ENVIRONMENT

The track record on environmental ethics for theological conservatives in the United States is not one of our points of strength, though it is far from the total loss often attributed by critics of evangelicalism. As Francis Schaeffer argued, "a truly biblical Christianity has a real answer to the ecological crisis."[66] There are understandable reasons why conservative Christians were not at the center of the ecological movement even when they participated. Some of the reasons for the limited cooperation were political, some were sociological, and some were theological. There are varying degrees of legitimacy in the resistance.

The theological objections were not primarily about environmental ethics itself, but about association with progressive theologies. Historian Evan Berry notes, "As the cult of nature made strong inroads

---

[63.] Paul and Anne Ehrlich, *The Betrayal of Science and Reason* (Washington, DC: Island Press, 1996), 26–28.

[64.] E.g., Klein, *On Fire*, 137–48 (see introduction, n. 7).

[65.] Klein, *On Fire*, 271.

[66.] Schaeffer, *Pollution and the Death of Man*, 5:47.

into mainstream American religious life, it met with careful resistance from clerical authorities and theological conservatives."[67] In light of the polarized attitudes driven in part by the 1925 Scopes trial, there was a greater openness to the spiritualization of nature among progressive theologians and clergy and thus an opposing resistance to environmental ethics by theological conservatives as a result of that spiritualization. Many religious leaders were "anxious about the potential of nature worship to erode the theological foundations of Christianity, especially with respect to the idea of a personal savior."[68] Their concerns were often warranted.

Evangelical Concerns

One major worry of evangelicals has been that environmentalism will lead people away from an orthodox faith, and there are many examples which appear to prove that true. As Mark Stoll notes, "A high proportion of leading figures in environmental history had religious childhoods. . . . Curiously, few (and after 1900, hardly any) were churchgoers as adults."[69] It is not clear where the division between correlation and causation should be drawn and which direction the arrow should point. I will not endeavor to solve that riddle here. I will simply observe that the fears of many theological conservatives were not unfounded, even if they were imprecise or resulted in an improper response.

Given the signs of theological drift among many environmentally engaged Christians, open resistance to environmentalism does not seem unwarranted. However, to be fair to mid-twentieth century evangelicals, their responses to environmentalism were not entirely negative. David Larsen argues,

Although evangelicals have often been painted as opposed to environmentalism, very nearly the opposite is the case as mainstream evangelical leaders proved surprisingly receptive to the claims of environmentalism. Nevertheless, evangelical interest in this issue tended to wax and wane along with the wider culture,

---

[67.] Berry, *Devoted to Nature*, 152.

[68.] Berry, 153.

[69.] Stoll, *Inherit the Holy Mountain*, 2.

to be articulated through the ambiguous language of steward-ship, and to be confined by characteristic evangelical impulses leading them to prefer personal over structural action, to seek specifically evangelical solutions to environmental problems, and to focus on what were deemed to be the spiritual pitfalls of the wider environmental movement. An evangelical minority com-posed of anti-environmental "minimizers" and "otherworldly apocalypticists" has repeatedly been misconstrued by the wider culture as the representative voice of the evangelical movement.[70]

Larsen's dissertation provides extensive documentation from evan-gelical periodicals of people writing in support of environmentalism.[71] There are fewer books on the environment until the 1990s and onward by theological conservative Christians than by more liberal-leaning Christians.[72] However, the primary cause of that does not seem to be a total lack of interest or wholesale rejection of environmental causes.[73]

It seems sometimes what is considered "anti-environmentalism" is actually a reflection of differences of opinion about what necessary actions should result from a robustly biblical environmental ethics. Katharine Wilkinson documents the balanced approach many evan-gelical leaders and individual churchgoers have taken. She notes that there has been a general growth in interest in creation care. However, she argues that some forms of environmentalism from an evangelical perspective are "overtly anthropocentric" because "some Christians criticize secular environmentalism for inverting the ranks of creation and equalizing incommensurate beings."[74] Nevertheless, Wilkinson tends to be more positive toward those who hold their theology firmly while trying to balance ethical concerns.

[70.] David Larsen, "God's Gardeners: American Protestant Evangelicals Confront Environmental-ism, 1967–2000" (PhD diss., University of Chicago, 2001), 4.

[71.] See, for example, the fifty years of essays in *Christianity Today* recently published as a collected volume: *Stewards of the Earth* (Bellingham, WA: Lexham, 2022).

[72.] Robert Booth Fowler, *The Greening of Protestant Thought* (Chapel Hill, NC: The University of Chapel Hill Press, 1995), 13–19.

[73.] Henry describes the difference in goals between conservative and liberal Protestants and then helps explain the difference in social emphases, including in publishing. Carl F. H. Henry, "Evangeli-cals in the Social Struggle," in *Architect of Evangelicalism* (Bellingham, WA: Lexham, 2022), 43–44.

[74.] Katharine Wilkinson, *Between God and Green: How Evangelicals Are Cultivating a Middle Ground on Climate Change* (New York: Oxford University Press, 2012), 34.

In contrast, critics like Roger Gottlieb argue "religious environmentalism and fundamentalism will always be in opposition."[75] Gottlieb lumps all believers concerned with orthodoxy into the "fundamentalist" category, as he defines a fundamentalist as someone who "cannot accept a world in which all traditions, including his own, have become a matter of choice."[76] It is thus only in a desperate grab for legitimacy in a changing world that "the fundamentalist grasps at a vision of an eternally fixed and universally true source of authority to stem the tide."[77] Alvin Plantinga describes this use of the term as "something like 'stupid sumbitch whose theological opinions are considerably to the right of mine.'"[78] Sometimes it is a wonder that theologically conservative Christians become involved in environmentalism at all since amid the friendly cooperation there are frequent rebuffs leveled at those not willing to agree on other issues. Such concerns are often rejected out of hand as merely part of a self-invented culture war.

Environment and the Culture Wars

Stoll explains apparent evangelical disengagement from creation care in this way: "In the late 1970s, conservatives declared what they termed a culture war and opposed most liberal initiatives (including environmentalism), along with homosexuality and abortion, in the name of family and traditional values."[79] This matches Gottlieb's explanation that "fundamentalism arises when people are threatened by dramatic and seemingly uncontrollable change" where traditional beliefs are "undermined by secularism, women's rights, technology, consumerism, and increased encounters with people of different cultures."[80] This is not unlike how the self-described evangelical climate scientist Katharine Hayhoe describes resistance to climate science among evangelicals as the result of fear. She writes, "Societal change is happening faster today than at any time in our lifetimes, and many are afraid they're already

---

[75.] Roger Gottlieb, *A Greener Faith: Religious Environmentalism and Our Planet's Future* (New York: Oxford University Press, 2006), 223.

[76.] Gottlieb, 221.

[77.] Gottlieb, 222.

[78.] Alvin Plantinga, *Knowledge and Christian Belief* (Grand Rapids: Eerdmans, 2015), 55.

[79.] Stoll, *Inherit the Holy Mountain*, 7.

[80.] Gottlieb, *A Greener Faith*, 221.

being left behind. That fear drives tribalism."[81] Given the real hostility toward orthodox Christians by many in society, such fears are not entirely unjustified.[82] Even if fear is a driver for limited enthusiasm toward environmentalism among some conservatives, religious and irreligious, it is not clear those concerns are unwarranted. Evangelical attitudes toward environmentalism have been impacted by real overlap between the green movement and other, less acceptable, social movements.[83]

Hayhoe notes that "climate change touches every single one of the issues that fill the headlines."[84] That has sometimes been a point of ridicule by those on the political right, but the pervasiveness of climate in media streams is not entirely coincidental: it has been encouraged by climate activists. As Naomi Klein declares,

> When it comes to climate action, it's abundantly clear that we will not build the power necessary to win unless we embed justice— particularly racial but also gender and economic justice—at the center of our low-carbon policies. *Intersectionality* . . . is the only path forward. We cannot play "My crisis is more urgent than your crisis"—war trumps climate; climate trumps class; class trumps gender; gender trumps race.[85]

For Klein, to work for environmental good, one has to sign on to the whole package of "justice" as she defines it. Klein also advocates for propaganda to overtake every channel of communication.[86] As Jacques Ellul notes, "Propaganda must be total. The propagandist must utilize all of the technical means at his disposal."[87] This sort of blending of issues and open propagandization helps explain the rise of the resistance to environmentalism among some social conservatives. In

[81]. Hayhoe, *Saving Us*, 6 (see introduction, n. 2).

[82]. George Yancey, *Hostile Environment: Understanding and Responding to Anti-Christian Bias* (Downers Grove: IVP, 2015), 14–22.

[83]. For example, Kim A. Lawton, "Is There Room for Prolife Environmentalists?," in *Steward of the Earth* (Bellingham, WA: Lexham Press, 2022), 72–76.

[84]. Hayhoe, *Saving Us*, 127.

[85]. Klein, *On Fire*, 194.

[86]. Klein, 271–78.

[87]. Jacques Ellul, *Propaganda: The Formation of Men's Attitudes* (New York: Vintage, 1965), 9.

particular, the association of abortion with environmentalism remains problematic.[88]

The SBC and the Environment

The Southern Baptist Convention (SBC) is now known as one of the most socially and theologically conservative denominations in the United States, but before a strenuous effort toward theological renewal in the late 1970s and early 1980s, the SBC was more closely aligned to many moderate to liberal mainline Protestant denominations. This included advocacy for social issues like the environment. The interest level of the SBC closely mirrors the US sociopolitical attitudes about controversial issues, like abortion and the environment. The approach of the SBC has varied based on the theological leanings of the those controlling the SBC as well as the nature of the ongoing cultural debate.

In 1967, the same year White published his essay denigrating orthodox Christianity, the messengers to the SBC approved a resolution that "commends to those married couples who desire it and who may be benefited by it, the judicious use of medically approved methods of planned parenthood and the dissemination of planned parenthood information."[89] Although this list does not explicitly include abortion, at the same time the Christian Life Commission (precursor to the Ethics and Religious Liberty Commission) called for Baptists to be open to many means of population control including "abortion, sterilization and contraceptives to the unmarried."[90] Meanwhile a sociology professor at an SBC-affiliated college published *The Case for Compulsory Birth Control.* The thesis of that volume is consistent with the title. Chasteen openly argues for abortion[91] and even predicts intersectionality by presenting a therapeutic vision of sex.[92] He also declares "the cancer of runaway population growth has eaten away both heart and soul of the body politic," which leads him to conclude that "we are on

---

[88.] See Andrew Spencer, "Three Reasons Why Evangelicals Stopped Advocating for the Environment," in *Stewards of Creation* (Bellingham, WA: Lexham Press, 2022), 254–61.

[89.] Southern Baptist Convention, "Resolution on the Population Explosion," December 1, 2020, https://www.sbc.net/resource-library/resolutions/resolution-on-population-explosion/.

[90.] Aaron Weaver, "Baptist Environmentalisms" (PhD diss., Baylor University, 2013), 112.

[91.] Chasteen, *The Case for Compulsory Birth Control,* 155–60 (see chap. 1, n. 24).

[92.] Chasteen, 184–89.

the verge of anarchy."[93] Therefore, even increasing crime and police brutality was the fault of overpopulation.[94] Many socially progressive issues have been clustered under an environmental heading,[95] which has proved to be unhelpful to the best interests of creation.

Environmentalism as a Progressive Shibboleth

During the mid-twentieth century, the environmental movement was more of a common-cause issue than a polarizing issue. Gross pollution in the 1960s was a unifying issue. In 1969 the Cuyahoga River burning caught national attention and became a rallying point for environmentalism and helped launch the first Earth Day in 1970. It was originally a bipartisan event.[96] Meanwhile, more than a decade of lobbying against indiscriminate pesticide use, led by Rachel Carson, eventually resulted in the ban of DDT in 1972.[97] It was the Republican president Richard Nixon who created the Environmental Protection Agency and called for a commission to study the relationship between the rising population and American prosperity.[98] The commission's report, *Population and the American Future*, published in 1972, helped cement environmentalism as a progressive political issue in the minds of many American Christians. The committee returned with recommendations, including legalization of abortion and government funding of contraceptive distribution.[99]

In light of this conflation of so many progressive policies with environmentalism, it is little wonder that conservative resistance—including among theologically conservative evangelicals—grew through the '70s and '80s. Thus, though Nixon had authorized the study of

---

93. Chasteen, 33.

94. Chasteen, 34–36.

95. Chasteen, 3–22.

96. Around this time there was a major electoral shift that closely paralleled the increasing polarization of the culture war that muddies any account of history that relies too heavily on political parties. See James Davison Hunter, *Culture Wars: The Struggle to Define America* (New York: Basic Books, 1991), 272–81.

97. United States Environmental Protection Agency, "DDT – A Brief History and Status," December 1, 2020, https://www.epa.gov/ingredients-used-pesticide-products/ddt-brief-history-and-status.

98. Byron W. Daynes and Glen Sussman, *White House Politics and the Environment* (College Station, TX: Texas A&M University Press, 2010), 66–83.

99. Commission on Population Growth, *Population and the American Future* (Washington, DC: United States Government Printing Office, 1972), 78.

population growth, he quickly distanced himself from its outcome.[100] Indeed, that commission's report may have been one of the major factors solidifying the politically progressive bent of the environmental movement. It isn't simply that evangelicals initially chose the culture war and identified the environment as victim, but that significant, vocal environmentalists seem determined to wage a war on principles derived from a Christian worldview. In reality, evangelical interest in the environment has always followed cultural trends but has been consistently resistant to doctrinal erosion.[101]

Increasing Evangelical Engagement

For example, despite the opposition to population control as part of the environmental movement, there was a fairly consistent effort among evangelicals to engage in environmental ethics. Francis Schaeffer entered the debate in 1970 with his *Pollution and the Death of Man*, which was intended as an open rebuttal to the calls for doctrinal devolution by Lynn White Jr. and Richard Means. In 1980, a significant coalition of evangelicals published *Earthkeeping: Christian Stewardship of Natural Resources*.[102] This was the first book-length treatment on environmental ethics since Schaeffer's initial entry.[103] The volume was updated in 1991 with the same substantive message.[104] Evangelical engagement in creation care picked up significantly in the 1990s and into the early 2000s.[105] When the market crashed in 2008, there was an observable reduction in interest in the environment all around as financial concerns became more prevalent. There was a similar lull among evangelicals at that time.

There are times when critics look at large, amorphous religious

---

[100.] Derek S. Hoff, "'Kick That Population Commission in the Ass': The Nixon Administration, the Commission on Population Growth and the American Future, and the Defusing of the Population Bomb," *Journal of Policy History* 22, no. 1 (2010): 24.

[101.] Loren Wilkinson, "Fifty Years of American Evangelical Thinking about the Gospel and Creation," in *Stewards of the Earth*, ix–xvii.

[102.] Loren Wilkinson, ed., *Earthkeeping: Christian Stewardship of Natural Resources* (Grand Rapids: Eerdmans, 1980).

[103.] Larsen, "God's Gardeners," 176.

[104.] Loren Wilkinson, ed., *Earthkeeping in the Nineties: Stewardship of Creation* (Grand Rapids: Eerdmans, 1991).

[105.] Wilkinson, *Between God and Green*, 18–26.

movements like evangelicalism and ascribe moral failure to their existence because they did not lead as champions of historically significant movements. This is often as much about perception and the reality that large groups are often very diverse in their interests. Sometimes evangelicals are credited with significant energy and importance in the abolition movement of the nineteenth century.[106] It is certainly to the credit of many Northern Christians with historically evangelical theology that they were active and vocal in pursuing the end of slavery. However, history shows that many Southern Christians with very similar beliefs were on the opposite side of the issue. What history is less likely to record is the fact that the vast majority of believers of every stripe probably gave little consideration to major reform movements because they were focused on their daily lives and because the main focus of most faithful congregations is often the propagation of the gospel.[107] For good or ill, daily life keeps most Christians from being active campaigners for any cause.

When churches or parachurch ministries become more focused on something other than their central identity as Christians, they lose focus on the gospel. Sometimes the result is success in their new main endeavor and growth numerically. However, often those organizations lose their momentum because they no longer have the energy that originally animated them.[108] This does not mean that Christians should not engage in social causes or that churches should shy away from teaching how the implications of sound theology lead to specific social perspectives. Evangelicals have been a part of many of the major social issues that were common in their day, including creation care and the abolition of slavery, but the nature of evangelicalism as centered on the proclamation of the gospel of Christ ensures that other purposes will tend to remain secondary. For some critics, this is the tragic flaw of evangelical theology. However, it is a feature and not a bug. It should come as no surprise that a movement defined by its

---

[106.] Donald Dayton with Douglas Strong, *Rediscovering an Evangelical Heritage: A Tradition and Trajectory of Integrating Piety and Justice*, 2nd ed. (Grand Rapids: Baker, 2014), 95–105.

[107.] Henry, "Evangelicals in the Social Struggle," 36–52.

[108.] Peter Greer and Chris Horst, *Mission Drift* (Minneapolis: Bethany House, 2014), 67–76.

theology (or theological method) is most noted for that rather than its political and social engagement.[109]

CONCLUSION

This chapter provides some context for the religious aspects of environmental ethics, especially those focused on how evangelicals in the United States fit into the ongoing debate. Environmentalism can be a false religion. However, the dangers of the environmental movement need not preclude all environmental interest, if it is built from a sound theology. The environmental debate since the Industrial Revolution has always included religious elements but has recently shifted to a more materialistic perspective with an ideological bent. The shift of the environmental movement from its original moral foundations of Western Civilization has resulted in the issue becoming clumped with others. That clumping has increased mistrust of environmentalists by theologically conservative Christians, even as their general interest in creation care has followed the tide of the cultural conversation.

KEY TERMS

Aldo Leopold
Anthropocentrism
Conservationism
Consumerism
Dualism
Gifford Pinchot
John Muir
Lynn White Jr.
Modernity
Preservationism
Rachel Carson

[109.] Thomas Kidd, *Who Is an Evangelical?* (New Haven: Yale University Press, 2019), 4–6.

STUDY QUESTIONS

1. Is environmental degradation in the West especially the fault of Christianity? Why or why not?
2. What are some differences between conservationism and preservationism?
3. How has the tendency to lump loosely related cultural issues together impacted Christian environmentalism?
4. Why is it normal for evangelical interest in cultural topics to vary as the broader culture's interest changes?

PART TWO
A THEOLOGY FOR CREATION CARE

CHAPTER 3

A Theology for Creation Care

In Ethiopia amid the dry fields tilled by families trying to feed themselves and make a living, there remain patches of ancient forest surrounding Orthodox churches. The forests are "like clothes surrounding the church at the center" and are a part of the architecture of the churches themselves.[1] In a country that has largely been deforested to make room for fields, these forests remain because of the theology of believers who maintain the property—they value the respite from the sun and the verdant beauty they experience as they approach their houses of worship.[2] The swaths of green that surround these Ethiopian churches are much different from the acres of bubbling asphalt that often surround suburban churches in the United States, many of them confessionally orthodox. But both expressions of faith have a great deal in common with each other. Both differ greatly theologically from the progressive seminary students who confess their "climate sins" to plants in chapel.[3] Theology matters, but it does not always translate into consistent practice.

Readers may legitimately wonder how some of the diverse understandings of creation care have developed from the Christian tradition. How can the same tree produce fruits that seem so different? Often the difference is caused by someone attempting to graft another competing worldview into Christianity.[4] For example, some approaches to environmentalism that are labeled Christian really grant ultimate authority to science rather than Scripture.[5] Though such ethics may use Christian

---

[1.] Alejandra Borunda, "Ethiopia's 'Church Forests' Are Incredible Oases of Green," *National Geographic*, January 18, 2019, https://www.nationalgeographic.com/environment/article/ethiopian-church-forest-conservation-biodiversity.

[2.] Sarah Hewitt, "The 'Sacred Forests' of Northern Ethiopia," BBC, May 21, 2019, https://www.bbc.com/travel/article/20190520-the-sacred-forests-of-northern-ethiopia.

[3.] Veery Huleatt, "Progressive Seminary Students Offered a Confession to Plants. How Do We Think about Sins against Nature?," *Washington Post*, September 18, 2019, https://www.washingtonpost.com/religion/2019/09/18/progressive-seminary-students-offered-confession-plants-what-are-we-make-it/.

[4.] See my discussion of ecotheology in Spencer, *Doctrine in Shades of Green*, 41–85 (see introduction, n. 21).

[5.] Fowler, *The Greening of Protestant Thought*, 79 (see chap. 2, n. 72).

terminology, sometimes they have little connection to the vibrant streams of biblical orthodoxy that flow through the Christian tradition.

Too much that passes for Christian thinking on topics is simply a form of the prevailing culture's reasoning with some Bible verses or traditional theological terms salted in. This is a form of syncretism. Such approaches are an example of attempting to have cake and eat it too. The result is usually ethics that are not consistent with the Christian tradition and not really acceptable to those outside of it, either. It is a compromise that satisfies no one.

Authentic Christianity should be weird to the surrounding world.[6] To those outside the church, the gospel is either a stumbling block or foolishness (1 Cor 1:23). As much as we long for acceptance by the surrounding culture, there is no concession that will make Christianity palatable to the rest of the world except abandonment of the gospel. Therefore, a Christian ethics of creation care cannot be built by taking a non-Christian approach to ecology and economics and trying to fit it into Christian orthodoxy.[7] We must seek to determine the questions the world around us is asking, then explore how we can answer those questions using God's Word in light of the historical understanding of the community of faith. This is the only approach that will arrive at authentically Christian answers to thorny cultural questions.

This chapter argues that doctrine should be consistent even as topics for concern change in culture because ethics proceeds from theology, not the reverse. It then outlines a basic understanding of four key doctrines that form the framework for this volume and help answer the questions that pertain to environmental ethics.

SHIFTING TOPICS, STEADY DOCTRINES

The culture around us is constantly changing. New topics of concern arise on a regular basis as technology advances. We cannot escape the

---

[6.] Russell Moore, *Onward: Engaging the Culture without Losing the Gospel* (Nashville: B&H, 2015), 28–46.

[7.] For an attempt to balance the ethical concerns of Christianity with a robust understanding of economics, see Victor V. Claar and Robin J. Klay, *Economics in Christian Perspective: Theory, Policy, and Life Choices* (Downers Grove: IVP Academic, 2007), 89–107; Brent Waters, *Just Capitalism: A Christian Ethic of Economic Globalization* (Louisville, KY: Westminster John Knox), 203–17.

culture we live in, no matter how high we try to build our figurative monastery walls by unplugging from cable and avoiding "worldly" entertainment. In fact, when Christians do remove themselves from culture by becoming isolationists, they often miss opportunities to provide a defense for the hope that is within us (1 Pet 3:15). Christians need to have real, gospel-saturated answers for the most important questions culture is asking, and these answers must be consistent with the historical Christian faith.

Chameleon Christianity

One way Christians can fail in trying to answer common cultural questions is by continually adapting Christianity to the surrounding culture.[8] This has been the approach of liberal theologians in the West for several generations. One huge problem with this approach is that the demands of the gospel entail obedience in every aspect of our lives. There is not one square inch of the world about which we can declare, "Mine!"[9] God's gospel demands all of it. Another problem is that culture is always changing, so attempts to adapt Christianity to culture inevitably leave little real Christianity after a few generations. When Christians try to accommodate culture, they fall into the trap of being "tossed to and fro by the waves and carried about by every wind of doctrine, by human cunning, by craftiness in deceitful schemes" (Eph 4:14 ESV).

Christians who are legitimately attempting to answer the questions of the prevailing culture can fall prey to the biases of the people with whom they are attempting to share the gospel. Those who compromise the Christian faith to "reach" the culture rarely do so out of an evil motive. The father of liberalism, Friedrich Schleiermacher, did not intend to destroy Christianity but was trying to save it by eliminating the elements that were offensive to modern believers.[10] However, there

---

[8.] Contextualization is a complex topic that exceeds the bounds of this book. For a helpful overview of models of contextualization, see Timothy Tennent, *Theology in the Context of World Christianity* (Grand Rapids: Zondervan Academic, 2007), 195–217. For a deeper discussion of methods of contextualization, see Stephen B. Bevans, *Models of Contextual Theology* (Maryknoll, NY: Orbis, 2002).

[9.] See Abraham Kuyper, "Sphere Sovereignty," in *Abraham Kuyper: Centennial Reader*, ed. James D. Bratt (Grand Rapids: Eerdmans, 1998), 488.

[10.] Alec Ryrie, *Protestants: The Faith That Made the Modern World* (New York: Viking, 2017), 240–44.

wasn't much left of historical Christianity in the version he finally espoused. The Social Gospel advocate Walter Rauschenbusch claimed his project of replacing the gospel presented in Scripture with the Social Gospel was initiated because he believed that "theology needs periodic rejuvenation."[11] He was hoping to save Christianity from its focus on outdated doctrines that, in his mind, did not match the ethical concerns of his day. Again, what Rauschenbusch outlined has little to connect it to the faith of generations before, except some common terminology he has redefined and the name Christian, which means much less than it did before his revisions. A Christian ethic must not abandon the fundamental truths of Scripture in an attempt to provide a culturally acceptable ethics. What results from that abandonment is usually neither accepted by culture nor recognizable as Christian.[12]

Doctrinal Stability

Instead of getting caught up in the vortex of changing culture, Christians are called to hold fast to truth. The most significant source of truth is God's self-revelation in Scripture. However, for the text of the Bible to answer contemporary questions, faithful readers of Scripture must transpose the text from the culture of its human authors to the context of its contemporary readers.[13] Thus, for example, though the Bible does not give specific instructions about the permissibility of using recreational marijuana, we understand the intoxicating effects of marijuana and the warnings against drunkenness and can transpose the biblical prohibitions into modern wisdom.[14] Transposition can be a difficult process, as many young musicians discover. It is adherence to faithful Christian doctrine that helps keep the church from drifting too far from truth in its efforts to transpose biblical wisdom. Every

---

[11] Rauschenbusch, *A Theology for the Social Gospel*, 12 (see introduction, n. 23).

[12] An engaging study of the sociological effects of liberalizing doctrine in mainline Protestant churches shows that such compromise to accommodate culture typically results in membership losses and weakened participation in denominations that deemphasize countercultural doctrine and ethics. Dean Hoge, Benton Johnson, and Donald Luidens, *Vanishing Boundaries: The Religion of Mainline Protestant Baby Boomers* (Louisville: Westminster John Knox, 1994), 180–202.

[13] John Frame, *The Doctrine of the Word of God* (Phillipsburg, NJ: P&R, 2010), 292–96.

[14] See Todd Miles, *Cannabis and the Christian: What the Bible Says about Marijuana* (Nashville: B&H, 2021).

Christian must do the work of transposing the teaching of our ancient Scriptures into ethics that sort out contemporary conundrums. This is fundamentally the process of hashing out doctrine.

Doctrine is not a special, academic section of Christianity set aside for pastors, elders, and seminary professors. Doctrines are the heart of the Christian faith and essential to keep our ethics in line with a biblical vision of the world.[15] As Dorothy L. Sayers argues,

> [Doctrines] are not a set of arbitrary regulations invented *a priori* by a committee of theologians enjoying a bout of all-in dialectical wrestling. Most of them were hammered out under pressure of urgent practical necessity to provide an answer to heresy. And heresy is . . . largely the expression of opinion of the untutored average man, trying to grapple with the problems of the universe at the point where they begin to interfere with daily life and thought.[16]

When Christians wrestle with contemporary ethical questions without an anchor in relevant orthodox doctrines, heresy is often the result. Theology precedes ethics, and a faithful theology helps Christians determine which doctrines are applicable to a particular ethical concern.

As we survey different ethical topics and seek to answer the particular errors of our day, often "under pressure of urgent practical necessity," our best source of assistance in countering the challenges of the world is the doctrines born out of a previous generation's struggles. As technology advances and Satan's tactics shift, there are always new issues to address. However, the sufficiency of Scripture promises that the theological perspective provided by the Bible will always be sufficient to arrive at a God-honoring answer.[17] We must rely on Scripture to answer life's pressing questions if we are to hold on to the principle of *sola Scriptura*, which animates and continues to invigorate the Protestant tradition.[18] At the same time, if we attempt to read Scripture

---

[15.] Rhyne R. Putman, *The Method of Christian Theology: A Basic Introduction* (Nashville: B&H Academic, 2021), 61.

[16.] Dorothy L. Sayers, "Creed or Chaos?" in *The Whimsical Christian* (New York: Macmillan, 1978), 41.

[17.] See Frame's explanation of the sufficiency of Scripture. John Frame, *Systematic Theology* (Phillipsburg, NJ: P&R, 2013), 618–29.

[18.] Frame, *Doctrine of the Word of God*, 571–74.

independently from believers in other times and places, we are likely to develop our own idiosyncratic readings based on the biases of our culture and time.[19] As C. S. Lewis argued, "Every age has its own outlook. It is specially good at seeing certain truths and specially liable to make certain mistakes. We all, therefore, need the books that will correct the characteristic mistakes of our own period. And that means the old books."[20] In this case, instead of reading classics from a previous generation, we must read the doctrines of previous generations to correct the failings of our own time. Our ethics must be a reflection on present problems from the vantage point of historical Christian theology.

Ethical responses to particular topics raised by changing cultural problems must be rooted in doctrines that are well seasoned by the careful reasoning of the saints who have preceded us. Although Calvin never dealt with questions about the rise in CO_2 levels and would have been unable to explain the problem with plastic in the ocean, he wrestled with issues of right and wrong, good stewardship, and a theological vision that valued the common good.[21] As we seek to ask today's questions, we remain most faithful to Christ when our doctrine does not shift, even when the topics of concern do. As the climate scientist Katharine Hayhoe argues, environmental ethics should be based on our values rather than in competition with our values.[22] Beginning our discussion with doctrines central to orthodox theology can help us remain faithfully Christian even as we wrestle with the urgent questions of our time.

THEOLOGY BEFORE ETHICS

A basic assumption of this project is that ethics flows out of theology. This has been the consistent approach of the Baptist tradition and,

---

[19.] Richard Lints, *The Fabric of Theology* (Grand Rapids: Eerdmans, 1993), 20–28. Also, Douglas Moo, "Creation and New Creation," *Bulletin for Biblical Research* 20, no. 1 (2010): 39–41.

[20.] C. S. Lewis, "On the Reading of Old Books," in *C. S. Lewis: Essay Collection and Other Short Pieces*, ed. Lesley Walmsley (London, UK: HarperCollins, 2000), 439.

[21.] For example, see John Calvin, *Sermons on the Ten Commandments* (Pelham, AL: Solid Ground Christian Books, 2011).

[22.] Hayhoe, *Saving Us*, 6 (see introduction, n. 2).

indeed, of the orthodox Christian tradition. Everyone wrestling with ethics is working out their theological system in practical application because what matters most to us is what motivates us to act in one way instead of another. Theology (or at least a particular controlling philosophy) is what determines that value and what range of actions are acceptable to achieve it.

The heart of any ethics is its *summum bonum*, its greatest good.[23] As we will discuss in chapter 5, the *summum bonum* of all creation (whether we acknowledge it or not) is to glorify God.[24] The Westminster Shorter Catechism focuses on this as the chief end of humanity by stating that we are "to glorify God, and to enjoy him forever."[25] Any orthodox Christian ethics must acknowledge *summum bonum* as the main goal of its reasoning. An ethics is deficient that does not see that the purpose of all human activity and existence is the glory of the triune God (1 Cor 10:31).[26] A faithful Christian ethics is *theocentric*—that is, focused on God—and is committed to doctrines, whether or not they are helpful to the cause of the day.

One of the fundamental efforts of liberal theology is the abandonment of doctrines that do not seem practical.[27] Movements like the Social Gospel were originated to unseat historical beliefs from their place of significance in Christianity. This was not a result of malice, but of improper theological belief about the essence of Christianity and the nature of salvation. Walter Rauschenbusch attempts to do this by arguing "theology is the esoteric thought of the Church."[28] He asserts, "It is clear that our Christianity is more Christian when religion and ethics are viewed as inseparable elements of the same single-minded and whole-hearted life, in which the consciousness of God and the consciousness of humanity blend together."[29] This assertion itself is not entirely false since right action (orthopraxy) should necessarily accompany right belief (orthodoxy), as the apostle James himself argued

---

[23] G. E. Moore, *Principia Ethica* (New York: Barnes and Noble, 2005), 186–87.

[24] See Christopher Wright, *The Mission of God* (Downers Grove: IVP Academic, 2006), 404–6.

[25] "The Westminster Shorter Catechism," Q1, in Van Dixhoorn, *Creeds, Confessions, & Catechisms*, 411 (see introduction, n. 5).

[26] Liederbach and Lenow, *Ethics as Worship*, xii–xxv (see chap. 1, n. 16).

[27] Olson, *The Story of Christian Theology*, 550–51 (see chap. 1, n. 28).

[28] Rauschenbusch, *A Theology for the Social Gospel*, 15.

[29] Rauschenbusch, 14.

(Jas 2:14–26). However, Rauschenbusch reveals that his Social Gospel is offering salvation by works, which is not an ethical assertion, but a profoundly doctrinal one that serves to distort his entire ethics away from the pursuit of known and lived truth to the pursuit of a *summum bonum* dependent on the surrounding culture.[30] Rauschenbusch assumes that his basically orthopraxic ethics can be retained without orthodox theology. However, the heirs of Rauschenbusch's theological revisionism often look much more like the paganized culture around them than anything consistent with the Christian tradition.[31]

In contrast, a faithful Christian ethics must properly begin by identifying its basic doctrinal assumptions before explaining how that theology answers the ever-changing questions the surrounding culture asks. John Frame's definition of theology emphasizes the close connection between ethics and doctrine. He writes that theology is "the application of the Word of God by persons to all areas of life."[32] He further clarifies that application "is the use of Scripture to meet some human need."[33] In other words, the work of theology is to answer the basic, real, and practical questions that humans have. Thus, "all theology is ethics."[34]

Starting at the broadest level of systematic theology to discover what Scripture says about a particular topic would be excessively time consuming and often results in exploring doctrines that have little to do with the topic of ethical concern. There are certain doctrines within theology that more closely relate to topics like the human-creation relationship. These doctrines will be the focus of the theological discussion in this volume.

FOUR DOCTRINAL QUESTIONS

Four questions are central to nearly every argument about the environment, whether Christian or not. Those questions are, (1) What are the sources of authority for environmental ethics? (2) Why does creation have value? (3) What is the human role in creation? (4) What

---

[30.] Rauschenbusch, 15.

[31.] Daniel Heimbach, *Fundamental Christian Ethics* (Nashville: B&H Academic, 2022), 193–95.

[32.] Frame, *The Doctrine of the Knowledge of God*, 81.

[33.] Frame, 83.

[34.] John Frame, *The Doctrine of the Christian Life* (Phillipsburg, NJ: P&R, 2010), 5.

is the end goal or final state of the created order, and how does it come about? These questions can be addressed under the heading of four key doctrines: revelation, creation, anthropology, and eschatology.[35]

These four questions rise from the various discussions on environmental ethics. People who write on and discuss environmental ethics seem to naturally gravitate toward the same topics. For example, in a 1992 essay on creation care, Millard Erickson identifies four common charges against Christianity:

1. The call to have dominion over the earth, in Genesis 1:28, entails treating the earth as being important only to support the good of the human being. This therefore leads to exploitation and rape of the earth.
2. Christianity has condoned modern science and technology's exploitation of the earth.
3. Christianity has promoted a dualism, according to which the natural or physical or the secular is of less value, or even is negative in character, compared with the spiritual or the otherworldly.
4. Belief in the second coming, which will usher in Christ's complete and perfect reign, effectively removes any reason for us to be concerned about ecology.[36]

These four accusations from various sources draw on four doctrinal questions. The first accusation relates to the place of humans within creation. The second deals with Christian epistemology, specifically how modern science has allowed the despoilation of earth. This relates to the doctrine of revelation. The third accusation deals with Christianity's valuation of creation. The fourth attacks Christian eschatology as a cause of being uninterested in this world.

It would be impossible to entirely eliminate from consideration all

---

[35.] For non-Christian alternatives, essentially the same topics are considered. However, in a materialist perspective, for example, they would be considered under different headings, such as epistemology (for sources of authority), nature, humanity, and thermodynamics.

[36.] See Erickson's summary of White's complaint in Millard J. Erickson, "Biblical Theology of Ecology," in *The Earth Is the Lord's: Christians and the Environment*, ed. Richard D. Land and Louis Moore (Nashville: Broadman Press, 1992), 36–37. Note that J. Simmons ascribes these critiques to the doctrinal headings of anthropology, ethics, cosmology, and eschatology. J. Aaron Simmons, "Evangelical Environmentalism: Oxymoron or Opportunity?", *Worldviews* 13, no. 1 (2009): 41n1.

other doctrines besides these four. In fact, as Northcott and company show in *Systematic Theology and Climate Change*, environmental ethics can be looked at through a number of doctrinal headings.[37] However, a careful reading of the essays in *Systematic Theology and Climate Change* reveals that even as the authors are discussing doctrines other than those here highlighted as key for environmental ethics, they are largely seeking to answer the same four doctrinal questions. The centrality of the doctrines of revelation, creation, anthropology, and eschatology is evident in non-theological treatments of the topics as well.

An Example of the Four Doctrinal Questions

In 2006, E. O. Wilson, Pulitzer Prize winner and Harvard biologist, published a volume addressing a hypothetical Southern Baptist pastor. The late Wilson, a secular humanist raised as a Christian, argues for Southern Baptists and secular humanists to work together to save the planet. According to Wilson, the environment is a common cause for cooperation, despite worldview differences. Wilson's introduction shows there are four main points of contact between his worldview and the Southern Baptist's that form the basis of communication.

Wilson begins with the question of revelation as a source of moral authority. He describes the pastor as "a literal interpreter of Christian Holy Scripture."[38] Illuminating his perception of tension between science and Scripture, he notes the pastor seeks special revelation while he, the biologist, is satisfied with "the glory of the universe revealed at last."[39] Despite this differing approach, both he and the Christian can find universal value in nature.[40] For Wilson, this is because nature "serves without discrimination the interests of all humanity."[41] He argues the

---

[37] Michael Northcott and Peter Scott, eds., *Systematic Theology and Climate Change* (New York: Routledge, 2014). Northcott et al. use ten doctrinal headings, but they all seem to point back to, or at least rely heavily on, revelation, creation, anthropology, and eschatology.

[38] Edward O. Wilson, *The Creation: An Appeal to Save Life on Earth* (New York: W. W. Norton & Co., 2006), 3.

[39] Wilson, 4.

[40] For a more in-depth view of Wilson's attitude toward science, through an overtly scientistic epistemology, see E. O. Wilson, *Consilience: The Unity of Knowledge* (New York: Alfred A. Knopf, 1998). The response by Wendell Berry makes an excellent pairing: Wendell Berry, *Life Is a Miracle: An Essay Against Modern Superstition* (New York: Counterpoint, 2000).

[41] Wilson, *The Creation*, 4.

pastor should desire to save the earth because "each species . . . is a masterpiece of biology, and well worth saving."[42] For Wilson, nature has value on both instrumental and aesthetic grounds. Of course, Wilson's own approach seems to presuppose some sort of designer (else how is something a masterpiece?), which seems to undermine the consistency of his humanism.[43]

Despite the points of agreement Wilson highlights, he also inadvertently highlights disagreement. For example, Wilson assumes an evolutionary view of humanity.[44] As an evolutionary biologist, this is not surprising, but Wilson does not reflect on the doctrinal implications of his approach.[45] Specifically, it undermines any distinction between humanity and the rest of creation.[46] This reflects Wilson's assumptions about both the authority of science and the role of humans within nature. Furthermore, Wilson actively seeks to undermine any sort of Christian eschatology. For Wilson, the vision of a destruction of the created order results in apathy toward the creation.[47] Thus, he believes that doctrine should be abandoned. The four doctrinal contact points highlighted here put differing ideas into relief, making discussion about the actual basis for disagreement clearer.

Wilson's appeal to the supposed Southern Baptist pastor is unlikely to be effective because he smuggles too many of his assumptions into the argument. However, his attempt to reach across ideological lines demonstrates there are discernable touch points of concern for environmental ethics within Christianity. Wilson provides evidence of doctrinal questions that appear to be central items of concern for creation care.

CONCLUSION

Ethics is fundamentally theological. As we pursue culturally significant concerns related to environmental ethics, we must begin our

---

[42.] Wilson, 5.

[43.] Compare Berry, *Life Is a Miracle*, 27–29.

[44.] Wilson, *The Creation*, 4.

[45.] Elsewhere Wilson mocks Southern Baptists for rejecting evolution, which he calls "the most important revelation of all!" Wilson, *Consilience*, 6.

[46.] E. O. Wilson, *On Human Nature* (Cambridge, MA: Harvard University Press, 1978), 1–13.

[47.] Wilson, *The Creation*, 6.

ethical reflection in Scripture with a desire to answer questions that fall under the doctrinal headings revelation, creation, anthropology, and eschatology. This approach amplifies our resources so that historical treatments of these doctrines that fall within the orthodox tradition can help prevent us from erring in our interpretation of Scripture and being overly influenced by our own cultural context.

The next four chapters will use the four doctrinal headings with the identified questions to develop a theological perspective for environmental ethics. The goal is to explore historical Christian doctrines to see how they shape a theology of creation care.

KEY TERMS

Anthropology
Creation
Eschatology
Revelation
Summum Bonum

STUDY QUESTIONS

1. What is the proper relationship between theology and ethics?
2. How does the unchanging nature of truth impact our approach to ever-changing cultural concerns?
3. What are the four doctrinal questions that relate most consistently to environmental ethics?
4. Are there additional questions you believe to be important for environmental ethics? What questions seem the most significant for other ethical topics, like wealth and poverty, medical ethics, and human sexuality?

CHAPTER 4

Sources of Moral Authority

Standing before the Diet of Worms in April of 1517, Martin Luther stated, "Unless I am convicted by Scripture and plain reason . . . my conscience is captive to the Word of God."[1] This was a bold rejection of the human authorities of his day that put Luther's life at risk. It also serves as a clear example for contemporary believers of Luther's conviction of the truthfulness and supreme authority of the Bible. Any system of theology or ethics that places a source of authority over the canon of Scripture is insufficient. *Sola Scriptura*—Scripture alone—is one of the central tenets of the Protestant Reformation and should be a guiding theme for faithful Christian ethics.

At the same time, *sola Scriptura* was never intended to mean Scripture *only* or the Bible without any other information. Even Luther's fiery statement before the Diet of Worms affirms the place of "plain reason" in working through the content of the Bible. We cannot apply Scripture to contemporary issues and arguments without considering various data from outside the Bible. A faithful Christian ethics must place God's special revelation in Scripture above any other source. At the same time, moral decision-making must also account for the faithful Christian tradition, for proper human reasoning, and for our own experiences as Christians.[2]

This chapter argues that there is objective truth and that Scripture is the supreme authority for determining questions of faith and life. However, God has graciously provided other sources of truth so that gifted men and women who are not Christian often discover valuable truths about the world, which should be considered for incorporation into our understanding of reality. Nevertheless, Christians must push back against scientism, which is an ideology that grants ultimate authority to current scientific findings. In particular, Christians must recognize scientism's failings to deal with the limits of science and the

---

[1] As quoted in Roland Bainton, *Here I Stand* (Nashville: Abingdon, 1950), 185.

[2] Ken Magnuson, *An Invitation to Christian Ethics: Moral Reasoning and Contemporary Issues* (Grand Rapids: Kregel, 2020), 70–74.

unchanging nature of Christian doctrine. This is, in short, a chapter about epistemology.

AUTHORITY AND WAYS OF KNOWING

Our culture has an ongoing crisis of epistemology.[3] If there is one philosophical topic that would be beneficial to people living in this world at this time, especially Christians, it is the study of how we know what we know. The topic of this chapter, which emphasizes the authority of Scripture amidst different ways of knowing in an information-saturated world, is not simply a theological topic, but part of a broader philosophical one. What is often pitched as a competition between irrational faith and evidence-based, careful scientific method is in many cases actually a battle of competing epistemologies.

Throughout history, the vast majority of Christian theologians have relied on some form of propositionalism. According to George Lindbeck, "For a propositionalist, if a doctrine is once true, it is always true, and if it once false, it is always false."[4] Christians have historically understood truth anchored in timeless realities. The pervasive epistemology of our time is a far cry from stolid propositionalism espoused through much of church history.[5] Zygmunt Bauman describes the prevailing epistemology of the world as "liquid modernity." This is, perhaps, the essentially modern attitude toward truth. As Bauman notes, "A hundred years ago 'to be modern' meant to chase 'the final state of perfection'—now it means an infinity of improvement, with no 'final state' in sight and none desired."[6] Within this conception of reality, truth, goodness, and beauty are accepted as changing with the times.[7] The propositionalist rejects that claim.[8]

---

[3] Bonnie Kristian, *Untrustworthy: The Knowledge Crisis Breaking Our Brains, Polluting Our Politics, and Corrupting Christian Community* (Grand Rapids: Brazos, 2022), 1.

[4] George Lindbeck, *Nature of Doctrine: Religion and Theology in a Postliberal Age* (Louisville: Westminster John Knox, 2009), 2.

[5] David Wells, *No Place for Truth: Or Whatever Happened to Evangelical Theology?* (Grand Rapids: Eerdmans, 1993), 279–82.

[6] Zygmunt Bauman, *Liquid Modernity* (Malden, MA: Polity, 2012), ix.

[7] This is not to say that style or aesthetic preferences do not change over time. Francis Schaeffer, "Art and the Bible," in *The Complete Works of Francis A. Schaeffer* (Wheaton: Crossway, 1983), 2:404–5.

[8] See the critique of modernity's lack of affirmation of the universality of truth in David Wells, *No Place for Truth* (Grand Rapids: Eerdmans, 1993), 53–92.

The limits of this volume do not allow for detailing the lengthy and convoluted intellectual history of thinking and attitudes toward truth. However, it is impossible to proceed with any discussion seeking to expound truth without making some basic assumptions about the footing of the conversation. For the ardent, orthodox Christian L. S. Chafer asserts, "The inspiration of the Scriptures are assumed. . . . As a chemist will make no advance in his science if he doubts or rejects the essential character of the elements which he compounds, so a theologian must fail who does not accept the trustworthiness of the Word of God."[9] This discussion begins with a belief in the trustworthiness of Scripture. The following pages will set out a doctrine of Scripture that is helpful in developing a robust, God-honoring approach to creation care.

SPECIAL REVELATION

For Protestants, and more particularly for confessional Baptists, there is no source of moral authority higher than the inspired Word of God. The Baptist Faith and Message 2000, the confessional statement of the Southern Baptist Convention, affirms that "all Scripture is totally true and trustworthy. It reveals the principles by which God judges us, and therefore is, and will remain to the end of the world, the true center of Christian union, and the supreme standard by which all human conduct, creeds, and religious opinions should be tried."[10] This position is not unique to Southern Baptists or the modern era but is consistent with the understanding of the nature of the Bible held by many in church history.[11] Scripture is inspired, inerrant, authoritative, and sufficient. The truthfulness and authority of Scripture are at the heart of a theological perspective for environmental ethics.

The purpose of special revelation is for God to reveal his unchanging character to his creation both directly (as through the incarnation

---

[9.] Lewis Sperry Chafer, *Systematic Theology*, vol. 1 (Dallas: Dallas Seminary Press, 1947), 7.

[10.] "Baptist Faith & Message 2000," SBC, https://bfm.sbc.net/bfm2000/#i-the-scriptures.

[11.] See D. A. Carson, ed., *The Enduring Authority of the Christian Scriptures* (Grand Rapids: Eerdmans, 2016); Carl F. H. Henry, ed., *Revelation and the Bible* (Grand Rapids: Baker, 1958); Kevin Vanhoozer, *Biblical Authority after Babel: Retrieving the* Solas *in the Spirit of Mere Protestant Christianity* (Grand Rapids: Brazos, 2016).

and the words of Scripture that clearly tell us what God is like) and indirectly (by recording God's working in events that have transpired through history). Scripture is the primary source of special revelation for Christians living in the world today.

Sufficiency of Scripture

Scripture is sufficient, which means it contains "the whole counsel of God concerning all things necessary for His own glory, man's salvation, faith and life."[12] As the Baptist Faith and Message 2000 notes, "Scripture has God for its author, salvation for its end, and truth, without mixture of error, for its matter." Furthermore, "All Scripture is a testimony to Christ, who is Himself the focus of divine revelation."[13] The primary function of Scripture is to provide the data necessary for salvation by grace through faith in Christ. What it says about other matters is true, but Scripture is not comprehensive. As Robert Letham notes, "The Bible does not contain all truth. It is not a scientific textbook."[14]

For data about climate change, for example, we will need to look beyond the pages of Scripture. The Bible is the norming norm of our faith, but we apply the norms of Scripture to data obtained externally to Scripture. The Bible has the necessary information for "faith and life," so the reasoning we perform based on the data and the ethical conclusions we draw from the data must be governed by what the canon of Scripture reveals about God.

Living faithfully in a world so technologically and culturally different from the world of the biblical authors is a challenge. There is a constant tension in the Christian life as we seek to read the events of the world through the lens of Scripture. On one hand, we affirm that "the instruction of the LORD is perfect, renewing one's life; the testimony of the LORD is trustworthy, making the inexperienced wise" (Ps 19:7). As well, Peter wrote, "His divine power has given us everything required for life and godliness" (2 Pet 1:3), which in the context of the chapter seems to rely strongly on the written Word of God. On the other hand,

---

12. "The Westminster Confession of Faith," 1.6, in Van Dixhoorn, *Creeds, Confessions, & Catechisms*, 186 (see introduction, n. 5).

13. "Baptist Faith & Message 2000," https://bfm.sbc.net/bfm2000/#i.

14. Robert Letham, *Systematic Theology* (Wheaton: Crossway, 2019), 200.

God also reveals truth outside the pages of Scripture (Ps 19:1–6; Rom 1:19–20). Therefore, we cannot retreat to the content of the canon of Scripture, claiming, "God said it, I believe it, that settles it," without looking at the objective truth God reveals through his creation. As John Frame argues, "If we exclude the use of extrabiblical information, then ethical reflection is next to impossible."[15]

Ethics and Extrabiblical Information

While the truthfulness of Scripture never changes, circumstances of its readers do. This means that while the eternal principles of the Bible never change, the application of those principles may.[16] This may sound doubtful to some, but an example will provide clarification. Let's accept that the traditional interpretation of the sixth commandment (Ex 20:13) includes not simply avoiding taking innocent life, but also "to protect them from harm as much as we can, and to do good even to our enemies."[17] But our ability to apply this principle depends on information from outside of Scripture.

For example, there is a complex history to the use of asbestos in buildings. It is effective at mitigating fires and thus seems a wise choice to fulfill the sixth commandment. However, the risks associated with disturbed asbestos fibers are significant. As we have come to find out, asbestosis and mesothelioma are serious conditions, which risk people's lives. There is no known safe exposure threshold for exposure to asbestos. So, is using asbestos to protect people compliance with or a violation of the sixth commandment?

In the late nineteenth and early twentieth centuries, thousands of innocent people died in building fires each year. In that context the use of asbestos to mitigate fires was an obvious choice for safety. It was the only substance known to be as durable and flexible for the necessary uses. However, as Rachel Maines argues, "After 1965, in part due to the success of the fire-safety system that included asbestos, short-term fire

---

[15.] Frame, *Doctrine of the Christian Life*, 164 (see chap. 3, n. 34).

[16.] Frame provides a detailed application of this concept through his triperspectival approach to ethics in Frame, *Doctrine of the Christian Life*, 166–68.

[17.] "The Heidelberg Catechism," Q107, in Van Dixhoorn, *Creeds, Confessions, & Catechisms*, 325. (see introduction, n. 5)

safety moved into the background of discussions of the material, and its long-term health hazards were generally treated as if they were the only safety consideration associated with asbestos."[18] The ethical reasoning about the safety of asbestos shifted drastically as the circumstances shifted.

This dramatic change in perspective warrants two observations. First, we need to be very careful in making moral judgments about history because we often have more information than those making the original decision. "Of course, asbestos is bad," we can say because millions of dollars have been spent in studying its effects and the problem it was intended to solve has been reduced. And yet, though it is impossible to say how many thousands of people have been saved by the use of asbestos in buildings, it is very likely to be orders of magnitude greater than those affected by asbestos-related diseases.[19] The second observation is that it is obviously impossible for anyone to make a moral evaluation of asbestos usage without a great deal of data that comes from outside the pages of Scripture.

Though we need information outside of Scripture to have the data to make a moral evaluation, the sixty-six books of the canon of Scripture have everything we need to build the framework upon which that moral determination is made.[20] However, Scripture does not provide us with the empirical data we need to apply the moral framework God prescribes. For that, we need other true information about the world, which is a form of general revelation.

GENERAL REVELATION

A vast quantity of true information exists outside of the realm of special revelation. Some theologians seem to limit the role of general revelation to specifically apologetic function for the existence and nature of God.[21] This, indeed, is a primary function of general revelation as it is exemplified in Scripture. General revelation is when "the heavens

---

[18.] Rachel Maines, *Asbestos and Fire: Technology and the Body at Risk* (Rutgers, NJ: Rutgers University Press, 2005), 155.

[19.] Maines, 12–13.

[20.] Herman Bavinck, *Reformed Ethics: Created, Fallen, and Converted Humanity*, vol. 1 (Grand Rapids: Baker Academic, 2019), 25–30.

[21.] For example, Wayne Grudem, *Systematic Theology* (Grand Rapids: Zondervan, 1994), 121–24;

declare the glory of God" (Ps 19:1). It is also the basis of the judgment of God against those who have not heard the gospel "since what can be known about God is evident among them, because God has shown it to them. For his invisible attributes, that is, his eternal power and divine nature, have been clearly seen since the creation of the world, being understood through what he has made" (Rom 1:19–20). General revelation is God's self-disclosure of his character in all of creation. It is accessible to all humanity apart from Scripture due to their basic rational abilities.[22]

With a broad understanding of God's providence within creation, we may understand general revelation to include "revelation in all objects of human knowledge."[23] Such revelation may point more or less directly toward the existence and nature of God. In some sense, then, even a Dickens novel may be considered a form of general revelation because it points toward the creativity imbued within humanity as part of the *imago Dei*.[24] General revelation may be broadly defined as truth that points to the order and design of the universe, which reflects the character of God, that is found outside of Scripture.

General revelation comes through observation of creation, but it also comes through tradition, reason, and experience. Together with Scripture, these three forms are often referred to as the Wesleyan quadrilateral. While none of them bear the same authority as the content of the Bible, they contribute to our understanding of God through the world. Our character is shaped by the communities we have been placed in, the minds God has given us, and the events God has seen fit for us to experience. We need Scripture to interpret them rightly, but the God who works through history has seen fit to use the world around us to communicate truth to us.

In the Dutch Reformed tradition, the universal availability of some truth is often referred to as common grace.[25] Common grace begins

---

Charles Ryrie, *Basic Theology: A Popular Systematic Guide to Understanding Biblical Truth* (Chicago: Moody, 1981), 33–34.

[22.] Russell Moore, "Natural Revelation," in *Theology for the Church*, 2nd ed., ed. Daniel Akin (Nashville: B&H Academic, 2014), 67.

[23.] Frame, *Systematic Theology*, 690.

[24.] Frame, 689.

[25.] Craig Bartholomew, *Contours of the Kuyperian Tradition: A Systematic Introduction* (Downers Grove: IVP Academic, 2017), 36–45.

with the concept of total depravity, which holds that the order of creation has been disrupted as a result of sin. Regeneration is part of the process of reordering human desires and the human mind to properly understand God's moral order in the universe. Due to the work of the Holy Spirit, Christians can comprehend spiritual truths that have been given to us by God but have been hidden from the world, because we have the mind of Christ (1 Cor 2:14–16).[26] Common grace, however, sustains the world so that non-Christians can know many true things about the moral order of the universe that even those with a renewed mind do not understand. One need not be Christian to discover new truths about the cosmos that bring glory to God.

The concept of common grace should lead Christians to anticipate that non-Christians can arrive at non-salvific truths about the world that we have not yet discovered.[27] This means that while we hope there are Christians doing science, we do not seek to establish a separate, Christian science.[28] The primary difference between Christian engagement in scientific endeavors will not typically be the methodology used, but the goal behind it. Since scientific data will not typically be specifically Christian in nature, we must consider the appropriate relationship between the authority of science and the authority of Scripture.

SCIENCE AND SCIENTISM

At the extreme of the spectrum of scientific authority is *scientism*. Philosopher J. P. Moreland defines scientism as "the view that the hard sciences provide the only or at least a vastly superior knowledge of reality compared to other disciplines."[29] E. O. Wilson calls this "the Ionian Enchantment," which relies on "a conviction, far deeper than

---

[26] Frame discusses the role of the Spirit in confirming the truths of Scripture through faith. Frame, *Systematic Theology*, 676–79.

[27] Abraham Kuyper, "Common Grace in Science," in *Abraham Kuyper: A Centennial Reader*, ed. James Bratt (Grand Rapids: Eerdmans, 1998), 441–60.

[28] See C. S. Lewis, "Christian Apologetics," in *Essay Collection and Other Short Pieces* (London: HarperCollins, 2000), 150–51.

[29] J. P. Moreland, *Scientism and Secularism: Learning to Respond to a Dangerous Ideology* (Wheaton, IL: Crossway, 2018), 205.

a mere working proposition, that the world is orderly and can be explained by a small number of natural laws."[30] He goes on to state that "science is a continuation on new and better-tested ground to attain the same end [as religion]. If so, then in that sense science is religion liberated and writ large."[31] Empirical science is the supreme, if not the only, pathway to true knowledge about the world. This is a view that has been popularized by some celebrity scientists as the only rational way to view the world.

Somewhat tongue in cheek, the astrophysicist and science popularizer Neil DeGrasse Tyson once proposed the creation of a country called Rationalia, where all decisions were made solely based on evidence.[32] Authority in Rationalia rests on the concept of empiricism, that observable facts that are testable and repeatable are the only reliable way to understand the world. This reduces all decisions to a form of utilitarianism. For example, Tyson states in his ground rules:

In Rationalia, if you want to fund art in schools, you simply propose a reason why. Does it increase creativity in the citizenry? Is creativity good for culture and society at large? Is creativity good for everyone no matter your chosen profession? These are testable questions. They just require verifiable research to establish answers. The debate then ends quickly in the face of evidence, and we move on to other questions.[33]

This may pass the initial test of being a reasonable approach. After all, why would we not want to make sure we get the desired result from our efforts and investments? It would seem that this sort of approach is just common sense. Missing from Tyson's discussion is how the values are determined. The final clause in his proposed ground rules for Rationalia reveals more of the problem:

---

[30] Wilson, *Consilience*, 4.

[31] Wilson, 6.

[32] See the helpful discussion in Alan Jacobs, *How to Think: A Survival Guide for a World at Odds* (New York: Currency, 2017), 83–88.

[33] Neil DeGrasse Tyson, "In Rationalia, if you want to fund art in schools, you simply propose a reason why," Facebook, June 29, 2016, https://www.facebook.com/notes/10158921216171613/.

In Rationalia, you could create an Office of Morality, where moral codes are proposed and debated. What moral codes would the citizens of Rationalia embrace? That is, itself, a research project. Countries don't always get it right, of course. And neither will Rationalia. Is slavery moral? The USA's Constitution thought so for 76 years. Should women vote? The USA's Constitution said no for 131 years.[34]

We may accept that slavery is immoral and that it is a moral good that both men and women vote; these are baseline cultural assumptions of the modern world. What is the empirical evidence that can prove that, though? Empirical evidence can show what *is* but not what *ought to be*. It might be proved through observation that race-based chattel slavery increases the feeling of misery of those who are enslaved. However, on a purely rational basis, that only matters if there is an external value of justice that sees minimizing human suffering as a moral good. These are value judgments that must function outside of the empirical system.

This form of materialistic reductionism is not solely the realm of celebrity scientists like Neil DeGrasse Tyson, but has also come from the views of eminent scientists like Stephen Hawking. In an interview with Ira Flatow on NPR's *Science Friday*, Hawking states:

> I believe there are no questions that science can't answer about the physical universe. Although we don't yet have a full understanding of the laws of nature, I think we will eventually find a complete unified theory. Some people would claim that things like love, joy, and beauty belong to a different category from science and can't be described in scientific terms. But I think they can all be explained by the theory of evolution.[35]

Science, therefore, can answer all questions in the material universe—which is often assumed to be the sum of the universe—and thus empiricism should be the reigning epistemology and Science

---

[34.] Tyson, "In Rationalia, if you want to fund art in schools, you simply propose a reason why."

[35.] Ira Flatow, "Stephen Hawking Looks Back," *Science Friday*, September 13, 2013, 0:40–1:13, www.sciencefriday.com/segments/stephen-hawking-looks-back/.

(with a capital *S*) is the supreme method for gaining information and ruling the world.

The problem of values remains in Hawking's scientism, just as it does in Tyson's. So does the problem of the concept of Science itself. In scientism, Science is the proper source of norms and the governing force behind social decision. The trouble is that Science itself is not a reified whole. Science, as well, "is unintelligible without a freely acting first cause such as God or man."[36] But such freedom cannot exist within the boundaries of the naturalistic worldview because the cause must be the natural system, not some external immaterial force. There is tension within scientism and perhaps a self-contradiction.[37]

Additionally, the accepted scientific method sometimes cannot be achieved. For example, one satirical study published in the *British Medical Journal* documents the inability to conclude that parachutes are effective in stopping death due to falling because the "search strategy did not find any randomised controlled trials of the parachute."[38] Strangely, no one was willing to see if there was a difference in outcome of a free fall without the parachute. The authors suggest this leads to two possible conclusions: "The first is that we accept that, under exceptional circumstances, common sense might be applied when considering the potential risks and benefits of interventions. The second is that we continue our quest for the holy grail of exclusively evidence based interventions and preclude parachute use outside the context of a properly conducted trial."[39] The authors of the study are pushing readers to accept that though there may not be a study, there are some things that may indeed be true. However, for scientism, each new set of studies becomes Science, which must be obeyed until new Science disrupts that in an apparently objective dialectic cycle of eternal progress. The conclusion we must draw is that Science does not provide perfectly objective access to truth.

[36.] Michael Gillespie, *The Theological Origins of Modernity* (Chicago: University of Chicago Press, 2008), 258.

[37.] C. S. Lewis, *Miracles*, rev. ed. (New York: HarperCollins, 1974), 17–36.

[38.] Gordon Smith and Jill Pell, "Parachute Use to Prevent Death and Major Trauma Related to Gravitational Challenge: Systematic Review of Randomised Controlled Trials," *BMJ* 327:7429 (December 20–27, 2003): 1459.

[39.] Smith and Pell, "Parachute Use," 1460.

SCIENCE AS OBJECTIVE TRUTH

Thomas Kuhn did much to undermine belief in science as a settled truth in his seminal work, *The Structure of Scientific Revolutions.* Kuhn studied the history of science and uncovered the pattern of revolutions in scientific thinking. Scientific thinking does not advance in a smooth, linear fashion, but in periodic revolutions as new discoveries are made that upend old paradigms. These paradigms control the progress of science because they determine what questions are asked, what experiments run, and what data is accepted as legitimate or excluded as "noise." Thus, two scientists with different paradigms can arrive at vastly different conclusions even given access to the same materials. When a preexisting scientific paradigm is not in place, a "current metaphysic," "another science," or "personal and historical accident" determines what bits of information are accepted as facts.[40] How science is presently understood both results from and controls the interpretation of new experimental data. Therefore, real scientific information is not objective truth as much as it is the currently accepted best explanation for the available data.

The reality of scientific revolutions and changing paradigms should not cause us to doubt many of the things that experimental research has given us—the proper conclusion is not that science is false and the Bible is true. However, Kuhn's work should put some of the overarching claims of scientism into perspective and lead to epistemic humility for those claiming to make predictions and moral declarations in the name of science. Today's consensus may well change. As the famed scientist and sometimes curmudgeon Erwin Chargaff noted in 1978, "Nowadays, scientific tradition hardly reaches back for more than three or four years. The proscenium looks the same as before, but the scenery keeps on changing as in a fever dream; no sooner is one backdrop in place than it is replaced by an entirely different one."[41] Science is an attempt to describe objective reality, but it is an inappropriate avenue for pursuing static truths about reality.

[40.] Thomas Kuhn, *The Structure of Scientific Revolutions* (Chicago: University of Chicago Press, 2012), 17.

[41.] Erwin Chargaff, *Heraclitean Fire: Sketches of a Life before Nature* (New York: Rockefeller University Press, 1978), 82.

SCIENCE AND SCRIPTURE

There can be no final conflict between truth discovered through general revelation and that given in Scripture. Assuming true revelation is describing one authentic reality, when there are apparent conflicts between special and general revelation, there are only three possibilities: (1) one or both of the sources are wrong about the fact in question; (2) the two sources are describing two different phenomena; (3) one or both of the sources are being misread for any number of reasons.

There is often a great rush to attempt to reconcile new ideas from culture or science to Christianity. However, as Francis Schaeffer warns,

> It must be understood that there is no automatic need to accommodate the Bible to the statements of science. There is a tendency for some who are Christians and scientists to always place special revelation (the teaching of the Bible) under the control of general revelation and science, and never or rarely to place general revelation and what science teaches under the control of the Bible's teaching. That is, though they think of that which the Bible teaches as true and that which science teaches as true, in reality they tend to end with the truth of science as more true than the truth of the Bible.[42]

All Protestant traditions began with a close reliance on Scripture, and most people engaged in environmental ethics recognize that science itself has contributed greatly to the environmental crisis as we know it. However, as the political scientist Robert Fowler notes, "Whether this fact is acknowledged or not, science often appears to be the ultimate authority among some Protestant environmentalists."[43] This contributes to the desire to adapt Christian doctrine to the perceived objective truths of contemporary science.

[42.] Francis Schaeffer, "No Final Conflict," in *The Collected Works of Francis A. Schaeffer* (Wheaton: Crossway, 1982), 2:140.

[43.] Fowler, *The Greening of Protestant Thought*, 5.

Reconciling Scripture and Science

In an essay about the religious ramifications of finding rational extraterrestrial life, C. S. Lewis points out the fickleness of trying to reconcile popular trends to the unchanging truths of Christianity:

> Each new discovery, even every new theory, is held at first to have the most wide-reaching theological and philosophical consequences. It is seized by unbelievers as the basis for a new attack on Christianity; it is often, and more embarrassingly, seized by injudicious believers as the basis for a new defence.
>
> But usually, when the popular hubbub has subsided and the novelty has been chewed over by real theologians, real scientists and real philosophers, both sides find themselves pretty much where they were before.[44]

American fundamentalist L. S. Chafer expresses similar confidence in the bedrock truths of Christianity as expressed in Scripture:

> Science is ever shifting and subject to its own revisions, if not complete revolutions. It reflects with a good degree of accuracy the progress from generation to generation of human knowledge. In the field of science, no human author has been able to avoid the fate of obsolescence in later periods; yet the Divine Records have been so framed that there is no conflict with true science in this or any age of human history.[45]

The basic lesson here is for Christians to be patient when new data or theories arise under the flag of science and to wait for the issue to settle out. As Lewis notes, most supposedly world-altering innovations are not as world altering as initially thought. As Schaeffer argues, quick reconciliation is dangerous because those who take both science and Scripture seriously tend to lean toward the authority of the more recent form of revelation. And as Chafer observes,

---

[44] C. S. Lewis, "Religion and Rocketry," in *Essay Collection and Other Short Pieces* (London: HarperCollins, 2000), 231–32.

[45] Chafer, *Systematic Theology*, 1:34.

agreeing with Thomas Kuhn, science itself tends to change over time. This is as likely to be true for scientific theories of cosmogony as for theories of human sexuality, political order, eugenics, or any other novel innovations that are trendy in our day.

Careful Engagement

Patience does not imply a refusal to engage with new ideas, however. The contemporary Christian, seeking to participate in culture as a Christian, must never ignore places where traditional orthodoxy seems to conflict with the ways of the world. C. S. Lewis argues,

> The man who yields to that temptation will, of course, never progress in Christian knowledge. For obviously the doctrines which one finds easy are the doctrines which give Christian sanction to truths you already knew. . . . It is just the same here as in science. The phenomenon which is troublesome, which doesn't fit in with current scientific theories, is the phenomenon which compels reconsideration and thus leads to new knowledge. Science progresses because scientists, instead of running away from such troublesome phenomena or hushing them up, are constantly seeking them out. In the same way, there will be progress in Christian knowledge only as long as we accept the challenge of the difficult or repellent doctrines.[46]

Lewis makes it clear that his target of criticism is "a 'liberal' Christianity which considers itself free to alter the Faith whenever the Faith looks perplexing or repellant."[47] However, the same might be said of forms of doctrinal orthodoxy that fail to reasonably engage in questions raised by the culture of the day due to concerns that it might lead away from an earlier conception of the faith.

Confidence in the faith once for all delivered to the saints and the Scriptures through which it has been delivered should enable the well-equipped Christian to thoughtfully engage with any topic

---

[46.] C. S. Lewis, "Christian Apologetics," in *Essay Collection and Other Short Pieces* (London: HarperCollins, 2000), 149.

[47.] Lewis, "Christian Apologetics," 149.

as a thoroughly orthodox believer. Theories about climate change should no more threaten our faith than the discovery of antibiotics, provided we seek to understand the world through Scripture rather than make Scripture conform to a particular understanding of the world.

CONCLUSION

This chapter has outlined an approach to moral authority that views the canon of Scripture as the final authority on all matters of faith and life. The original manuscripts of the Bible are inerrant, and the text we have is a faithful rendition of that text. God has graciously given general revelation, which can teach us many things about creation. The challenge of our age is to appropriately esteem the information gained from scientific experimentation and philosophical reasoning without undermining the supreme authority of Scripture.

KEY TERMS

Common Grace
Epistemology
General Revelation
Scientism
Special Revelation
Sufficiency of Scripture

STUDY QUESTIONS

1. What is the main purpose of God's self-revelation through Scripture?
2. How are general and special revelation similar and distinct?
3. What are some examples of moral decisions that require extra-biblical information?

4. How does common grace support the value of scientific data for moral decisions when it is evaluated through the lens of Scripture?
5. What are the dangers of scientism, and how have they affected moral decision-making in our day?

CHAPTER 5

The Value of God's Creation

An athlete's leg immediately after they have had a cast removed for a broken ankle is a disappointing sight. After months of crutches or scooting along awkwardly, the leg will look scrawny and typically a lot paler than the other, healthy leg. The muscle on the leg wasted away as the injured leg was confined by the cast and underused. Similarly, as Gavin Ortlund argues, "Creation is a frequently underdeveloped, atrophied doctrine."[1] Some theologically conservative systematic theologies deal with the doctrine of creation as part of anthropology.[2] In other cases, the doctrine has been reduced to a topic of apologetic debate about the age of the earth.[3]

This chapter considers some of the core truths of the doctrine of creation to answer another question fundamental to creation care: Why does creation have value? It begins by defining different terms used for the created order, offering definitions that will be useful for the balance of this volume. Then it bounds the discussion to the question of value so that debates about creationism and the usefulness of creation as an apologetic tool do not distract us from the main point of discussion. The chapter then explores different types of value creation has, which is the crux of the argument. Finally, it discusses the impact of sin on the value of creation and the twin dangers of pantheism and dualism.

NATURE, ENVIRONMENT, OR CREATION?

What does the word *creation* actually mean? Depending on the author, there can be a range of meanings in the words *creation*, *nature*, and

---

[1] Gavin Ortlund, *Retrieving Augustine's Doctrine of Creation: Ancient Wisdom for Current Controversy* (Downers Grove: IVP Academic, 2020), 15.

[2] For example, Ryrie, *Basic Theology*, 180–88 (see chap. 4, n. 21); Elmer L. Towns, *Theology for Today* (Boston: Cengage Learning, 2001), 555–622; Chafer, *Systematic Theology*, 2:130–43 (see chap. 4, n. 9).

[3] For example, Chafer, *Systematic Theology*, 7:99–101.

environment. The term *creation* has a double meaning.[4] It often refers to God's creative act in forming and sustaining the world. This is the sense that John Frame offers in his *Systematic Theology*: "Creation is an act of God alone, by which, for his own glory, he brings into existence everything in the universe, things that had no existence prior to his creative word."[5] He focuses on the original creative act, electing to discuss God's continuing work in sustaining creation under the heading of *providence*. However, *creation* can commonly be used to discuss the *product* of God's generative work too. As Albert Wolters notes, "Creating activity and created order ought not to be confused."[6]

Creation is a loaded term in environmental ethics because it presumes a supernatural understanding of reality. It is unsurprising that many environmentalists default to the term *nature*, which has a more naturalistic sense.[7] To call the cosmos *nature* in a reductive sense means that "humans cease to be creatures of God made to share in the divine delight in the goodness and beauty of things. Instead, all things are reducible to amoral, material elements that can be manipulated to suit a variety of purposes chosen by us."[8] Some, like the late E. O. Wilson, argue that nature is the part of the cosmos unaffected by humanity. He writes, "Nature is that part of the original environment and its life forms that remains after human impact."[9]

Wilson's definition of nature constrains the created order and the place of humans within that order.[10] This sort of definition leads to disenchantment and abuse.[11] Instead of the supernaturally charged cosmos, this view argues that "we live in a universe, a cold, hostile place whose existence is a big accident, where humanity is temporarily animated 'stuff' that's ultimately meaningless and destined for the

---

[4.] Albert Wolters, *Creation Regained: Biblical Basics for a Reformational Worldview*, 2nd ed. (Grand Rapids: Eerdmans, 2005), 13–14.

[5.] Frame, *Systematic Theology*, 185 (see chap. 3, n. 17).

[6.] Wolters, *Creation Regained*, 13.

[7.] Notably, the use of *nature* is not confined to non-Christians. Francis Schaeffer used the term frequently, still believing strongly in special creation by God. See Francis Schaeffer, *Pollution and the Death of Man*.

[8.] Norman Wirzba, *From Nature to Creation: A Christian View for Understanding and Loving Our World* (Grand Rapids: Baker, 2015), 14.

[9.] Wilson, *The Creation*, 15 (see chap 3, n. 38).

[10.] Ironically, Wilson describes his naturalistic epistemology as coming from "the Ionian Enchantment." Wilson, *Consilience*, 3–7.

[11.] Berry, *Life Is a Miracle*, 7 (see chap. 3, n. 40).

trash heap."[12] This definition limits the boundaries of nature to that which can be seen, touched, or measured.

Since this is a book about how humans should tend to the product of the creative work of God, the term *creation* will generally be used to mean *created order* or *all the things that God created*. That, of course, includes all things "in heaven and on earth, the visible and invisible, whether thrones or dominions or rulers or authorities" (Col 1:16). Creation is everything God has made. As Schaeffer argues, "*All* things were equally created out of nothing. *All things, including man, are equal in their origin*, as far as creation is concerned."[13] An appropriate definition of creation, therefore, must include both human and nonhuman creation.

CREATIONISM AND APOLOGETICS

Christians can lose sight of the value God places on creation when they begin to focus on debates about creationism, especially with regard to the age of the earth,[14] and apologetics, where the beauty of nature is used to point people toward belief in God.[15] Both of these aspects of creation are worthy for debate, but when our view of creation is reduced *only* to a discussion of the existence and power of the Creator or the timing of the creation event, we miss the goodness of creation as creation.

Creationism and the Gospel

Often when creation comes up in a conversation about Christianity, people assume the point of discussion is going to be the age of the earth and whether humans evolved from apes. When I was in Naval Nuclear Power School, one of the main concerns of my non-Christian friends was how I could be concerned with splitting the atom when

[12.] Michael Cosper, *Recapturing the Wonder: Transcendent Faith in a Disenchanted World* (Downers Grove: IVP, 2017), 15.

[13.] Schaeffer, *Pollution and the Death of Man*, 5:28. Emphasis original.

[14.] Kenneth Keathley and Mark Rooker, *40 Questions about Creation and Evolution* (Grand Rapids: Kregel, 2014), 17–18.

[15.] Schaeffer, *Pollution and the Death of Man*, 5:23.

Christianity required a belief in a 6,000-year-old earth. My classmates had a tacit assumption that a belief in Young Earth Creationism was an essential Christian position.[16] They also assumed it was somehow an impediment to my ability to learn how to operate a nuclear reactor. In part, this was a means of establishing a defeater belief to isolate themselves from the gospel so they did not need to consider to the core truths of Christianity.[17] It was a challenge to convince them otherwise, and my efforts to do so likely clouded my ability to communicate the much more vital message of the gospel.

Whatever one does with the timeline of Genesis 1 and 2, the most important aspect of creation is that it comes from God. The power of God to create and his work in creation are among the most significant motivators for faith. It is on the basis of that faith that a theology for creation care must be developed. The age of the earth may well be debated, but God's special role as creator is an essential part of the Christian story.

In a 2013 article, the late British geneticist and Christian R. J. Berry argued that belief in creationism is necessarily an impediment to advocacy for proper stewardship of the environment. Berry thus argues that if Christians are going to be rightly concerned with creation care, they must simply adopt the common scientific understanding of an ancient earth with an evolutionary theory of life.[18] He claims that non-Darwinian theories of creation rely on dualism, which in turn causes apathy toward the well-being of the environment. His argument is essentially that to deny Darwinian theories of evolution is to stubbornly deny the validity of modern science, so there is little reason for further discussion.[19] More significantly, Berry elsewhere made extended arguments for evolution as the basis for environmentalism.[20] It seems it is the creationist position, not the discussion itself, that

---

16. This assumption is not without grounds, as some Christian confessions include a six-day creation as an article of faith. See "The Westminster Confession of Faith," 4.1, in Van Dixhoorn, *Creeds, Confessions, & Catechisms*, 181 (see introduction, n. 5).

17. Tim Keller, *The Reason for God: Belief in an Age of Skepticism* (New York: Dutton, 2008), 92–95.

18. R. J. Berry, "Disputing Evolution Encourages Environmental Neglect," in *Science & Christian Belief* 25, no. 2 (2013): 113–30.

19. Berry, 127–30.

20. R. J. Berry, *Ecology and the Environment: The Mechanisms, Marrings, and Maintenance of Nature* (West Conshohocken, PA: Templeton Press, 2011).

Berry most fervently opposed. However, Ortlund's underlying point is worth considering: endless debates over the timing and duration of the initial process of creation *ex nihilo* tend to distract Christians from the implications of the doctrine of creation.[21]

This is not to say that discussions about creationism cannot be fruitful or are unimportant to discipleship. However, the controversial aspects of discussions about creationism, theistic evolutionism, and other theories of origin tend to distract from the thorough consensus Christians ought to have about the goodness of creation and what that means to our daily lives. Whenever creation happened and however long it took, orthodox Christians should all be able to agree that God created through Christ (Col 1:16), God owns all of creation (Ps 89:11), and God has entrusted humans to be active in creation for his glory (Gen 1:26–30).

Creation and Apologetics

Even a focus on creation as an apologetic tactic can lead to an improper view of nature. Francis Schaeffer cautioned his readers, "Nature has become merely an academic proof of the existence of the Creator, with little value in itself. Christians of this outlook do not show an interest in nature *itself.* They use it simply as an apologetic weapon, rather than thinking or talking about the real value of nature."[22] Schaeffer was not arguing that Christians stop using the wonder of creation as an apologetic. This would be to undermine a portion of Paul's own methodology in Lystra (Acts 14:8–18) and, more famously, in his discourse on Mars Hill (Acts 17:16–31), not to mention the whole of Scripture itself, which begins with a declaration of wonder at God's creative power.

One of the tragedies of the rise of modern scientific thinking has been a loss of wonder at the created order as humans try to explain it away. As Erwin Chargaff notes, "All great scientific discoveries . . . carry . . . an irreversible loss of something that man cannot afford to lose."[23] That loss is a sense of wonder. So wrote the romantic poet

---

[21.] Ortlund, *Retrieving Augustine's Doctrine of Creation*, 15–17.

[22.] Francis Schaeffer, *Pollution and the Death of Man*, 5:23 (see chap. 2, n. 20). Emphasis original.

[23.] Chargaff, *Heraclitean Fire*, 104 (see chap. 4, n. 41).

William Wordsworth: "We murder to dissect."[24] Once humans have dissected something and understand its constituent parts, there is a natural tendency to lose the sense of awe at it. Wonder at the goodness of creation points to the character of God.[25]

We dare not miss the way that creation testifies to God's character (Rom 1:19–20). Job's worship in response to God's whirlwind tour of creation's majesty is appropriate (Job 40:1–41:34). The beauty of the world affirms the innate sense people have that there is a God, and it illustrates the truthfulness of the Christian story.[26] The inborn idea that there is a right way and a wrong way to live that is largely shared across cultures is evidence of the existence of a common creator.[27] All of these are true and part of how creation clearly reveals God's nature. A proper understanding of the value of creation depends on recognizing the relationship between the creator and his creation.

THE VALUE OF CREATION

The first chapter of Genesis is abundantly clear that God values his creation. Seven times we read of the goodness of creation in God's eyes (Gen 1:4, 10, 12, 18, 21, 25) with the final description of the value of creation being "very good" (1:31). There is little doubt that God values creation. How we sort through the value of creation is exceedingly important, as will become abundantly clear in a later discussion of pantheism. God declares creation to be good, but it is not good because he declares it so. Creation is not good because God labels it so; God labels creation good because it is so.[28]

Where, then, does the goodness of creation come from? Though God sees the goodness that existed before he describes it, that goodness only exists because he made it so. Just as Christ the Creator existed before

---

[24] William Wordsworth, "The Tables Turned," line 28, in *Selected Poetry of William Wordsworth*, ed. Mark Van Doren (New York: Modern Library, 2002), 80.

[25] Peter Kreeft, *Doors in the Walls of the World: Signs of Transcendence in the Human Story* (San Francisco: Ignatius, 2018), 7–25.

[26] Gregory E. Ganssle, *Our Deepest Desires: How the Christian Story Fulfills Human Aspirations* (Downers Grove, IL: IVP Academic, 2017), 89–100.

[27] C. S. Lewis, *Mere Christianity* (San Francisco: HarperSanFrancisco, 1952), 3–27.

[28] Wright, *The Mission of God*, 398–99 (see chap. 3, n. 24).

all things, so the goodness of God predates the creation of the world
(Col 1:17). The goodness of creation is derivative of God's goodness.

Common Categories of Value

To sort out the subtle categories of value, I will use a vocabulary borrowed from non-Christian philosopher C. I. Lewis. According to Lewis,
there are three categories of value. The first is *intrinsic* value, which
is native to an object for its own sake.[29] According to Lewis, nothing
exists in this category, but for Christians this is the category in which
God alone exists. Something that has *intrinsic* value would have value
if it existed and nothing else did. Thus, the triune God, who alone is
self-existent,[30] is the only entity who would (and did) have value with
nothing else to value him.

The second category of value in Lewis's system is *instrumental* value,
which describes the usefulness of an object to a subject. For example,
paper money has very little worth due to its raw materials but can
have a great deal of instrumental value because it is useful to us to
gain other needed things. In most conversational discussion of value,
especially in economics, instrumental value is often the only category
under consideration.

Some environmental ethicists only recognize two categories of value:
intrinsic and instrumental.[31] This is problematic because, simplistically
speaking, it leaves only two options: either an object is of unassailable
worth or it is reducible to its usefulness. Both are problematic for
different reasons. If all created objects have only instrumental value,
then there need be only economic considerations for their utilization.
There is little room for the dignity of humans or even a concern for
the welfare of animals apart from their work. And yet, God seems to
value both humans and animals for more than their practical value

---

[29.] C. I. Lewis, *An Analysis of Knowledge and Valuation* (La Salle, IL: Open Court, 1946), 382.
Though Lewis's value theory was published in the first half of the twentieth century, it continues
to be cited in discussions of value theory as useful.

[30.] The theological term for this is *aseity*. See Frame, *Systematic Theology*, 405–6.

[31.] David Schmidtz, "Value in Nature," in *The Oxford Handbook of Value Theory*, ed. by Iwao
Hirose and Jonas Olson (New York: Oxford University Press, 2015), 383. Another reading of the
intrinsic and instrumental bifurcation in theological context can be found in Jame Schaefer, "Valuing Earth Intrinsically and Instrumentally," *Theological Studies* 66 (2005): 783–814.

(cf. Matt 10:29). Therefore, using only the category of instrumental value to describe the worth of creation is problematic.

Because of a desire to elevate nature above its mere instrumental value, some environmentalists have ascribed intrinsic value to objects in nature. However, when intrinsic value is assigned equally to all natural objects, it makes decision-making about utilization of resources impossible.[32] Ahumanist Patricia MacCormack illustrates this, arguing "the rights of any entity [are] based on not what it is but that it is."[33] If intrinsic value is assumed, it is impossible to choose between cutting down a tree to clear land for building a hospital and lives that might be saved by constructing that hospital. MacCormack's solution is to call for "the cessation of reproduction toward the end of the human as a parasitic detrimental species."[34] The only solution to pollution is for the rational agent to cease to exist. Intrinsic value affirms the futility of this world, rejecting hopeful solutions to environmental problems. At the same time, intrinsic value also opens up opportunities for pantheism because of a belief in the self-worthiness of natural objects. A third category of value is, therefore, warranted.

Inherent Value

C. I. Lewis provides a helpful third category of value between intrinsic and instrumental, which he calls *inherent* value.[35] Inherent value describes the goodness of a physical object based on its proper orientation to that which imparts value to it.[36] In other words, inherent value considers both the value of the existence of an object and its fulfillment of a purpose. For example, a painting may have little instrumental value because it could be used to momentarily feed a

---

[32.] Sahotra Sarkar, *Biodiversity and Environmental Philosophy: An Introduction* (New York: Cambridge University Press, 2005), 57.

[33.] MacCormack, *The Ahuman Manifesto*, 14 (see introduction, n. 16).

[34.] MacCormack, 16.

[35.] Some philosophers use the terms *inherent* and *intrinsic* interchangeably. E.g., J. Baird Callicott, "Intrinsic Value, Quantum Theory," in *In Defense of the Land Ethic* (Albany: State University of New York Press, 1989), 160. Others attempt to differentiate between *intrinsic1* and *intrinsic2*, which generally correspond to Lewis's categories of *intrinsic and inherent*. E.g., Sarkar, *Biodiversity* and *Environmental Philosophy*, 53–54. My goal is to define terms clearly and consistently in my own work, not to attempt to critique the selected vocabulary used by others.

[36.] Lewis, *Analysis of Knowledge and Valuation*, 115.

flame or be wedged in a crack to stop a draft, but it has a great deal of inherent value because it may point to the genius of the mind that imagined it and the skill of the hands that painted it. Consider that if it were taken only for its practical usefulness, the Mona Lisa has little worth. Inherent value includes aesthetics but also transcends it because it looks beyond beauty toward the creator of the beauty.

For Christians, the inherent value of da Vinci's portrait rests in wonder at the God-created mind and skill that rendered the image.[37] Considering what that small painting by da Vinci points toward, the classic work of art is priceless and draws hundreds of thousands of visitors to the Louvre each year. It is the inherent value of the *Mona Lisa* that draws people, not its usefulness or its value apart from those who value it.[38]

Creation has both inherent and instrumental value. It is useful for building houses, feeding other parts of creation, and generating wealth. Creation also has a nonnatural purpose that it fulfills, at least partially, by pointing people toward the Creator (Rom 1:18–20). By the definitions borrowed from C. I. Lewis, creation does *not* have intrinsic value, because it is not self-existent and would not have any worth apart from someone to value it.

This somewhat lengthy discussion on categories we can assign to different types of value may seem like a philosophical abstraction, but it matters. At the same time, these categories, while helpful, are not absolute, and others may use the words differently. For example, in his book on environmental ethics, *Pollution and the Death of Man*, Francis Schaeffer uses the term "intrinsic" for creation.[39] It is clear from the context that he is not ascribing the sort of independent value to the created order that would be implied by a more rigorous definition of *intrinsic*, such as is offered in this chapter. This merely reinforces the importance of offering and demanding clear definitions in reading and dialoguing with others.

[37.] Bruce Riley Ashford and Craig G. Bartholomew, *The Doctrine of Creation: A Constructive Kuyperian Approach* (Downer's Grove: IVP Academic, 2020), 251–56. See also Francis Schaeffer's approach to the value of art in Schaeffer, "Art and the Bible," *Collected Works of Francis A. Schaeffer* (Wheaton: Crossway, 1983), 2:394.

[38.] The idea of inherent value pointing to the goodness of God resonates with "transposition" as described in C. S. Lewis, "Transposition," in *Essay Collection and Other Short Pieces*, 267–78.

[39.] Schaeffer, *Pollution and the Death of Man*, 5:51. Similarly, Mark Liederbach and Seth Bible, *True North: Christ, the Gospel, and Creation Care* (Nashville: B&H Academic, 2012), 37–41.

VALUE OF CREATION IN CHURCH HISTORY

This basic framework for valuing creation is not a novel innovation, however. We can find it in the Christian tradition as far back as Augustine, though the terminology is quite different.[40] In *The Nature of the Good*, Augustine argues that the triune God exists in a unique category of value that is unlike the created order. Creation's value, which is entirely different from God's, is derived from its relationship to the Creator.[41] The degree to which an object is valuable in this sense is determined by its fulfillment of the purpose for which God designed it.[42] These are the categories of intrinsic and inherent value.

Augustine approached the same idea in a slightly different way in *On Christian Teaching*. Here he argues that only God is to be enjoyed, noting that "to enjoy a thing is to rest with satisfaction in it for its own sake."[43] This is distinctly different from objects that are to be "used," which in Augustine's language means to utilize an object for the enjoyment of something that ought to be properly enjoyed. To utilize an object for an incorrect purpose, or to enjoy something other than God, is to abuse it. Only God is to be supremely valued. The created order can be useful in serving and glorifying God. It is sinful to mix up those categories of value.[44] The duty of the Christian is to honor the purpose of God's creation.

Perhaps the most helpful treatise on the purpose of creation is Jonathan Edwards's essay, *A Dissertation on the End for Which God Created the World*. This short work is a careful, step-by-step, logical explanation of the reason for God's original and ongoing creative work. The essence of Edwards's message is that God created the world for his own glory. This purpose of creation helps to undergird the inherent value of creation. As Edwards notes, "Because

---

[40.] For a helpful introduction to Augustine's doctrine of creation, see Ortlund, *Retrieving Augustine's Doctrine of Creation*. See also Rowan D. Williams, "'Good for Nothing'? Augustine on Creation," *Augustinian Studies* 25 (1994): 9–24.

[41.] Augustine, *The Nature of the Good*, in *The Works of Saint Augustine*, vol. 19 (Brooklyn: New City Press, 1990), 325.

[42.] Augustine, *Nature of the Good*, 327.

[43.] Augustine, *On Christian Teaching*, trans. by R. P. H. Green (New York: Oxford University Press, 2008), 4.4.

[44.] Oliver O'Donovan, "*Usus* and *Fruitio* in Augustine, *De Doctrina Christiana I*," in *Journal of Theological Studies* 33, no. 2 (1982): 361–97.

[God] infinitely values his own glory, consisting in the knowledge of himself, love to himself, and complacence and joy in himself; he therefore valued the image, communication, or participation of these in the creature."[45] In other words, God values his creation because it reflects his glory back toward him. This is the essence of the idea of the inherent value of creation.

Herman Bavinck, writing well before the specific question of environmentalism had raised its head in popular conversations, argues:

> The theory that creation is grounded in God's goodness and has for its final end the salvation of man, is also at variance with reality. The universe is not, certainly, exhausted by its service to humanity and must therefore have some goal other than utility to man. The pedestrian utilitarianism and the self-centered teleology of the eighteenth century have been sufficiently refuted.[46]

For Bavinck, the purpose of creation is to bring glory to God because he willed it to exist. It is distinct from God and thus cannot have intrinsic value. Though he does not use the term, Bavinck affirms the inherent value of creation.

C. I. Lewis's vocabulary is helpful for a robust discussion of the value of the created order, but the concept is one that is rooted in the Christian tradition. A proper understanding guards against an overvaluation of the created order while preventing the unthinking misuse of it. It also helps us to understand how creation can retain its goodness despite the effects of sin on creation through the fall of man.

SIN AND THE FALL

Any discussion of the goodness of creation must be accompanied by a consideration of the impact of the sin of humans. The untainted goodness of the created order did not last long.[47] When Adam chose

---

45. Jonathan Edwards, *The End for Which God Created the World*, in *The Works of Jonathan Edwards*, vol. 1 (Peabody, MA: Hendrickson, 2003), 120.

46. Herman Bavinck, *Reformed Dogmatics* (Grand Rapids: Baker Academic, 2006), 1:433

47. There is significant debate among faithful Christians whether there is "some sort of mysterious

to disobey God and eat of the tree of the knowledge of good and evil, he incurred God's just wrath. The result was banishment from the garden, but also, as both a form of discipline and as a blessing, the earth was cursed as well.

God's words to Adam in Gen 3:17–19 are particularly significant to our understanding of the value of creation. The key phrase is in verse 17: "the ground is cursed because of you." Often this is taken to mean that God somehow is punishing creation in lieu of Adam and Eve or that it sums up his making childbirth painful (v. 16) and work more difficult (v. 19), but another reading of the verse, particularly in the context of the broader narrative of Scripture, may indicate this cursing of the ground is as much "for thy sake" (KJV) as it is "as a result of what you did." In other words, creation was cursed to help remind humans that this sinful condition is not the way it is supposed to be by pointing to the need for redemption.[48]

There is no question that creation's curse significantly impacts our understanding of suffering and our hope of redemption. Paul made this perfectly clear in Rom 8:18–25. Creation groans as in the pains of childbirth—an allusion to Eve's pain in Gen 3:16—and it was subjected to futility "because of him who subjected it, in hope" (Rom 8:20 ESV).[49] The word *hope* here implies there is a purpose beyond the suffering itself. In other words, God was not simply punishing humanity by making things harder or, to borrow Paul's anthropomorphic metaphor, by making creation a substitutionary sacrifice for human sin. Instead, there is a symbolic purpose for the curse.

The world around us reminds us that things are not the way they ought to be.[50] It points us toward the need for righteousness. When

---

ontological change in the very makeup of creation itself." Douglas J. Moo and Jonathan A. Moo, *Creation Care: A Biblical Theology of the Natural World* (Grand Rapids: Zondervan, 2018), 103. For example, Bauckham argues that the futility of Rom 8:20 exceeds the frustration of work in Gen 3:17 and should be understood to "mean that, because of human sin, God set creation on course for un-creation." Bauckham, *The Bible and Ecology*, 97. In context, it appears he is trying to defend a natural continuity of creation before and after the fall, which he claims more specifically later in the volume (160). The divide seems to be based on theories of human origin and acceptance of contemporary theories of evolution.

[48.] John Frame, *Nature's Case for God* (Bellingham, WA: Lexham Press, 2018), 44–47.

[49.] Thomas R. Schreiner, *Romans,* BECNT (Grand Rapids: Baker Academic, 2018), 436; Sandra L. Richter, *Stewards of Eden: What Scripture Says about the Environment and Why It Matters* (Downers Grove: IVP Academic, 2020), 12.

[50.] Williams highlights how a proper understanding of the effects of sin in creation help delineate

Adam sinned, God cursed all of creation: "The ground is cursed because of you. You will eat from it by means of painful labor all the days of your life" (Gen 3:17). The King James Version translates the first phrase as "cursed is the ground for thy sake." The modern translation is true, but there is theological significance in the older language. The ground was cursed because of Adam's sin but also for his good.[51] Instead of immediate death, the curse was a gift that points to the need for redemption.[52] The curse was for our sake.

Jesus's words in Luke 13:1–5 help explain what it means for creation to have been cursed for the sake of humanity. When the crowd began asking Christ about evil done against certain Galilean Jews whose bodies were desecrated by Pilate, Jesus pointed toward a natural evil—a bad thing that happened to "innocent" people without clear human agency—to show that one purpose of the effects of the fall is to lead people to repentance. The disruption of peace in the created order is ordained by God to remind us that all is not right with the world.[53]

Pilate's murder of the Galilean Jews was a very human evil perpetrated by a wicked ruler against his subjects. But Jesus also pointed to the collapse of the tower in Siloam (Luke 13:4), which fell and killed eighteen Jews who, according to Christ, were no worse sinners than anyone else. What he said in verse 5 is key to understanding the effect and purpose of sin in creation: "No, I tell you; but unless you repent, you will all perish as well." Natural evil is intended to remind us that this world is not as it should be, that we deserve worse than we have received, and therefore that we must turn from our own sin.

The effects of the fall did not wholly obscure God's purpose for creation; it merely redirected it. Paul explained to the Romans that even the cursed creation still reveals God's glory: "For what can be known about God is plain to them, because God has shown it to them. For his invisible attributes, namely, his eternal power and divine nature, have been clearly perceived, ever since the creation of the world, in

the need for and effects of redemption. Michael D. Williams, *Far as the Curse Is Found: The Covenant Story of Redemption* (Phillipsburg, NJ: P&R, 2005), 76.

[51.] Cornelis Vonk, *Opening the Scriptures: Genesis* (Grand Rapids: Christian's Library, 2013), 125–32. See also, Herman Bavinck, *Reformed Dogmatics*, 3:199–200; Louis Berkhof, *Systematic Theology* (Carlisle, PA: Banner of Truth, 2021), 260.

[52.] Frame, *Systematic Theology*, 858–59.

[53.] Frame, 283.

the things that have been made. So they are without excuse" (1:19–20 ESV). Creation's groanings are for freedom from the curse, which has redirected creation's goodness. Instead of simply glorifying God, creation now also serves to illuminate the deficiencies of the present age to sinful humans. Creation still has inherent value, even though it is sown with thorns and thistles, because it is fulfilling the purpose God has ordained for it. The promise of the future restoration of creation, which will be discussed in chapter 7, actually enables the current sin-infused state of creation to be a foil that will glorify God even more. That restoration began with the incarnation of God himself in the person of Jesus Christ.

INCARNATION AND RESTORATION

Perhaps the most hopeful indication of the continued value after the fall is that the second person of the Trinity, Jesus Christ, himself took on human flesh, taking part in the creation he had brought into existence (John 1:1–18). C. S. Lewis describes it as the central chapter of the history of the universe. The incarnation and subsequent resurrection of Christ is the piece of the story that brings new meaning out of the whole work and without which the story would not be complete.[54] When Christ "assumed the form of a servant, taking on the likeness of humanity" (Phil 2:7), he validated the goodness of the created order.

God himself became our great high priest, who is able to "sympathize with our weaknesses" because he was "tempted in every way as we are, yet without sin" (Heb 4:15). As Athanasius argues, Christ "has been manifested in a human body for this reason only, out of the love and goodness of His Father, for the salvation of us men." This sounds rather human centered, but Athanasius immediately makes it clear that all of creation was validated through the incarnation. He writes, "We will begin, then, with the creation of the world and with God its Maker, for the first fact that you must grasp is this: *the renewal of creation has been wrought by the Self-same Word Who made it in the beginning.*"[55] It is the incarnation of Christ, in part, that helps us understand. As Al

---

[54.] C. S. Lewis, "The Grand Miracle," in *Essay Collection and Other Short Pieces*, 3–9.
[55.] Athanasius, *On the Incarnation* (Crestwood, NY: St Vladimir's Seminary Press, 1977), 26. Emphasis original.

Wolters argues, "God does not make junk, and he does not junk what he made."[56] The incarnation is a pivotal moment in the timeline of the restoration of all creation, which Christ began on the cross and which will be brought to completion at his soon return. In the meanwhile, we are called to work for the restoration of creation from the effects of sin.

THE GOODNESS OF *SHALOM*

Chapters 9 and 10 will address practical aspects of environmental ethics and the proper relationship of humans with the rest of creation, but it must be abundantly clear what is and is not meant by the goodness of creation prior to the fall. The cosmos was very good and unspoiled by sin, but it was not complete. God's will is unchangeable. His intention was always for humans to cultivate the earth from a garden to a city, which is evidenced by John's vision of our heavenly dwelling being presented as a rich, abundant New Jerusalem (Revelation 21–22). Eschatological depictions of eternity all have one common theme, namely *shalom*.

As Cornelius Plantinga explains in his classic volume *Not the Way It's Supposed to Be,*

> The webbing together of God, humans, and all creation in justice, fulfillment, and delight is what the Hebrew prophets call *shalom*. We call it peace, but it means far more than mere peace of mind or a cease-fire between enemies. In the Bible, shalom means *universal flourishing, wholeness, and delight*—a rich state of affairs in which natural needs are satisfied and natural gifts fruitfully employed, a state of affairs that inspires joyful wonder as its Creator and Savior opens doors and welcomes the creatures in whom he delights. Shalom, in other words, is the way things ought to be.[57]

The goal is, therefore, not to attempt to return creation to a state prior to human influence, but to pursue the flourishing of the whole creation.[58]

[56.] Wolters, *Creation Regained*, 49.

[57.] Cornelius Plantinga, *Not the Way It's Supposed to Be: A Breviary of Sin* (Grand Rapids: Eerdmans, 1995), 10.

[58.] Wolters, *Creation Regained*, 77.

When a concern for *shalom* permeates the development of technology, expansion of human settlements, and production of consumer goods, then we will have taken a significant step toward recognizing the goodness of creation. Francis Schaeffer writes,

> Christians, of all people, should not be the destroyers. We should treat nature with an overwhelming respect. We may cut down a tree to build a house, or make a fire to keep the family warm. But we should not cut down the tree just to cut down the tree. . . . To do so is not to treat the tree with integrity.[59]

Schaeffer then goes on to explain that housing developments that bulldoze all the trees to save a small amount of money create a neighborhood that is "less human in its barrenness, and even economically it is poorer as the topsoil washes away. So when man breaks God's truth, in reality he suffers."[60] The pursuit of the moral order within creation is the pursuit of *shalom*. And, within the fallen world that we occupy, our goal should be to seek the flourishing of creation. This requires incredible thoughtfulness about every aspect of our daily lives. Though it increases concern for creation, the idea of *shalom* guards us from worshipping the creation rather than the Creator because it seeks the proper order of that relationship.[61]

THE DANGERS OF PANTHEISM

God is both transcendent and immanent at the same time. He is uncreated and totally distinct in nature from the created order. At the same time, God intimately relates to creation. He made it. He owns it. He sustains it. And, most significantly, God came down and participated in creation through the incarnation. Both God's transcendence and his immanence reinforce the importance of caring for creation. Significantly, they also create boundaries for creation care that should prevent Christians from heading toward neglect on one side or nature worship on the other side.

---

[59] Schaeffer, *Pollution and the Death of Man*, 5:44.
[60] Schaeffer, *Pollution and the Death of Man*, 5:44.
[61] Bavinck, *Reformed Dogmatics*, 1:438–39.

The balance between transcendence and immanence is a constant source of tension in the history of Christian tradition. Recent trends in modern theology have tended to emphasize the immanence of God in creation; thus, they have often tended toward pantheism or panentheism.[62] These errors are deadly to Christian orthodoxy. Unfortunately, pantheism is sometimes touted as a means to make Christianity more ecologically friendly.[63] The threat of pantheism has tended to make orthodox Christians leery of creation care and those who advocate for it.

Pantheism includes the belief that matter is divine.[64] It is a belief system more often present in Eastern mystical religions. Panentheism is the belief that the divine is in matter, but is not limited to the material world.[65] For proponents of environmentalism, belief in a direct link between the matter of the world and the divine provides obvious motivation for preserving the environment.[66] (Recall that Lynn White Jr. argued the Christian idea of the transcendence of God was the cause of environmental degradation.[67]) If God is in a flower, then to kill a flower is to kill a part of the divine. In a real sense, pantheists and panentheists actually worship nature.

There are logical problems with believing in the divinity of matter. For example, humans must eat something to survive, and the consumption even of plants requires the death of something. By arguing for creation's intrinsic value, pantheism and panentheism remove the ability to debate between the existence of different living things. In theory, it is not clear why, or if, a tree can be cut down to build a home or heat it if the tree is part of the divine or infused with divine nature. Since this is unworkable in theory, it has enabled in practice the abuse of the environment even in pantheistic cultures. John Gatta notes, "Well before the industrial era, parts of China and Japan had suffered deforestation and erosion—sometimes in appreciable measure,

[62.] Olson, *The Story of Christian Theology*, 550 (see chap. 1, n. 28). For a clear example of this, see Gretel Van Wieren, *Restored to Earth: Christianity, Environmental Ethics, and Ecological Restoration* (Washington, DC: Georgetown University Press, 2013), 78–80.

[63.] Means, "Why Worry about Nature?," 5:71–76 (see chap. 2, n. 19).

[64.] James W. Sire, *The Universe Next Door: A Basic Worldview Catalog*, 2nd ed. (Downers Grove, IL: IVP, 1988), 140–41.

[65.] Timothy R. Phillips and Dennis L. Okholm, *Welcome to the Family: An Introduction to Evangelical Christianity* (Wheaton: Bridgepoint, 1996), 27–30.

[66.] See Van Wieren, *Restored to Earth,* 78–80.

[67.] White, "The Historical Roots of Our Ecological Crisis," 131–35 (see chap. 2, n. 15).

because so much timber had been cut for the construction of large Buddhist temples."[68]

There are also obvious theological problems with pantheism and panentheism for the orthodox Christian.[69] These beliefs undermine the Creator-creature distinction. It confuses perfect, eternal existence of the divine with the material reality that is around us. In the end, movements that attempt to elevate the value of nature end up diminishing its value because it depersonalizes the conception of the divine. There is little accountability for morality, justice, or love when the divine is simply a cosmic energy or the matter that makes up the world.[70] As Paul noted, those who deify nature "exchanged the truth of God for a lie, and worshiped and served what has been created instead of the Creator, who is praised forever" (Rom 1:25). As Robert Letham summarizes, "In both cases [of pantheism and panentheism], [God] has been dethroned, and humanity is the master."[71]

A Christian environmental ethics must therefore recognize a sharp distinction between the Creator and his creation. A value structure that recognizes the inherent value of creation instead of the intrinsic value of creation helps make this differentiation. Thus, in Augustine's conception of worth, only God is to be enjoyed and to attempt to find ultimate value in the created order is to abuse it. Avoiding panentheism and pantheism is a healthy step toward orthodoxy and a proper valuation of creation, but Christians must also avoid the opposite error associated with Gnostic dualism.

THE DANGER OF GNOSTIC DUALISM

If panentheism and pantheism overemphasize the immanence of God to creation, some forms of dualism overstress the difference between the creature and the Creator. In light of one error, our basic human instinct is to toggle to the opposite stance. However, to do so will cause us to fall into an error in some ways as dangerous as the deification

---

68. Gatta, *Making Nature Sacred*, 22 (see chap. 2, n. 18).

69. Bavinck, *Reformed Dogmatics*, 1:408–15.

70. See Frame, *Doctrine of the Christian Life*, 63–66 (see chap. 3, n. 34).

71. Letham, *Systematic Theology*, 52–53 (see chap. 4, n. 14).

of nature. Gnostic dualism is a philosophical orientation that sees the chief problem of humanity as being embodied in creation and that salvation, as it were, is to be freed from material existence.[72] This sort of negative attitude toward creation has been a temptation to Christians throughout church history.[73]

To be clear, orthodox Christianity recognizes various forms of dualism.[74] There is a difference between spirit and matter. Humans are not *only* spirit or *only* body. We are both.[75] Even if someone dies in a flaming car wreck and their body is entirely consumed by the blaze, their soul lives on apart from their body. The parable of Lazarus and the rich man (Luke 16:19–31) illustrates this idea. Paul, too, reminded the Corinthian church that one can be "away from the body and at home with the Lord" (2 Cor 5:8). At the same time, our bodies are significant since we will receive physical, resurrection bodies when Christ comes again (1 Cor 15:35–49). Neither spirit nor matter can be discounted by Christians as unworthy aspects of God's creation.[76]

The dualisms evidenced in a biblical Christian theology are different from other forms of dualism, including Gnostic dualism. As critics like Rosemary Radford Ruether note, there are harmful forms of dualism that denigrate the material creation, sometimes leading to its abuse. These dualisms have, at times, found their way among Christian thinkers.[77] Augustine is sometimes described as an arch-dualist because there are points (particularly in his sexual ethics) where earlier Neoplatonic influences seem to retain some sway. However, Bradley Green convincingly argues, "While Augustine does affirm a type of matter-spirit dualism . . . it is important to see that for Augustine

---

[72] See John Frame, *A History of Western Philosophy and Theology* (Phillipsburg, NJ: P&R, 2015), 89–96.

[73] For a rebuttal of Cartesian dualism, which is distinct but which carries some similarities with Gnostic dualism, see R. Lucas Stamps, "A Chalcedonian Argument Against Cartesian Dualism," *The Southern Baptist Journal of Theology* 19, no. 1 (2015): 53–66.

[74] For a discussion of the idealistic dualism of Plato and how it has influenced (or resonated) with the Christian tradition, see Sean M. McDonough, *Creation and New Creation: Understanding God's Creation Project* (Peabody, MA: Hendrickson, 2017), 110–40.

[75] Moreland, *Scientism and Secularism*, 86–95 (see chap. 4, n. 29).

[76] Jame Schaefer, *Theological Foundations for Environmental Ethics* (Washington, DC: Georgetown University Press, 2009), 65–66.

[77] Rosemary Radford Ruether, "Religious Ecofeminism: Healing the Ecological Crisis," in *The Oxford Handbook of Religion and Ecology*, ed. Roger S. Gottlieb (New York: OUP, 2006), 363–67.

this is a *limited* dualism. Both matter *and* spirit are good, although Augustine sees the spiritual as superior."[78]

There is little question that there is a hierarchy between matter and spirit, as Christ himself urged his disciples to fear God "who can destroy both soul and body in hell" and not to fear those "who kill the body but are not able to kill the soul" (Matt 10:28). Similarly, Jesus asked, "For what will it profit a man if he gains the whole world and forfeits his soul?" (Matt 16:26 ESV). There is a difference between matter and spirit, and while both are good, there are degrees of value.

Some Christians significantly undervalue the goodness of creation as a result of this difference. This often comes with an eschatological dimension, which is evidenced in hymns like "This World Is Not My Home," "I'll Fly Away," and "The Gospel Ship." All of these songs reflect a strong desire for being in God's presence, but they implicitly teach an escapist mentality that sees the world as something to leave behind without adequately considering how God can be glorified even as we eat and drink (1 Cor 10:31). Creation has inherent value, so our understanding of the differences between matter and spirit, creation and Creator, ensouled humanity and brute animal should never cause us to diminish the goodness of God's creation.

CONCLUSION

Other than the doctrine of revelation, which answers the basic question of the source of authority, the doctrine of creation is the most important doctrine for a Christian environmental ethics. If the value of creation is reduced to its material benefits for humans, then dominion can quickly turn to domination, and use can become abuse. At the same time, without establishing the distinction between intrinsic value and inherent value, creation care can quickly lead to nature worship. This chapter has examined the value in creation and how that has been explained in church history. It has also examined common terminology for the value of creation and argued that creation has both inherent

---

[78.] Bradley Green, *Colin Gunton and the Failure of Augustine* (Eugene, OR: Pickwick, 2011), 132. Emphasis original.

and instrumental value. In addition, this chapter has warned of the dangers of pantheism and dualism.

The goodness of creation should drive us to care for it. That is why this doctrine is so essential to a Christian environmental ethics. Since God created the world for his own glory, we should be actively engaged in helping creation fulfill its purpose.

KEY TERMS

Dualism
Incarnation
Inherent Value
Instrumental Value
Intrinsic Value
Panentheism
Pantheism
Shalom

STUDY QUESTIONS

1. Why are the differences between *inherent* and *intrinsic* value significant for environmental ethics?
2. What is *shalom,* and how does it shape the goal of environmental ethics?
3. What are the dangers of *pantheism* and *panentheism*? How does Scripture show that God is distinct from creation?
4. How can dualism negatively influence a theological perspective for creation care? Is all dualism bad?
5. Why did God create the world?
6. In what ways does the fall impact the value of creation?

CHAPTER 6

Anthropology and Stewardship

Shift, the scheming ape in C. S. Lewis's book *The Last Battle,* represents the essence of humanity as wearing clothes and exploiting the rest of creation. To sell his dominance over the other talking animals, the monkey wore "a scarlet jacket which did not fit him very well, having been made for a dwarf. He had jeweled slippers on his hind paws which would not stay on properly because, as you know, the hind paws of an Ape are really like hands."[1] When others questioned his humanity, Shift asserted, "I'm a Man. If I look like an Ape, that's because I'm so very old: hundreds and hundreds of years old. And it's because I'm so old that I'm so wise. And it's because I'm so wise that I'm the only one Aslan is ever going to speak to."[2] So trousers are the symbol of wisdom, and supposed wisdom is the justification for abusive domination. This is an appallingly thin answer to an important question.

One of the central worldview questions is, What does it mean to be human?[3] For a theology of creation care, we must ask more specifically, What is the proper role of humanity within the created order? The question is how humans fit within the web of creation. We seem different than the rest of creation, but it is not always clear in what ways. This has been a perennial concern throughout the modern era, particularly since Darwin began to cast the nature of humanity in doubt.[4] It remains a valid question whether humans are an alien species whose impact always mars creation, or whether we are servants of creation sent to care for its every need, or something in between. We must wrestle with all of these questions as we seek to discern the place of humans within the created order.

[1.] C. S. Lewis, *The Last Battle* (New York: HarperTrophy, 1984), 32.

[2.] Lewis, 35.

[3.] See Ronald Nash, *Life's Ultimate Questions: An Introduction to Philosophy* (Grand Rapids: Zondervan, 1999), 17.

[4.] C. S. Lewis, "*De Descriptione Temporum,*" in *Selected Literary Essays* (London: Cambridge University Press, 1969), 7.

Wendell Berry points out that this is a fundamentally religious question. He notes,

> The question of human limits, of the proper definition and place of human beings within the order of Creation, finally rests upon our attitude toward our biological existence, the life of the body in this world. . . . These are religious questions, obviously, for our bodies are part of the Creation, and they involve us all in the issues of mystery. But the questions are also agricultural, for no matter how urban our life, our bodies live by farming; we come from the earth and return to it, and so we live in agriculture as we live in flesh.[5]

Some environmentalists seek to answer this question apart from overt appeals to religious language. But it is impossible to separate the doctrine of humanity from other basic religious and philosophical conceptions of reality.[6] We are, therefore, fully justified in exploring the topic from a traditionally Christian perspective, whatever those committed to supposedly neutral humanistic points of view may claim.

As we explore these questions, it will become clear from Scripture that humans have a special place within creation. Men and women were created in the image of God. Humanity has been given a unique role in the created order, with both privilege and responsibility. In some sense, humans are lords of creation, but our lordship is really a stewardship for the Creator King (Psalm 115). As stewards we have the right to consume the fruit of nonhuman creation with a clear conscience within proper limits. We also have the responsibility to tend the garden of creation and to bring it into healthy production. Stewardship bears with its limits: limits driven by the responsibility of management without ownership and reinforced by the unknown timeframe of the owner's return. Humans have unquestionably struggled to live up to our stewardship responsibilities since the fall of humanity, which raises doubts about the connection between the vocation of stewardship and our unique role as humans.[7]

---

[5] Wendell Berry, *The Unsettling of America: Culture and Agriculture* (Berkeley: Counterpoint, 2015), 101.

[6] For example, Wilson, *On Human Nature*, 1–13 (see chap. 3, n. 46).

[7] Richard Bauckham, *Living with Other Creatures* (Waco: Baylor University Press, 2011), 14–62.

UNIQUENESS OF HUMANITY

For most of human history, the distinctness of the human race from other animals seemed self-evident. Most religions describe humans as being specially created by the divine, recognizing the obvious differences between human and nonhuman creatures. In the late nineteenth century when Charles Darwin published his controversial book *The Descent of Man*, the assumed distinctiveness of humanity took a blow. He argued natural selection applies to humans as well as to the lower animals and that humans were genetically descended from a common ancestor with apes.[8] The main difference between the human and ape was considered to be behavior and brain size, caused by humans winning the evolutionary lottery, so to speak.

For decades after Darwin, the definition of human was expressed in utilitarian terms. Humans were animals that used tools. Though this definition certainly did not satisfy many Christians who argued for God's special creation of humanity as a distinct species, it at least recognized the categorical difference between humans as "higher" creatures and animals as lower. Even this distinction was exploded, however, based on the studies of Jane Goodall, whose embedded research with primates in central Africa revealed that chimpanzees used sticks as tools to poke ant hills in order to gather the insects for food.[9] Research into animal communication and emotional behaviors has continued to shift the definition of humanity so that many now assume humans are not distinct from animals but merely at a higher point on certain spectrums of evolved capability.[10]

It is true that research into animal behavior has significantly undermined the categorical distinctions between human and nonhuman living beings. Yet, as we consider the fact that the tool use of chimpanzees and the communication among dolphins confuse categories once assumed to define humanity, we can still recognize that the degree of competence of humans within those categories is orders of magnitude different than the most advanced animal. There is an enormous distance between a pocket calculator and a stick used for poking ant hills. The

---

[8.] Berry, *Ecology and the Environment*, 144–48 (see chap. 5, n. 20).

[9.] Jane Goodall, *In the Shadow of Man* (Boston: Houghton Mifflin, 1971), 239–41.

[10.] Wilson, *On Human Nature*, 15–70.

range of concepts communicated in human language far exceeds the complexity of information transmitted by nonhumans in their barks, clicks, squawks, and gestures. Moreover, as Alasdair MacIntyre argues, humans alone are capable of self-reflection and critique.[11]

As Christians, we are led by Scripture to understand the place of humanity as being uniquely made in the image of God. All the land animals were made from the earth in response to God's spoken word (Gen 1:24–25). The description of the creation of humanity reflects a more intimate, personal involvement as "The LORD God formed the man out of the dust from the ground and breathed the breath of life into his nostrils, and the man became a living being" (2:7). The first woman, too, was specially created by God from the flesh of the first man (1:21–22). Moses, the author of Genesis, documented a distinct divine focus on the origin of humanity.

The uniqueness of humanity is reinforced by the creation of humanity in the image of God (1:26–27). According to Herman Bavinck, "Nothing in a human being is excluded from the image of God. While all creatures display *vestiges* of God, only a human being is in the *image* of God."[12] What exactly it means for humanity to be made in the image of God has been the source of extensive debate throughout Christian history.[13] We exhibit the image of God, in part, when we exercise our vocations of creativity and stewardship.[14] The special position of humans is an honor bestowed by God, but it makes it more shameful when we fail to live up to God's creational ideal.

The Limited Value of Humans

Despite the elevated status of humans, the uniqueness of humanity does not translate to infinite value of any human. Such a concept presupposes the idea of *intrinsic* value, which was discussed in greater detail in chapter 5. Humanity is unique from the rest of creation;

[11.] Alasdair MacIntyre, *Ethics in the Conflicts of Modernity: An Essay on Desire, Practical Reasoning, and Narrative* (Cambridge, UK: Cambridge University Press, 2016), 224–28.

[12.] Bavinck, *Reformed Dogmatics*, 2:555 (see chap. 5, n. 46).

[13.] John Hammett and Katie McCoy, *The Doctrine of Humanity* (Nashville: B&H Academic, 2023), chapters 4 and 5. See also, Bavinck, *Reformed Dogmatics*, 2:533–54.

[14.] Christopher W. Morgan, *Christian Theology: The Biblical Story and Our Faith* (Nashville: B&H Academic, 2020), 188–89.

moreover, each human is precious; but this does not mean any human life has infinite value. Assertions of infinite value are useful for creating ethical dilemmas about trolleys, which seem designed by philosophers to reveal underlying utilitarianism in people's thinking. Infinite human value shares the difficulties of the intrinsic value in creation: it makes resolving conflicting moral decisions about human life impossible.

For example, if each human life was infinitely valuable, then no environmental cost would ever be too great to save the life of even one human. Could we level a forest to extract a trace chemical needed to save one person? If the life of one human is infinitely valuable, then how valuable is the comfort and temporary happiness of some? Society often functions as if human comfort is worth a great deal of environmental destruction, but that reflects the human tendency to sin as we live out the experience of the fall. We are unique as humans in creation, but we are still part of creation and must relate to creation by giving it the respect it deserves. As Francis Schaeffer notes, "We are separated from that which is the 'lower' form of creation, yet we are united to it. One must not choose; one must say both."[15] God created both the tree and the human for much the same purpose. As a result, humans must exercise the special role of steward of creation with both that unity and distinction in mind.

A Distinct Human Role

Humans alone in creation were given the authority over the rest of creation (Gen 1:28). God directly authorized the cultivation of crops and the husbandry of animals. Indeed, humans were made "little less than God" (Ps 8:5). God made humanity "ruler over the works of your hands . . . [and] put everything under his feet: all the sheep and oxen, as well as the animals in the wild, the birds of the sky, and the fish of the sea" (Ps 8:6–8). The purpose of this responsibility was to increase the "magnificence" of God's "name throughout the earth" (Ps 8:9). The authority to rule and the duty to glorify God are inseparable. As N. T. Wright argues, "God's design was to rule creation in life-giving

---

15. Schaeffer, *Pollution and the Death of Man*, 5:31 (see chap. 2, n. 20).

wisdom through his image-bearing creatures."[16] Failure to properly exercise authority over creation for God's glory is sin.[17]

Another critical difference between humans and animals is our fallenness, which sometimes leads us to abuse creation. As Wendell Berry argues, "Whereas animals are usually restrained by the limits of physical appetites, humans have mental appetites that can be far more gross and capacious than physical ones. Only humans squander and hoard, murder and pillage because of notions."[18] When Adam sinned, the ground was cursed on behalf of humanity (Gen 3:17–18). The curse also contains a promised blessing of God's future restoration of creation.[19] All of creation is affected by the fall, but it is humans that continue to knowingly exacerbate its effects. The call for humans, then, is not to live unthinkingly according to our fallen nature, but for born-again believers to be thoughtful as we steward God's creation by the Spirit until Christ restores it all from sin's pervasive pollution.

A CASE FOR STEWARDSHIP

Human responsibility within creation is sometimes described as stewardship.[20] A steward is someone who does not own something but has been given the authority and responsibility to manage on behalf of the owner. God gave humans authority over creation to "fill the earth, and subdue it" (Gen 1:28). He placed Adam in the garden of Eden to "work it and watch over it" (Gen 2:15).[21] As Sandra Richter argues, "In essence, woman and man are the embodiments of God's sovereignty in the created order."[22] When the stewardship responsibility of tending

---

[16.] N. T. Wright, *Surprised by Hope: Rethinking Heaven, the Resurrection, and the Mission of the Church* (New York: HarperOne, 2008), 103.

[17.] Liederbach and Lenow, *Ethics as Worship*, 412–14 (see chap. 1, n. 16).

[18.] Wendell Berry, "With Nature," in *Home Economics* (Berkeley: Counterpoint, 1987), 15.

[19.] Ashford and Bartholomew, *The Doctrine of Creation*, 228–29 (see chap. 5, n. 37).

[20.] E.g., Douma, *Environmental Stewardship*, 36–41 (see chap. 2, n. 17). For an argument against stewardship as a metaphor, see Richard Bauckham, *The Bible and Ecology* (Waco: Baylor University Press, 2010), 1–36. Another scholar argues for the use of *shepherd* as the predominant metaphor for the human relationship with creation, Donald McDaniel, "Becoming Good Shepherds: A New Model of Creation Care for Evangelical Christians" (PhD diss., Southeastern Baptist Theological Seminary, 2011).

[21.] Moo and Moo, *Creation Care,* 77–78 (see chap. 5, n. 47).

[22.] Richter, *Stewards of Eden,* 9 (see chap. 5, n. 49).

the garden is set alongside the command to fill the earth, it seems that "God's intention was for Eden to expand way beyond its borders."[23]

The human relationship with the rest of creation changed when Adam sinned, but implicit in that punishment for sin is the idea that the responsibility to work and watch over the earth remains (Gen 3:17–20).[24] Both Cain and Abel, in their own ways, continued to steward the earth as farmer and husbandman, respectively (4:2). Those early humans spiraled into greater and greater sin, not heeding the warning offered to them by the cursed earth. Therefore, "human wickedness was widespread on the earth and . . . every inclination of the human mind was nothing but evil all the time" (6:5). As a result, God chose to "wipe mankind . . . off the face of the earth, together with the animals, creatures that crawl, and birds of the sky" (v. 7). It was human sin that led to God's destruction of most of creation in the flood (cf. 2 Pet 2:5; 3:6).

After God used a massive flood to destroy most of life on earth, he renewed the mandate for humanity to "be fruitful and multiply and fill the earth" (Gen 9:1). God also established a new covenant with every living creature that "never again will every creature be wiped out by floodwaters; there will never again be a flood to destroy the earth" (v. 11). The ongoing stewardship relationship is made clear because humanity was given the command to fill the earth, but God also enacted a promise with every living creature. Hope arises out of futility. Creation longs for redemption, which will be consummated at some point in the future. In a very similar way, humans, too, long for the end of the effects of sin on earth (Rom 8:19–24). Meanwhile, humanity has an obligation to live holy, obedient lives to God as we long for Christ's return.

Most humans do not question the desire to master the world around us. We like having regular food sources, not having rivers overflow into our homes, and possessing the many comforts that are sometimes viewed as necessities in the West. We struggle with ruling over creation for God's glory. Paul reminded the Colossians that "whatever you do, in word or deed, do everything in the name of the Lord Jesus, giving thanks to God the Father through him" (Col 3:17). This is a parallel

---

23. Ashford and Bartholomew, *The Doctrine of Creation*, 187.
24. Wright, *The Mission of God*, 432–33 (see chap. 3, n. 24).

to his command to the Corinthians, "Whether you eat or drink, or whatever you do, do everything for the glory of God" (1 Cor 10:31). The command to rule over the earth for God's glory is not unique to the Old Testament, nor is having the goal of glorifying God as a central aspect of life unique to creation care.

Human stewardship is intended to reflect God's care for creation. It is a form of compassionate governance. God sustains creation, but he also cultivates creation. At least part of being made in the image of God includes this responsibility. God intended for humans to cultivate creation for his glory (Gen 2:15). We are stewards who are responsible for what God has left us until the inauguration of the new creation.

HUMANS AS PRODUCERS

Stewardship implies human responsibility—both conservation of the goodness of creation and also cultivation of creation. The new heavens and the new earth are depicted as a garden city, not an untamed wilderness (Rev 21:9–27).[25] Humans are both consumers and producers.

It is impossible to venture even into the shallows of environmental literature without bumping into concerns about human consumption. Thomas Malthus's concern for population growth was over human consumption, though his fear was for the well-being of humanity rather than the health of the ecosystem.[26] In the mid-twentieth century, Paul Ehrlich's concern was more plainly connected to human consumption: "The causal chain of the [environment's] deterioration is easily followed to its source. Too many cars, too many factories, too much detergent, too much pesticide, multiplying contrails, inadequate sewage treatment plants, too little water, too much carbon dioxide—all can be traced easily to *too many people*."[27] The pervasive antihuman bias has persisted over recent decades, and perhaps increased, despite Ehrlich's apocalyptic predictions being demonstrably disproved.[28]

25. Wolters, *Creation Regained*, 77–78 (see chap. 5, n. 4).
26. Thomas Robert Malthus, *An Essay on the Principle of Population* (New York: Oxford University Press, 1993), 12–15.
27. Paul R. Ehrlich, *The Population Bomb* (New York: Ballentine, 1968), 66–67.
28. Paul Sabin, *The Bet: Paul Ehrlich, Julian Simon, and Our Gamble over Earth's Future* (New Haven: Yale University Press, 2013).

Antihuman Bias

One example of the growing antihuman movement is the ahumanist movement, which sees the possibility of human extinction in a positive light. As Patricia MacCormack argues, "Human extinction can be understood as a good idea for ecosophical ethics and need not be considered 'unthinkable' but can be welcomed as affirmative of earth life."[29] MacCormack sees humans in a negative light because she views them as consumers and destroyers only. She writes, "Humans do not create symbiosis. Humans do not reciprocate. Humans use."[30] And if this is one's view, then the extinction or at least stringent control of human population makes a great deal of sense.[31] Tragically, as P. D. James depicts in her novel *The Children of Men* about humanity on the verge of extinction, the likely outcome of such an overwhelming sense of futility is environmental negligence and hopelessness.[32] In contrast, hope encourages care for creation.

Though we might agree that humans have often failed to have a positive impact on creation, it is not clear that such a relationship is impossible. Deep poverty, which often accompanies ecological degradation, can be a result of a failure of humans to live out our vocation as producers.[33] As Jane Jacobs argued in reference to the population-control movement of her day, "People are producers as well as consumers, and wherever poverty is deep and persistent, it is because a great deal of work is just not being done, because people are not producing."[34] Where environmental degradation is greatest, it is sometimes a sign that human stewardship has been exercised poorly or not at all.[35]

---

[29] MacCormack, *The Ahuman Manifesto*, 144 (see introduction, n. 16).

[30] MacCormack, 12–13.

[31] MacCormack's ahumanism is part of a broader set of movements that can be associated with deep ecology. Martin W. Lewis, *Green Delusions: An Environmentalist's Critique of Radical Environmentalism* (Durham, NC: Duke University Press, 1992), 28–30.

[32] P. D. James, *The Children of Men* (New York: Alfred A. Knopf, 1993).

[33] In some cases, the failure of stewardship is on the part of those who abuse their productive abilities to unjustly restrict the opportunities of others.

[34] Kent, "More Babies Needed, Not Fewer," 87 (see introduction, n. 20).

[35] So, for example, Hayhoe recognizes the need for energy to eliminate poverty but encourages the pursuit of sources other than fossil fuels. Hayhoe, *Saving Us*, 161–71 (see introduction, n. 2).

Wise Cultivation

For Christians, the call to care for creation is not simply to avoid consumption, but also to cultivate wisely. We are to "be fruitful and multiply" (Gen 1:28 ESV), which implies both procreation and creative invention. Both duties were carried out by humanity shortly after the fall, with the growth of human population in Cain and Abel (Gen 4:1–2), the construction of cities (v. 17), the invention of musical instruments (v. 21), and the discovery of metal implements (v. 22). Those exercises in human ingenuity were a response to God's command, were an application of the image of God, and were carried out with heavy labor because of sin. Stewardship is a vocation that must be exercised with care.

There is no room to discuss the doctrine of vocation in detail here, but our call to cultivate the earth is a call to work.[36] Work was a gift from God given to humans prior to the entry of sin into the world (Gen 2:5, 15). Work continues to be a gift from God because its frustration reminds us that the world needs redemption (Gen 3:17) and because it is part of the order God ordained in creation (Ps 104:23). As the preacher argued in Ecclesiastes, "There is nothing better for a person than to eat, drink, and enjoy his work. I have seen that even this is from God's hand" (2:24). And yet work is perverted because it becomes about accumulation of goods that become the property of others without appropriate gratitude toward God's goodness (Eccl 2:26). The human call to produce, create, innovate, and cultivate remains a part of our duty to be stewards of all creation. But that calling has limits.

THE LIMITS OF HUMANITY

The limits of humanity's role in the created order are contained in our stewardship responsibility. A steward has authority to care for what was left in trust, with the expectation that it will be used according to the owner's wishes, improved upon, and returned to the owner when

---

[36.] Helpful resources on the doctrine of vocation and the call to work include Daniel M. Doriani, *Work: Its Purpose, Dignity, and Transformation* (Phillipsburg, NJ: P&R, 2019) or Benjamin Quinn and Walter Strickland, *Every Waking Hour: An Introduction to Work and Vocation for Christians* (Bellingham, WA: Lexham, 2016).

requested. Matthew 25:14–30 illustrates the role of steward: the master left the servants with varying amounts to invest, with the expectation it would be returned when the master returned. In the case of that parable, two of the servants increased the amount they were given, but one of them buried it in the dirt. Given that the point of that metaphor is salvific, there is no servant in the story who squandered the investment with careless living, but the text is clear that good stewardship means using resources wisely and making things better for the owner of the resources.

Problems with Population Control

God is the owner of all creation because he made it all (Ps 24:1–2). As we have seen, humanity was given the command to be fruitful and multiply while spreading across the earth (Gen 9:7). I've heard it humorously stated that the command to be fruitful and multiply may be the only one of God's commands humanity has really followed. We've gone from a population of eight in Genesis 9 to roughly 8 billion, with no real endpoint in sight. For some environmentalists, the sheer number of humans is the primary problem.

Several decades ago, one formerly Southern Baptist sociologist wrote, "The basic cause of pollution and waste is simple: too many people."[37] His proposed solutions include mandatory birth control. However, more recently, the evangelical climate advocate Katharine Hayhoe notes that population control measures are often proposed by "male theorists in rich countries with low birth rates."[38] She urges readers to evaluate consumption patterns as a means to control impact on the environment. Protesting the injustice of many attempts at population control, the abortion supporter Betsy Hartmann writes, "The countries where birth rates remain relatively high have among them the lowest carbon emissions per capita on the planet."[39] In other words, the problem is consumption, not population. However, rather than deal

---

[37] Chasteen, *The Case for Compulsory Birth Control*, 15 (see chap. 1, n. 24).
[38] Hayhoe, *Saving Us*, 147.
[39] Betsy Hartmann, *Reproductive Rights and Wrongs: The Global Politics of Population Control*, 3rd ed. (Chicago: Haymarket, 2016), xi.

with the question of stewardship of resources, advocates of population control focus on the number of people using resources.[40]

Biblical Limits

Limits of human activity are both explicit and implicit throughout Scripture. The initial mandate to subdue the earth and rule over non-human animals included the expectation it was to be maintained for food, not wantonly destroyed (Gen 1:28–30). More explicitly, Gen 2:4–6 records the barrenness of creation before humans were created, and Gen 2:15 is a purpose statement for Adam's stewardship of the garden of Eden. All of these make plain that increasing the flourishing of creation should be a primary goal of human cultivation. However, Adam's stewardship is frustrated as he has to scratch out existence from the thorn-infested ground. In none of those calls is there any right to dominate or strip the goodness out of creation. In warfare, the Israelites were told not to clear-cut fruit trees because they were useful for food (Deut 20:19–20). There is both a strategic element to this and an ecological one. Even the non-food-bearing trees were only to be cut down for the purpose of building siege works. Clear-cutting to make the area desolate was not an approved tactic, even in the total war authorized by God.[41]

The most obvious limits on human stewardship in Scripture are those regarding agricultural practices of Sabbath.[42] In contemporary Christian discussions of Sabbath, there is often a focus on human activity on the seventh day, which is encouraged by the frequent conflict between Jesus and the Pharisees about Sabbath rules (e.g., Luke 14:1–6; Matt 12:1–14). Jesus's message about the Sabbath is sometimes taken to indicate that the fourth commandment (Deut 5:12–15) was set aside in the New Testament, along with the ceremonial law.[43] However, Jesus did not tell his hearers that the Sabbath was eliminated as a principle of the moral law but that the cultural rules of the day had distorted

40. See Ehrlich, *The Population Bomb*, 15–68.
41. Richter, *Stewards of Eden*, 60–63.
42. Moo and Moo, *Creation Care*, 96–97.
43. R. Albert Mohler, *Words from the Fire: Hearing the Voice of God in the 10 Commandments* (Chicago: Moody, 2009), 78–86.

the practice of Sabbath. Thus, as Jesus said, "The Sabbath was made for man and not man for the Sabbath" (Mark 2:27). Sabbath was an eternal principle of rest that God intentionally wove into creation.

Sabbath was more than a temporary cultural marker for Israel, as evidenced by God punishing his people for not honoring the practice (Ezek 20:15–16). Ezekiel explained that the purpose of the Sabbath was not simply to inhibit economic activity but to serve as a cultural marker of God's people (20:12).[44] The ongoing significance of Sabbath for Christians is demonstrated by the letter to the Hebrews, where we see that "a Sabbath rest remains for God's people" (Heb 4:9). There is a great deal of debate about the proper application of the practice of Sabbath, which exceeds the space limits of this chapter, but my own position is that there should be a pattern of rest and work in the Christian life that demonstrates a reliance upon God as our provider. It is a sign of hope. The failure of our culture and many Christians to cease from economic striving is a sign of a weak faith and often greed. It is also a sign of poor stewardship because one of the positive impacts of Sabbath was rest for the farm animals and the land itself. God gave creation the Sabbath as a gift of rest in an exhausting, fallen world.

HUMANITY AND THE FALL

Every possible relationship of humanity was disrupted by sin, including our relationship with the rest of creation.[45] The patterns of this world reflect attempts to repair those relationships. So, for example, Francis Bacon, in his classic volume *The New Organon*, summarizes his view of modern science and the fall:

> For by the Fall man declined from the state of innocence and from his kingdom over the creatures. Both things can be repaired even in this life to some extent, the former by religion and faith, the latter by the arts and sciences. For the Curse did not make the creation an utter and irrevocable outlaw. In virtue of the sentence

---

[44.] Gilbert Meilaender, *Thy Will Be Done: The Ten Commandments and the Christian Life* (Grand Rapids: Baker Academic, 2020), 90–91.

[45.] Schaeffer, *Pollution and the Death of Man*, 5:38.

"In the sweat of thy face shalt thou eat bread," man, by manifold labors (and not by disputations, certainly, or by useless magical ceremonies), compels the creation, in time and in part, to provide him with bread, that is to serve the purposes of human life.[46]

For Bacon, the goal of science was to compel the creation to serve the purposes of human life.[47] Bacon's sentiment about the role of science as the human opportunity to reverse the fall is representative of attitudes that drove technological development. Such an attitude drove many innovations that have reduced human suffering, but as we see in Bacon's own comment, the attempts to push back the fall by science and technology, apart from the values provided by "religion and faith," will go off in the wrong direction.[48]

As we have seen in a previous chapter, the inherent value of creation is based on it fulfilling God's main purpose, which is to glorify him. Certainly, that includes providing resources necessary to sustain human life and society, but the purpose of creation for Bacon and the purpose outlined in a more holistic view of Scripture are several degrees apart. There is a difference between the modern Western understanding of humanity and that of Scripture.

Sin and Human Power

Scripture is clear that sin has infected the human heart so that it is deceitful and wicked (Jer 17:9). This has led the human race, in general, to pursue the conquest of creation rather than stewardship, as is evidenced by Bacon's instrumental view of creation. Far from leading humanity to freedom and absolute comfort, however, the conquest of creation has in some very clear ways made humanity's plight worse. On one hand, it is undeniable that the rise of the vast majority of humanity from near-starvation levels of poverty to amazing prosperity is a good thing.[49] The cost of that improvement has been significant

---

46. Francis Bacon, *The New Organon* (Cambridge: Cambridge University Press, 2000), 221.
47. See Gillespie, *The Theological Origins of Modernity*, 37–40 (see chap. 4, n. 36).
48. Bauckham's discussion of Bacon and the impact of his thought on the environment are insightful: Richard Bauckham, *Living with Other Creatures: Green Exegesis and Theology* (Waco: Baylor University Press, 2011), 47–58.
49. Arthur C. Brooks, *The Road to Freedom: How to Win the Fight for Free Enterprise* (New York:

for creation broadly and, more specifically, for the freedoms endowed upon humanity by the Creator. As C. S. Lewis argues, "What we call Man's power over Nature turns out to be a power exercised by some men over other men with Nature as its instrument."[50] This is a form of futility.

Through eugenics, control of property, and superior technology, humans have power over each other and later generations. Technology—creation shaped by humans for some purpose beyond its natural powers—is a critical way that some humans wield the power of creation against other humans. It concentrates power in the hands of fewer and fewer. Lewis goes on,

> Man's conquest of Nature, if the dreams of some scientific planners are realized, means the rule of a few hundreds of men over billions upon billions of men. There neither is nor can be any simple increase of power on Man's side. Each new power won *by* man is a power *over* man as well. Each advance leaves him weaker as well as stronger. In every victory, besides being the general who triumphs, he is also the prisoner who follows the triumphal car.[51]

If you wonder whether this is so, consider how many happy hours have been interrupted by cell phone calls and texts from an employer. On a larger scale, consider how dependent society is on the electrical grid and how difficult it would become if the grid was disrupted. Both technologies have positive uses, no doubt, but this has shifted more control to the employer whose regular paychecks keep the lights on, the corporations who operate the generators and maintain the grids, or a few terrorists who can threaten to disrupt a nation with a snippet of malicious code.

The image of God makes possible the creation of technologies to push back the effects of the fall. The effects of the fall make the corruption of those efforts to increase human misery probable. Lord Acton is famously quoted as saying, "Power tends to corrupt, and absolute

---

Basic Books, 2012), 69–80.

[50.] C. S. Lewis, *The Abolition of Man* (San Francisco: HarperSanFrancisco, 1974), 55.

[51.] Lewis, 58.

power corrupts absolutely."[52] It is possible to debate whether there is a causal effect of power, but there is little question that increased power magnifies the consequences of the corruption of the human soul and the domination of creation.

Distortions of Human Rationality

Perhaps the most significant effect of the fall on humanity is the distortion of rational human capability. This distortion is evident in the inability of unregenerate humans to see God's goodness in all of creation. "Instead, their thinking became worthless, and their senseless hearts were darkened" (Rom 1:21b). After all, it did not take long for Cain to kill Abel and Lamech to become a polygamist bragging about seeking disproportionate revenge (Genesis 4). The human ability to properly reason has been distorted.

Bacon, and others of that era, thought conquering human limits would lead to human perfection, which is a central element of the myth of progress.[53] Some limits are part of the design of God's creation and not always something to overcome.[54] It is the distortion of the goodness of creation due to the fall that humans should strive against. Creation itself seems to be groaning, not just under the curse of thorns and thistles, but also under the growing moral failures of humanity to recognize realistic limits and curb the cumulative impact of sinful abuse of creation. A large part of contemporary stewardship is an attempt to solve the central problem of conforming the whole of our existence to reality, to recognize the limits of our reason, to establish boundaries for the use of nature, and to seek to work toward substantial healing of creation as we await Christ's return.

The fall of humanity misdirected all human relationships. The goal of human culture should not be to conquer nature so that it serves human purposes, but to redirect creation back toward the *shalom* that it was intended for. It is difficult to determine exactly what such holistic

---

[52.] John Dalbert-Acton, *Historical Essays and Studies* (London: MacMillan, 1907), 504.

[53.] Gillespie, *The Theological Origins of Modernity*, 8; Louis Dupre, *The Enlightenment and the Intellectual Foundations of Modern Culture* (New Haven, CT: Yale University Press, 2004), 202.

[54.] Kelly M. Kapic, *You're Only Human: How Your Limits Reflect God's Design and Why That's Good News* (Ada, MI: Brazos, 2022), 12–15.

flourishing should look like—and in this scientific exploration can be a great help, when informed by proper values—but we can get some sense of the proper role of humanity within creation by looking to the example of Christ.

CHRIST AS EXAMPLE

In debates about Christ's role in salvation history, there have been attempts to reduce his earthly ministry from one of substitutionary atonement to one that is a moral example to humanity.[55] Paul's reminder of the central truth of Christianity is worth considering when those ideas arise: "Christ died for our sins according to the Scriptures" (1 Cor 15:3b). At the core of Christ's earthly ministry was his death on the cross, which led to the substitutionary atonement—the heart of the gospel. It is spiritually bankrupt to reduce the life of Christ to a moral example.[56]

At the same time, Christ does serve as a moral example for humanity. Christ is our representative before the Father, "who has been tempted in every way as we are, yet without sin" (Heb 4:15). Paul exhorted the Corinthian believers to imitate him as he imitated Christ (1 Cor 11:1). There is no question of Christ's moral perfection, which means that his life bears examination as it pertains to his interaction with creation.

Christ's interactions with nature are in accord with the moral order of creation and are redemptive in nature. His first miracle was the acceleration of the process of water turning into wine at the wedding at Cana (John 2:1–11). This was in accord with the pattern of nature; grapes turn water to wine on a regular basis.[57] Christ's first miracle was also socially redemptive, saving host embarrassment. When Jesus calmed the storm on the Sea of Galilee with a word, he was demonstrating his lordship over creation, but it also was a sign of his redemptive power as he stopped a natural evil (Matt 8:23–27). Jesus

---

[55.] Stephen Wellum, "Behold, the Lamb of God," in *The Doctrine on Which the Church Stands or Falls,* ed. Matthew Bates (Wheaton: Crossway, 2019), 365–66.

[56.] Bavinck, *Reformed Dogmatics,* 4:384–85.

[57.] Lewis, *Miracles,* 221–22 (see chap. 4, n. 37).

healed many who came to him throughout his ministry, including Peter's mother-in-law and others in his hometown (Luke 4:38–44). Each of Christ's numerous recorded miracles is consistent with the order of creation, demonstrates his lordship of creation, and pushes back on the effects of sin and the fall.[58] They give a glimpse of life in the new heavens and new earth.[59]

The only possible exception to the redemptive nature of Christ's miracles is in the cursing of the fig tree (Matt 21:18–22; Mark 11:12–14, 20–25).[60] There are several interpretive possibilities for that event other than Jesus committing some sort of wanton ecological destruction. A full discussion of this event is beyond what is required here. It is sufficient to note that (a) Jesus merely accelerates the natural process of aging of the tree, (b) the likely intended message is the importance of being fruitful in this time, and (c) it clearly supports Christ's place as Lord over creation.[61]

Limitations of Temporal Lordship

Christ was a healer during his earthly ministry. He overtly exercised righteous, sinless dominion over nature. Christ lived as a perfect human, without sin. His ministry was one of redemptive power, and he has always had all the power needed to restore all of creation, even as he holds it all together (Heb 1:3). And yet, Christ's ministry on earth was not one of total, immediate repristination of nature. That is, Christ did not simply renew everything with a single word, as we might have hoped. Indeed, repristination is not a worthy goal because creation was meant to be cultivated by humanity for the glory of God.[62] Christ's example as the perfect human should serve to regulate our vision of creation care.

When we see Christ living on earth, we see a teacher who frequently used natural and agricultural examples in his teaching (Matt 13:1–33; 20:1–16; 21:33–45); he was in tune with his creation. We see him

---

[58] Lewis, 229–31.
[59] Wolters, *Creation Regained*, 74–75.
[60] Lewis, *Miracles*, 228–29.
[61] David Jones and Andrew Spencer, "Fate of the Creation in the *Eschaton*," *Southern Theological Review* 9, no. 1 (Spring 2018): 86n27.
[62] Wolters, *Creation Regained*, 77–78.

undo the effects of the fall on humans (Matt 8:1–4; 9:18–26; John 11:1–44); his ministry was redemptive in nature. We see him begin the process of cosmic reconciliation of all creation by paying the penalty for human sin (Col 1:15–20). His purpose was cosmic in scope. As we follow Christ's example, imitating his life to the best of our meager abilities, we can see the direction of Christ's ministry: redemption from the fall.[63] Of course, none of our actions will be perfectly righteous (Isa 64:6); we will not have a perfect understanding of God's nature, purposes, and plan (1 Cor 13:12); and we will continue to fall short of perfection in any number of ways (Rom 7:15–20). Christ exhibited an attitude toward creation that is worth emulating, though his unique role as creator and sustainer of the universe clearly differentiates the outcomes of his activities from our feeble efforts at restoration. However, Christ's example points Christians in the direction of a positive relationship with creation, one that seeks to embody what Francis Schaeffer calls substantial healing.

CONCLUSION

A biblical doctrine of anthropology helps place human efforts toward environmental ethics into perspective. Humans are called to be stewards of creation. It was created with a purpose, and it has inherent value inasmuch as it fulfills its purpose to glorify God. Our duty is not to repristinate creation—to make it as if we had never existed—because we are a part of creation. At the same time, we must recognize that throughout history, many human actions have unthinkingly harmed creation. The calling of the faithful Christian, seeking to live under the authority of Scripture, is to pursue stewardship of creation that reflects the goal of substantial healing. When directed toward redemption, human efforts are signposts toward the final disposition of the created order, which we will examine in the next chapter, which deals with the doctrine of eschatology.

[63.] Williams, *Far as the Curse Is Found*, 284–85 (see chap. 5, n. 50).

KEY TERMS

Anthropology
Fall
Sin
Stewardship
Technology

STUDY QUESTIONS

1. What role did God give humans in creation?
2. How does the term *stewardship* enable and limit human activity within God's creation?
3. Why is it important to understand humans as consumers and producers?
4. How has Francis Bacon's idea of conquering nature had a negative impact on Western culture's approach to the environment?
5. What can we learn from Christ's interactions with creation?

CHAPTER 7

Near and Distant Hope for God's Creation

On February 5, 1981, James Watt was grilled by a congressional committee due to his nomination for secretary of the interior in Ronald Reagan's administration. James Weaver, a representative from Oregon, praised Watt for his desire to continue sustainable-use policies for natural resources. Watt responded, "That is the delicate balance the Secretary of the Interior must have, to be steward for the natural resources for this generation as well as for future generations. I do not know how many future generations we can count on before the Lord returns, whatever it is we have to manage with skill to leave the resources for future generations."[1] Watt was known to be a Christian from the Pentecostal tradition, so his statement caused a firestorm.[2]

The controversy surrounding Watt's comments was driven by the selective quotation that made it to the public. Watt was quoted as saying simply, "I do not know how many future generations we can count on before the Lord returns."[3] This piece of the quote is now so firmly embedded in the cultural memes of environmentalism that it will likely be impossible to shake the assurance that Watt was encouraging wanton destruction of natural resources and abuse of creation.[4] In the minds of some, Watt's eschatology is the official eschatology of

---

[1.] Quoted in Ron Arnold, *At the Eye of the Storm: James Watt and the Environmentalists* (Chicago: Regnery Gateway, 1982), 75.

[2.] Mark Stoll, *Protestantism, Capitalism, and Nature in America* (Albuquerque: University of New Mexico Press, 1997), 190–92.

[3.] Bill Prochnau, "The Watt Controversy," *Washington Post*, June 30, 1981, https://www.washingtonpost.com/archive/politics/1981/06/30/the-watt-controversy/d591699b-3bc2-46d2-9059-fb5d2513c3da/.

[4.] For example, see H. Paul Santmire, *Nature Reborn: The Ecological and Cosmic Promise of Christian Theology* (Minneapolis: Fortress, 2000), 1; Steven Bouma-Prediger, *For the Beauty of the Earth: A Christian Vision for Creation Care* (Grand Rapids: Baker, 2001), 71–72.

conservative Protestant Christianity, and thus, Christians can be safely dismissed instead of debated.[5]

Although some might strongly disagree with Watt's regulatory approach, it is clear from his comments that he was expressing an interest in conservation of natural resources. Watt's eschatology included the fiery destruction of creation at the end of time, but since he did not know when that would be, he felt called to steward the resources well with the need for indefinite availability for humanity. For critics of Christianity, however, eschatology has remained one of the main points of concern.

The geographer Janel Curry-Roper writes, "I believe that eschatology is the most ecologically decisive component of a theological system. It influences adherents' actions and determines their views of mankind, their bodies, souls, and worldviews."[6] How we treat God's creation in the time between redemption purchased on the cross and redemption completed in the second coming depends a great deal on our vision of the final state of creation and the process of redemption. These are the critical aspects of eschatology this chapter takes up.

NARROWING THE SCOPE

Curry-Roper is right that eschatology is vital to a proper handling of ecology; indeed, it is an indispensable aspect of Christian theology.[7] However, some environmental critics of Christianity make the assumption that it is necessary for Christians to abandon the expectation of God's pending renewal of all creation. The argument is generally that such an eschatology tends to encourage Christians to become detached from this earth as a temporary dwelling and to see God's future action in renovating creation as cause for ignoring environmental stewardship.[8]

[5.] Watt later wrote a rebuttal of what he felt was a misrepresentation of his eschatology. James Watt, "The Religious Left's Lies," *Washington Post*, May 21, 2005, https://www.washingtonpost.com/archive/opinions/2005/05/21/the-religious-lefts-lies/c348908f-9c4a-4f73-ac88-603de131a06a/.

[6.] Janel Curry-Roper, "Contemporary Christian Eschatologies and Their Relation to Environmental Stewardship," *Professional Geographer* 42, no. 2 (1990): 159.

[7.] See, for example, Douglas Moo, "Nature in the New Creation: New Testament Eschatology and the Environment," *JETS* 49, no. 3 (September 2006): 449–88.

[8.] Wilkinson, *Between God and Green*, 59–60 (see chap. 2, n. 74).

After all, no hotel guest participates in remodeling, so if someone is going to come and redo all of the work, but better, in the future, then there is no reason to improve the environment now. If the thin eschatology that many critics ascribe to Christians was typical, then the criticism would be more generally true. Thankfully, that is not the case.

Theologian Michael Horton places eschatology at the heart of Christian theology. He argues, "Eschatology is not simply a concluding topic but an indispensable lens through which we come to understand the whole system of Christian faith and practice."[9] The word *indispensable* does not signify "only" or "primary," but it does indicate the power eschatology has to shape a hopeful theology for creation care. Eschatology is a central doctrine to Christianity, but as with the doctrine of creation, the public awareness of the doctrine tends to focus on the sensational and controversial elements rather than the vital core. In the case of eschatology, interest in the specific order and timing of events often consumes the bulk of the debate, leaving discussions about the broader eschatological vision offered by all of Scripture neglected. Without diminishing the value of careful study of end-times chronology, this chapter intentionally focuses on the narrative arc of Scripture, which helps inform a robust theology for creation care.

ESCHATOLOGY AS THE NARRATIVE ARC OF SCRIPTURE

The scriptural witness to eschatology is not limited to prophetic books in the Old Testament, select passages from the Gospels and Epistles, and the final eighteen chapters of Revelation. Rather, eschatology is woven throughout Scripture in the narrative arc of God's story. The story begins with creation, continues through the fall, turns dramatically with Christ's redemptive work on the cross, and culminates in the final restoration of heaven and earth at the end of this story, when a new chapter begins.[10]

As we saw in chapter 5, God spoke all of creation into existence.

[9.] Michael Horton, *The Christian Faith: A Systematic Theology for Pilgrims on the Way* (Grand Rapids: Zondervan. 2011), 906.

[10.] Wolters, *Creation Regained*, 69–78 (see chap. 5, n. 4).

Absolutely nothing exists that did not begin and is not owned and ordered by the God of the universe. When God created Adam, he was placed in the garden of Eden "to work it and watch over it" (Gen 2:15). Some theologians argue that God's expectation was for a growing population of humans to continue to expand the borders of Eden and develop the earth into a habitable space for humanity.[11] The vision here is not of paving paradise to put up a parking lot, as the old pop song describes it, but of building a civilization that honors the wonder and order of creation. In some sense, Adam's sin introduced a plot twist into the narrative arc of creation. As a result of the first man's disobedience to God's clear command, creation was cursed as a reminder that there is something wrong and that humans need a solution to their sin.

Adam and Eve were removed from the garden of Eden and pushed into the wilderness with the mandate to engage in toilsome labor to make a living (Gen 3:19). Sin quickly spiraled out of control, with Cain killing Abel (4:8), Lamech escalating revenge (4:23–24), and eventually the corruption of humanity's intentions and thoughts being so significant that God determined to press the figurative reset button (6:5–8). The flood, the preservation of creation through Noah and his ark, and the continuation of the mandate to steward creation after the flood are a foreshadowing of the greater narrative arc of Scripture (2 Pet 3:3–7). Peter explicitly linked the Noahic flood to the future of all creation, making the eschatological implications of even the first chapters of Genesis plain.[12]

The treasure map of eschatology begins in the garden, wanders through the wilderness, and ends in the garden city in the end of Revelation. The glorious New Jerusalem is a huge city made of precious materials and exquisite in its appearance. It is a holy city filled only with good thing, because "nothing unclean will ever enter it, nor anyone who does what is detestable or false, but only those written in the Lamb's book of life" (Rev 21:27). In this, New Jerusalem is like Eden because only holiness can enter, which is why God drove Adam from the garden and stationed a guard at the entrance (Gen 3:24). There is no mention of a guard in Revelation because once all of God's creation is renewed, there is no need for one.

[11.] See Ashford and Bartholomew, *The Doctrine of Creation*, 187 (see chap. 5, n. 37).

[12.] Wolters, "Worldview and Textual Criticism in 2 Peter 3:10," *WJT* 49 (1987): 408; Williams, *Far as the Curse Is Found*, 278–81 (see chap. 5, n. 50).

Similarities between Eden and New Jerusalem do not end at the purity of their residents, though. Both contain the tree of life (Gen 2:9; Rev 22:2). A river flows from within each (Gen 2:10; Rev 22:1). Just as Eden is a garden paradise, so is New Jerusalem paradisical. The greatest difference is that New Jerusalem is a city, fully cultivated and kept by the power of God for the glory of God. New Jerusalem will be the perfect fulfillment of the cultural mandate originally given to Adam and Eve.

The trajectory of creation was always from garden to garden city. Creating a city is not a concession God made due to human sin. It was God's design from the very beginning of creation. Therefore, though treacherous Cain "became the builder of a city" (Gen 4:17), the creation of the city was not itself sin. The heavenly city will bring the glory of the natural world together with the blessings of technology in a completed, sinless perfection. The vision of the culmination of history presented by Scripture is radically different than the preservationist vision of the natural world barren of the evidence of humanity. The new heavens and new earth are filled with humanity because the resurrection points to the coming renewal of all things.

RESURRECTION AND THE CREATED ORDER

According to Oliver O'Donovan, "Christian ethics depends upon the resurrection of Jesus Christ from the dead."[13] Furthermore, "In the resurrection of Christ creation is restored and the kingdom of God dawns."[14] By this account, the resurrection of Christ is the central aspect of all of ethics, especially an ethics of creation care.

Some retellings of the gospel focus on the redemption of humans alone, with personal salvation as the seemingly sole significant purpose of Christ's substitutionary death, burial, and resurrection.[15] It would be a mistake to lose sight of the centrality of personal redemption in

---

[13.] Oliver O'Donovan, *Resurrection and the Moral Order: An Outline for Evangelical Ethics*, 2nd ed. (Grand Rapids: Eerdmans, 2016), 13.

[14.] O'Donovan, 15.

[15.] See Greg Gilbert, *What Is the Gospel?* (Wheaton: Crossway, 2010), 23–36. For a somewhat broader, but consistently orthodox, evangelical understanding of the gospel, see Ray Ortlund, *The Gospel: How the Church Portrays the Beauty of Christ* (Wheaton: Crossway, 2014).

the gospel. After all, as Paul wrote, "For I passed on to you as most important what I also received: that Christ died for our sins according to the Scriptures, that he was buried, that he was raised on the third day according to the Scriptures" (1 Cor 15:3–4). He died for *our* sins—the focus of humanity as the cause for and a primary recipient of Christ's redemption is at the heart of the gospel.

Cosmic Redemption

However, the reconciliation Christ brings extends beyond the redemption of humanity. In Col 1:20, Paul said that God worked through Christ "to reconcile everything to himself, whether things on earth or things in heaven, by making peace through his blood, shed on the cross." In the following verses, he again highlighted the redemption of humans, but the cosmic aspect of Christ's redemptive work is no secret. John 3:16, that most famous of verses, states that "God loved the world." The word there for world is *cosmos*, not *gentes*, as one might expect if the message was intended solely for humanity.[16] God's love sees beyond humanity to the whole creation. James 1:18 reminds us that the elect have been saved "so that we would be a kind of firstfruits of his creatures."[17]

Paul again made this evident in Rom 8:19–22. In this passage an anthropomorphized creation "eagerly waits" (v. 19) the redemption of humanity. It was "subjected to futility" (v. 20), which connects with the curse that has warped the created order and is the cause of creation's groaning (v. 22). The key is Paul's declaration that "the creation itself will also be set free from the bondage to decay into the glorious freedom of God's children" (v. 21). The redemption of all creation has been set in motion by Christ's work on the cross, and it will be brought to completion when Christ comes again.[18] Christ's resurrection is a foretaste of the renewal of all creation.

Indeed, as O'Donovan notes, "It might have been possible, we could say, before Christ rose from the dead, for someone to wonder

---

[16.] Derek Carlsen, "Redemption versus the Fall," *Christianity and Society* 14, no. 3 (2005): 48.
[17.] Williams, *Far as the Curse Is Found*, 275–76.
[18.] Thomas Schreiner, *Romans* (Grand Rapids: Baker Academic, 1998), 434–39.

whether creation was a lost cause."[19] We know that creation is not a lost cause because Christ did, in fact, rise from the dead. Therefore, we anticipate the restoration of creation to bear some similarities to the resurrection from the dead.

Relative Continuity in Resurrection

The gospel accounts reveal to us that Jesus's body after his resurrection was substantially similar to his unglorified body. There was continuity between the form of Jesus's body so that, once he introduced himself, it was apparent to his disciples who he was (e.g., John 20:16). His resurrected body bore the physical marks of his death on the cross (e.g., John 20:20, 27). At the same time, there are differences between his body before and after the resurrection, which are illustrated by his ability to get through a locked door without forcing entry (John 20:19). There is both continuity and discontinuity.

No doubt due to some of the same questions that we tend to ask about the nature of the resurrection, Paul explained the change that happens in a resurrected body with a contrast in glory: "So it is with the resurrection from the dead: Sown in corruption, raised in incorruption; sown in dishonor, raised in glory; sown in weakness, raised in power; sown a natural body, raised a spiritual body. If there is a natural body, there is also a spiritual body" (1 Cor 15:42–44). This passage does not explain all of the details about our glorified bodies. That mystery may have to be experienced rather than explained. Paul's words do indicate we will have similar, but different, incorruptible bodies (1 Cor 15:50–53).

Given this change in the resurrection body paired with the anticipated similarity between the setting free of creation "from the bondage to decay into the glorious freedom of God's children" (Rom 8:21), we should anticipate similarities between the renewal of creation at the end of history and the renewal of our bodies in the resurrection, which brings into question our understanding of destruction as described by Scripture.

---

19. O'Donovan, *Resurrection and the Moral Order*, 14.

DESTRUCTION OR RENEWAL?

A common accusation against theologically conservative Protestants is that we expect the world to be consumed in a fiery conflagration at the end of history. This was the fear when James Watt made his statement about his uncertainty of the number of remaining generations. As it turns out, the fear was not entirely unfounded.[20] Hal Lindsey, in his infamous book *The Late Great Planet Earth,* writes that at the end of time, "Christ is going 'to loose' the atoms of the galaxy in which we live. No wonder there will be a great roar and intense heat and fire. Then Christ will put the atoms back together to form a new heaven and a new earth."[21] Dwight Pentecost is more careful in his language, speaking of the purging of creation,[22] but with a subsequent new creation. He writes, "By a definite act of creation God calls into being a new heaven and a new earth."[23] For both Pentecost and Lindsey, the view is of a destruction of the physical world in its present form with a radical re-creation event.

Pastor John MacArthur states his position more strongly, writing, "The intense heat will be so powerful that the earth and its works will be burned up. God's power will consume everything in the material realm—the entire physical earth—with its civilizations, ecosystems, and natural resources."[24] Larry Overstreet argues that when Peter wrote that heaven and earth will pass away, it means that "they shall be annihilated. In nuclear fission some waste products are always left over. But when God causes this catastrophic event, the destruction will be complete and total, far greater than any nuclear reaction that man has ever known."[25]

It is worth observing in both Lindsey and Pentecost that they leave some ambiguity in their descriptions of the destruction. Lindsey in particular makes it sound as if the material particles of creation will

---

[20] See Williams, *Far as the Curse Is Found,* 278–80.

[21] Hal Lindsey, *The Late Great Planet Earth* (Grand Rapids: Zondervan, 1970), 179.

[22] Dwight Pentecost, *Things to Come* (Findlay, OH: Durham, 1958), 551–53.

[23] Pentecost, *Things to Come,* 561.

[24] John MacArthur, *2 Peter and Jude,* MacArthur NT Commentary (Chicago: Moody, 2005), 124–25.

[25] Larry Overstreet, "A Study of 2 Peter 3:10–13," *BSac* 138 (1980): 365.

be disassembled and reassembled in a supernatural work of purging.[26] While this view is of a radical disruption of the present created order, it does not paint the image of total destruction that is sometimes assumed to be held by evangelical eschatology. This helps explain why many theologically conservative Christians do not actually see the environment "as fuel for the fire that is coming," as former White House Press Secretary Bill Moyers asserts.[27] However, MacArthur and Overstreet are much more explicit in their expectation of annihilation followed by *de novo* re-creation.

Text and Translation

The critical passage for some understandings of the earth being destroyed and subsequently re-created is 2 Pet 3:10. Though even Bart Ehrman, a consistent opponent of Christianity, agrees that textual variants make no difference to central doctrines of the Christian faith,[28] there is a textual variant in 2 Pet 3:10 that has influenced the doctrine of eschatology. In the King James Version, 2 Pet 3:10 reads:

> But the day of the Lord will come as a thief in the night in which the heavens shall pass away with a great noise, and the elements shall melt with fervent heat, the earth also and the works that are therein shall be burned up.

In contrast, the Christian Standard Bible states:

> But the day of the Lord will come like a thief; on that day the heavens will pass away with a loud noise, the elements will burn and be dissolved, and the earth and the works on it will be disclosed.

For the most part, these two verses read very similarly in English translations that were created some four centuries apart. However,

---

26. Lindsey, *The Late Great Planet Earth,* 179.

27. Bill Moyers, "Welcome to Doomsday," accessed April 29, 2022, https://billmoyers.com/2005/02/25/welcome-to-doomsday-march-24-2005/.

28. Bart Ehrman, *Misquoting Jesus: The Story Behind Who Changed the Bible and Why* (New York: HarperOne, 2005), 252.

there is a critical difference between the two that creates an important shade of meaning with eschatological implications.

The older translation states that the earth and the works on it will be "burned up," while the newer translation states it will be "disclosed." These terms are not synonyms. The first seems to contribute to the idea of a fiery destruction of creation, while the second has a revealing purgation through fire in view. So, why is there such a difference between the two?

There is actually a difference between manuscripts in 2 Pet 3:10 that makes a difference in translation. The *Textus Receptus*, which is the source for the KJV, contains the Greek word *katakaesetai*, a word meaning "will be burned up" or "destroyed." The *Codex Vaticanus* and *Codex Sianaticus* both contain the word *heurethesetai,* which can be rendered "will be found."[29] Al Wolters notes that every major critical edition of the New Testament text since the late nineteenth century uses the latter word because it exists in the earlier manuscripts.[30] The actual wording of this verse is, in the end, questionable. Metzger argues that the large number of textual variants and relative lack of consistency leave the wording somewhat uncertain; by his count, the majority of the variants tend to imply a dissolution of the present creation.[31] The question cannot be resolved based on textual analysis alone.

As Wolters argues, the notion of destruction in the 2 Peter 3 passage both relies upon and confirms a particular worldview, which presumes that creation is destined for destruction. This has been a common view in the English-speaking tradition because of the weight of the King James Version, which was based on the best texts available at the time. This destructionist view of creation has been codified in the popular American Christian imagination through songs like "This World Is Not My Home"[32] and "I'll Fly Away."[33] That worldview leads to statements

---

[29] Richard Bauckham, *Jude, 2 Peter,* Word Biblical Commentary (Waco: Word Books, 1983), 303.

[30] Albert Wolters, "Worldview and Textual Criticism in 2 Peter 3:10," *WTJ* 49, no. 2 (1987): 405–13.

[31] Bruce M. Metzger, *A Textual Commentary on the Greek New Testament* (Swindon, UK: United Bible Societies, 1971), 363–67.

[32] Albert Brumley, "This World Is Not My Home," in *Songs & Hymns of Revival,* ed. Jack Trieber (Santa Clara, CA: North Valley Publications, 2009), 485.

[33] Albert Brumley, "I'll Fly Away," in *The Baptist Hymnal* (Nashville: LifeWay Worship, 2009), 601.

like the one made by a fundamentalist blogger, "All of nature and everything man has created will be completely destroyed. . . . If the world is going to be 'dissolved,' there is no need for us to become too attached to it."[34] He relies on 2 Pet 3:10–11 for his evidence of this dissolution. No doubt, the author would claim Scripture drove his worldview, not the reverse. However, reading historical theology makes it clear that the influence goes both ways and that those who are least aware of their biases are most likely to be controlled by them.[35]

Destruction and the Canon

If there is evidence for both *destruction* and *revealing* in 2 Pet 3:10 based on textual research, then deciding which translation takes priority must rely on a broader understanding from the canon of Scripture. Based on the usage of some key terms from 2 Peter 3 in other places in the New Testament, the common reading of coming destruction may not be warranted. In addition to word studies, the direction of a biblical theology of creation points toward New Creation as a renewal rather than a brand-new replacement of the current outdated model. Using Scripture to interpret Scripture is vital to a proper understanding of the fate of the earth.

As Matthew Emerson writes in his provocatively titled article "Does God Own a Death Star?," one key point of confusion regards the phrase "pass away." He notes that ambiguity remains even with a canonical examination of the phrase because it elsewhere means "to speak of walking, going or coming." However, it can also be used to signify time passing or the mortality of humans. In 2 Cor 5:17, Paul used it to refer to our old sin nature passing away to be replaced by our new nature in Christ. It is used multiple times in the Gospels to refer to the fate of creation (Matt 5:18; 24:34–35; Mark 13:30–31; Luke 16:17; 21:22–23), but it isn't clear that annihilation of the current created order is in view in any of these instances.[36] It is helpful

---

34. RR2, "Bible Prophecy and Environmentalism," *Rapture Ready* (blog), accessed April 28, 2022 https://www.raptureready.com/2016/08/08/bible-prophecy-vs-the-environment/.

35. Richard Lints, *The Fabric of Theology: A Prolegomenon to Evangelical Theory* (Grand Rapids: Eerdmans, 1993), 14.

36. Matthew Y. Emerson, "Does God Own a Death Star?: The Destruction of the Cosmos in 2 Peter 3:13–13," *Southwestern Journal of Theology* 57, no. 2 (2015): 286–87.

to take a broader look at the fate of the earth at the end; something other than annihilation seems to be in order.

In the immediate context of 2 Peter 3, the Noahic flood is set up in contrast to the coming judgment (vv. 5–7). Certainly, there was judgment on the whole earth and a great deal of destruction as recorded in the flood narrative, but God preserved his creation and gave humanity a new call to cultivate it (Gen 9:1–7). Indeed, God made a covenant with all of creation, promising not to destroy the earth by flood again (v. 11). In a passage that seems to have some parallels to 2 Peter 3, the prophet Micah predicted the destruction of Samaria. He wrote about mountains melting like wax near fire (Mic 1:4), which is a stern judgment for idolatry, but the result is that Samaria will become "a planting area for a vineyard" (Mic 1:6). Once again, severe judgment results in renewal rather than disposal.

Fiery Purging

Creation will clearly be purged of evil. The ecological disruption caused in the sixth seal of Revelation, for example, is indicative of widespread damage to the created order (Rev 6:12–14). But Revelation depicts damage on the way to redemption of creation (Revelation 21–22). In many ways this appears to mirror the dissolution of the "elements" when the earth and the works on it will be disclosed (2 Pet 3:10).

The term *elements* here requires some exploration. For those of us who have had at least high school chemistry, the term *elements* brings to mind a periodic table, noble gases, and perhaps getting to use Bunsen burners with less than adequate supervision. The Greek term *stoicheia* has been used to refer to the four basic elements, heavenly bodies, or angelic powers, especially in later extra-biblical literature. However, five uses of the term in Scripture outside of 2 Peter 3 are taken to refer to false or immature moral principles (Gal 4:3, 9; Col 2:8, 20; Heb 5:12).[37] Thus, it is plausible to understand Peter to be arguing that the heavens will "pass away with a loud noise, the [immoral philosophies] will burn and be dissolved, and the earth and the works on it will be disclosed" (2 Pet 3:10). The coming fire is

---

[37.] Jones and Spencer, "Fate of the Creation in the *Eschaton*," 80–81 (see chap. 6, n. 61).

more like a refiner's fire, like what is described in Mal 3:2–4, which leads to reconciliation through judgment. This image seems to tie in better with the ethical implications Peter drew from the coming judgment on creation.

Peter wrote, "Since all these things are to be dissolved in this way, it is clear what sort of people you should be in holy conduct and godliness" (2 Pet 3:11). Overstreet, who argues for total annihilation of creation, states this means that "a separated life and conduct is to be led by the Christian with piety toward God."[38] The result of this view could be a lack of concern for the environment. However, if what is anticipated is a total, supernatural purging that lays wickedness bare, then "holy conduct and godliness" might include a robust earth-positive ethics that hopes for the renewal of God's creation.

NEW CREATION

In what sense are the new heavens and new earth actually new? In the Greek language, two words could be translated with the English word *new*. When Peter wrote of "new heavens and a new earth, where righteousness dwells" (2 Pet 3:13) as an aftermath to the cosmic conflagration of 2 Pet 3:10, he used the term *kainos*. This term has the general connotation of something that is superior, improved, or distinctive as relates to its quality. In contrast, the word *neos* would more generally be understood as something new in time, or, as we might say in English, *brand-new*.[39]

Neither understanding of the newness of creation cuts off the faithful from caring for creation well, but the different meanings could change the final goal of environmental stewardship.[40] As Gale Heide writes, "If this earth on which we live is going to be completely destroyed, as many evangelicals believe it is, then we have little more responsibility to it than to act as good stewards of the resources God has given us.

[38.] Overstreet, "A Study of 2 Peter 3:10–13," 366.

[39.] Jones and Spencer, "Fate of the Creation in the *Eschaton*," 83.

[40.] Douglas Moo offers a helpful textual survey of texts pointing toward the continuity of creation and new creation, with application pointed toward ecological stewardship. Moo, "Creation and New Creation," 39–60 (see chap. 3, n. 19).

But if this world has a future in God's plan, being renewed rather than re-created *ex nihilo,* then perhaps we have a much greater responsibility that to merely act as good managers."[41]

The consistent description of the newness of creation should shape our understanding of the nature of the destruction of creation as well as our care for it in the meanwhile. In Isaiah 24, the prophet described a renewed rather than re-created earth. He noted that "the Lord is stripping the earth bare and making it desolate" (v. 1), that it will be "totally plundered," and it "wastes away and withers" (v. 4). Toward the end of the same chapter, however, Isaiah's vision is that the "Lord of Armies will reign as king on Mount Zion in Jerusalem" (v. 23), which seems to point toward renewal and continuity rather than annihilation and re-creation.[42] Furthermore, in Isa 65:17–25, the imagery of the new creation is of redeemed continuity with the old creation, rather than something that is radically different in kind.[43]

Overstreet is correct when he argues that the *kainos/neos* distinction is not entirely conclusive. It is possible that something can be new in quality (*kainos*) and also new in time (*neos*).[44] He is certainly correct that the outcome for those who hold creation to be totally re-created is that "the believer looks forward to God and the new creation."[45] The same, however, is true of those who look forward to a renewal of all things. However, there is a subtle difference between the two words, which should push readers to understand creation as being renewed vice re-created when it is taken in context with the full account of the *eschaton.*[46]

As we have already seen, the descriptions of human resurrection seem to depict a more hopeful renewal of the human body. When the body is buried, what is sown into the ground is a seed (1 Cor 15:37). Seeds become new objects, but they are objects that bear a strong resemblance to the plant that produced them. Our resurrected bodies will therefore have some degree of continuity with our current flesh.

[41.] Gale Heide, "What's New about the New Heaven and the New Earth?," *JETS* 40, no. 1 (March 1997): 39.

[42.] Jones and Spencer, "Fate of the Creation in the *Eschaton*," 85–86.

[43.] Emerson, "Does God Own a Death Star?," 289.

[44.] Overstreet, "A Study of 2 Peter 3:10–13," 367.

[45.] Overstreet, 367.

[46.] Williams, *Far as the Curse Is Found,* 287–89.

We see this because Jesus himself was recognizable in his glorified, resurrected flesh, which bore the marks earned during his earthly life (Luke 24:36–43). Paul's argument in Rom 8:18–23 seems to make the renewal of humanity parallel to that of the renewal of creation. More clearly, perhaps, we see in Col 1:20 that Christ's work on the cross was effective in reconciling "everything to himself, whether things on earth or things in heaven."

When all these ideas are taken together, the image offered by Scripture is one of creation being purged by fire as a means of destroying the thorns and thistles from the curse. Then, creation is supernaturally restored to become a perfect home for the reconciled humans who will dwell in the presence of the Lord continually for eternity. This is the end point of the narrative of Scripture.[47]

We know the final state of creation; therefore, "it is clear what sort of people [we] should be in holy conduct and godliness as [we] wait for the day of God and hasten its coming" (2 Pet 3:11–12). What does it look like to live with holy conduct toward creation as we long for the coming of the final judgment? Francis Schaeffer described the proper response to creation's renewal as substantial healing, which extends to the way we live in every aspect of our lives.

Substantial Healing

Substantial healing puts creation care into the arc of biblical theology: creation, fall, redemption.[48] Cosmic redemption was set in motion by Christ's work on the cross (Col 1:15–20). It will not be completed until the divine action in the renewal of all creation when Christ comes again (2 Pet 3:11). In the meanwhile, the calling of humanity, especially Christians who have a hope of the redeemed creation from the pages of Scripture and the indwelling of the Holy Spirit, is to pursue redemptive actions that push back the effects of the fall.

Too many people live as if the status quo is good enough as they wait for Christ to come. They are too comfortable living in the fallen

---

[47.] Williams, 287–89.

[48.] Forrest Baird, "Schaeffer's Intellectual Roots," in *Reflections on Francis Schaeffer* (Grand Rapids: Zondervan, 1986), 54–61.

world and have become one with the world they are in. Schaeffer speaks strongly against those who are overly comfortable with this world:

> Abnormality stretches out on every side. It is possible to argue strenuously for the historicity of Genesis 3, and yet not to view life in the reality of the resulting abnormality. This is not just a theological statement to be maintained as theology; rather, we are to understand this all-reaching abnormality and live in the comprehension of what the present situation truly is. *I could not stand this world if this comprehension was not present.* In this world a person can only be complacent if he or she is young enough, has money enough, is well enough, and at the same time lacks compassion for those about him. As soon as we face reality, the obscenity of the present situation strikes us in the face.[49]

The distortions of the created order through injustice, pollution, disease, abject poverty, and other evils within the created order should be resisted as our knowledge and ability allow. We should be seeking substantial healing of the evils of the world. *Healing* is the final state that will be brought about by God's sovereign work. *Substantial* modifies that concept to what is within our capability at this time.

As Schaeffer notes, "When we use the word 'substantial,' we must recognize two things. The first is that there is the *possibility* of substantial healing, but the second is that 'substantial' does not mean 'perfect.'"[50] We humans continue to live with the effects of sin, though we are called to limit its effects and resist its increase in our lives (Rom 6:1–2). There will always be trade-offs. However, one of the implications of the gospel is that humans actively try to mitigate the effects of sin in the world.

Futility of Perfectionism

Since humanity lives in a fallen world, we cannot expect any action to lead only to desired consequences. There is a sort of tragic nature in our efforts toward creation care. As Noah Toly states, "That we must

---

[49.] Francis Schaeffer, "True Spirituality," in *The Collected Works of Francis A. Schaeffer* (Wheaton: Crossway, 1982), 3:374. Emphasis original.

[50.] Schaeffer, 3:327.

forgo, give up, undermine, or destroy one or more goods in order to possess or secure one or more other goods . . . is often obscured, but always present in modern environmental thought."[51] Substantial healing recognizes the reality that perfect restoration will not be achieved by humanity without final supernatural intervention.

Such a vision runs contrary to some approaches to environmental ethics, which seek repristination of nature. At the risk of oversimplification, some environmentalists hold that the goal of environmental ethics should be to restore environments to a prehuman condition. Patricia MacCormack argues for the end of human existence because "Humans do not create symbiosis. Humans do not reciprocate. Humans use."[52] Inasmuch as an argument can be found in MacCormack's manifesto, it depends on the assumption that the best state of the natural order would be some sort of ecological balance that did not include humanity. Her position is extreme but is evidence of the widening of the Overton window of environmental ethics.

MacCormack's misanthropy is driven by a common understanding of the impact of humans on the environment. Gretel Van Wieren notes, "Ecologists today understand ecosystem damage as not inherent to natural systems but as mostly the result of human activities."[53] That definition is not unreasonable, given the outsize impact humanity has had in much of the world, but by directly connecting "ecosystem damage" to "human activities" without presuming abuse or excess in those activities, it leaves little space for moral human action. This is consistent with the religious roots of American environmentalism, which tended to see preservation of wilderness as its primary goal, especially in the writing of John Muir.[54]

Muir's upbringing was in a Scottish Campbellite Christianity, a primitivist tradition that tended to have a negative view of human activity. Muir used a distinctly Christian theological vocabulary to communicate his spirituality of nature to an American population steeped in the Judeo-Christian tradition. Thus, when he argued against the creation

---

[51.] Noah J. Toly, *The Gardener's Dirty Hands: Environmental Politics and Christian Ethics* (New York: Oxford University Press, 2019), 25.

[52.] MacCormack, *Ahuman Manifesto*, 13 (see introduction, n. 16).

[53.] Van Wieren, *Restored to Earth*, 35 (see chap. 5, n. 62).

[54.] Berry, *Devoted to Nature*, 171–75 (see chap.1, n. 31).

of a reservoir in what is now Yosemite National Park, he wrote, "Dam Hetch-Hetchy! As well dam for water-tanks the people's cathedrals and churches, for no holier temple has been consecrated by the heart of man."[55] In this line of argumentation, wilderness is sacred because it is untouched by humanity and should be preserved thus to maintain its holiness. As historian Thomas Berry notes of the preservation movement, "Natural beauty and wild landscapes were moral necessities that required large-scale technological and legal interventions for their protection. Human manipulation provided the means to guarantee places to escape mechanistic civilization."[56] Of course, some of those well-intentioned interventions have had negative results. The necessity of trade-offs prevents repristination apart from human extinction.

The reusable shopping bag—in some circles the basic symbol of ecological responsibility—is typically a net negative for the environment. They are billed as an environmentally friendly alternative to disposable plastic bags, but as the New York Times reported, "An organic cotton tote needs to be used 20,000 times to offset its overall impact of production."[57] There is no question that the proliferation of plastic bags is a problem, but the solution has created a new problem. There are often other forms of injustice threatened for ecological goods. For example, in recent years minerals that are necessary for clean energy (like the antimony needed for batteries to make solar energy possible) have been found on lands owned by the Nez Perce tribe. Mining operations necessary for the good of the global environment could result in damage to the local ecology and disruption of land considered sacred by the tribe.[58] There are trade-offs between good things, like the protection of the earth and honoring indigenous lands. There are no simple solutions to ecological degradation. It is futile to believe we can attain perfection through our efforts. However, there is hope in the concept of substantial healing.

Substantial healing completes the ideas described in the land ethic of Aldo Leopold. It recognizes the tension between human impact

---

[55.] John Muir, The Yosemite (New York: The Century Co., 1912), 262.

[56.] Berry, Devoted to Nature, 172.

[57.] Grace Cook, "The Cotton Tote Crisis," New York Times, August 24, 2021, https://www.nytimes.com/2021/08/24/style/cotton-totes-climate-crisis.html.

[58.] Jack Healy and Mike Baker, "As Miners Chase Clean-Energy Minerals, Tribes Fear a Repeat of the Past," New York Times, December 27, 2021, https://www.nytimes.com/2021/12/27/us/mining-clean-energy-antimony-tribes.html.

on creation and the goal of proper functioning of the created order. Leopold summarizes his ethical system: "A thing is right when it tends to preserve the integrity, stability, and beauty of the biotic community. It is wrong when it tends otherwise."[59] Leopold's vision of environmental ethics will conflict with a robust vision of substantial healing because its sole focus is on the environment, while substantial healing is an attempt to bring restoration to all of creation. Therefore, the land ethic can be turned simply into NIMBYism—"not in my back-yard," the resistance of changes to one's own locality—because building *anything* new will doubtless disrupt the ecosystem in that local area. That, among other potential problems, leads ecologist Lawrence Slobodkin to describe Leopold's approach as "nonsense."[60] The land ethic sets out in a positive direction, but it falls short of a faithful Christian ethic because it devalues the role of humanity within nature.

Instead, Christians will find the principle of substantial healing helpful as part of a fully orbed understanding of stewardship, especially as related to the environment. Substantial healing recognizes that human impact is not foreign to the created order. Indeed, as Richter argues with respect to God's original design for creation, "Progress would not necessitate pollution. Expansion would not require extinction."[61] Humans were intended to build, develop, and invent, but always at creation's pace and in harmony with God's design. Our lives, therefore, must be conformed to God's order for creation in our daily practices. Chapters 9 and 10 will explore some of the complexity of the practical application of creation care in the lives of Christians.

CONCLUSION

Christian eschatology rightly points toward our hope in the coming renewal of all things. A desire to live a holy life in every aspect of our existence flows from that hope of a creation purged of sin and renewed in righteousness. Our lives, therefore, should seek to embody substantial

---

[59.] Leopold, *A Sand County Almanac*, 262 (see chap. 2, n. 56).

[60.] Lawrence B. Slobodkin, *A Citizen's Guide to Ecology* (New York: Oxford University Press, 2003), 174.

[61.] Richter, *Stewards of Eden*, 11 (see chap. 5, n. 49).

healing as we attempt to live in light of the coming restoration in the fallen, sinful world. This is the duty of the individual Christian.

At the same time, a Christian eschatology also leads to the anticipation that God's direct action in creation will be necessary to set things right. Though we long for the coming restoration, Scripture is clear that God alone can renew creation. After all, it is his curse that is being purged from the created order, once it is no longer needed to remind humanity of their need for a savior. Eschatology both encourages and directs creation care for the faithful Christian, making it an essential doctrine to consider when navigating environmental ethics.

KEY TERMS

Destruction
Elements
Eschatology
Eschaton
Extinction
Renewal

STUDY QUESTIONS

1. Why is eschatology a central part of a Christian worldview?
2. How does destructionist eschatology impact one's understanding of stewardship of God's creation?
3. What is the fate of the earth at the end of time based on the balance of the witness of Scripture?
4. Why is substantial healing an important part of stewardship of God's creation?
5. How does perfectionism undermine biblical stewardship?

PART THREE
THE PRACTICE OF CREATION CARE

CHAPTER 8

The Church
and the Environment

Behind my local church building in Monroe, Michigan, there is a one-acre plot that has been turned into a wildflower field. This is a project that I proposed, thinking it would be a pet project for me, but which has become a point of interest for the congregation. When I was looking for a way to till the soil, someone volunteered to bring an old tractor and some rusty farm equipment. Someone else has expressed a desire to mow a path around it to allow people to walk near the flowers. A wildflower field, sown in part to encourage pollinators and improve the environment, has become a project for the church. Is this effort part of the church's mission? Is it a distraction from the mission? Or is it just something nice to do that really doesn't matter?

This chapter explores the balance between individual and social ethics in recent evangelical Christian history. It then explores the mission of the church, shifting to a particular understanding of the mission to argue for the church as a pilot plant. The chapter then moves to consider the real danger of mission drift, which is often made possible by putting social engagement, rather than the gospel, at the center of an organization's focus.

INDIVIDUAL AND SOCIAL ETHICS

Evangelical ethics through much of the twentieth century focused strongly on personal ethics over social ethics. This fact is not particularly surprising to those familiar with the battles of the late nineteenth and early twentieth centuries. The significant debates over the truthfulness of Scripture are often the focus of evangelical history.[1] However, the

---

[1.] See Harold Lindsell, *The Battle for the Bible* (Grand Rapids: Zondervan, 1976).

nature of Christian ethics has also been a significant debate in the United States since the Civil War. Liberal Protestants tended to see ethics as primarily a social concept, as witnessed by Walter Rauschen- busch's concept of the Social Gospel.[2] In reaction to this, orthodox Protestants tended to retreat from social ethics to personal ethics. In some ways, ethics in the conservative, evangelical tradition has been inconsistent. Evangelicals believe Scripture is universally true but have often argued for primarily personal application through ethics.

The internal tension in evangelical ethics can be seen in the writ- ings of Carl F. H. Henry. In 1947 he wrote *The Uneasy Conscience of Modern Fundamentalism*, which argues for theologically conservative Protestants to have a greater interest in social ethics.[3] However, his most significant text in ethics is *Christian Personal Ethics*, published in 1957.[4] Henry was consistent in his thinking and was publicly engaged through his founding of *Christianity Today*. According to Henry, it is perfectly logical that evangelicals are more concerned with theological truths than social activism because that aligns with the goals of the movement.[5] That personal ethics were prioritized over social ethics in print and in practice, whether fairly represented or not, tends to encourage the idea that evangelicals are largely disengaged from social interest, including care for creation. This tension is not unique to evangelicals, however.

There is tension in the very fabric of American culture between concepts of individualism, freedom, personal rights, and collective action.[6] It has been present from the very founding of the nation and continues today. We are a nation largely descended from the second sons who had the courage and desire to get on the boat to seek for- tunes across the water. Now we are trying to build a stable society in a geographically and socially diverse land. This tension helps to explain

---

[2]. Walter Rauschenbusch, *Christianity and the Social Crisis in the 21st Century* (New York: HarperOne, 2007), 3–8.

[3]. Carl F. H. Henry, *The Uneasy Conscience of Modern Fundamentalism* (Grand Rapids: Eerd- mans, 1947).

[4]. Carl F. H. Henry, *Christian Personal Ethics* (Grand Rapids: Eerdmans, 1957).

[5]. Carl F. H. Henry, "Evangelicals in the Social Struggle," *Christianity Today*, October 8, 1965, 43–44.

[6]. This is well depicted in Robert Bellah et al., *Habits of the Heart: Individualism and Commit- ment in American Life* (New York: Harper & Row, 1985).

the present polarization in culture, with an increasingly empty political and social center. At least, this is the common perception of the situation. However, that perception seems to be grounded in national-level politics. There are signs that, at the local level, the degree of polarization is much less extreme.[7] It is hard to agree on policies that will directly influence the lives of over 300 million people whose geography, social location, and economic opportunities vary drastically. However, local communities are much quicker to recognize the need for a new sidewalk along a dangerous road or the effects a polluted river is having on the local population of fish.

Atomistic Individualism

The predominant shift in the culture of the United States has been toward an atomistic individualism.[8] Conservatives often lament Justice Anthony Kennedy's comment in the *Planned Parenthood v. Casey* case that self-determination is essential to the American way. He wrote, "At the heart of liberty is the right to define one's own concept of existence, of meaning, of the universe, and of the mystery of human life."[9] This was spoken in the context of a case that helped abortion continue as a legal practice in the United States for more than fifty years. However, those loudest in lament over abortion sometimes fail to see how some versions of libertarian economic freedom can also have a damaging effect on community and other individuals. There is no moral equivalence between the direct killing of a preborn baby and the unthinking destruction of local ecology in pursuit of a few percentage points, increase in efficiency and profit, but the results can trend in the same direction. The latter is often less carefully evaluated.

Critics of evangelicalism sometimes attack the ill-defined movement for imparting individualism because of the correlation between political and theological conservativism and the focus in evangelical theology

---

[7.] See the examples in James Fallows and Deborah Fallows, *Our Towns: A 100,000-Mile Journey into the Heart of America* (New York: Vintage Books, 2019).

[8.] Alan Noble, *You Are Not Your Own: Belonging to God in an Inhuman World* (Downers Grove: IVP, 2021), 156–60.

[9.] Supreme Court of the United States, *Planned Parenthood of Southeastern Pennsylvania v. Casey,* Legal Information Institute of Cornell Law School, June 29, 1992, https://www.law.cornell.edu /supct/html/91-744.ZO.html.

on the salvation of the individual.[10] Even for the most ardent defenders of evangelicalism, it is impossible to deny the creeping individualism in American churches. The question is whether individualism is the fruit of evangelical theology or the result of insufficient resistance to modern Western culture. The latter is a better explanation. If anything, evangelical theology continues to be distorted by the influences of modernity; modernity has not been significantly shaped by evangelical theology. For example, as a reaction to theological liberalism and its emphasis on universal salvation, many evangelicals tend to neglect the concept of cosmic redemption. The response to a very modern theological drift has created an unhelpful response in the focus of teaching among American evangelicals.

Universalism and Cosmic Redemption

Universal salvation is a common theme of theological liberalism.[11] In the modern calculus, the very word *salvation* is redefined from traditional, orthodox meaning. Thus, Walter Rauschenbusch writes, "When we submit to God, we submit to the supremacy of the common good. Salvation is the voluntary socializing of the soul."[12] He then argues for salvation of super-personal forces: "The salvation of the composite personalities, like that of individuals, consists of coming under the law of Christ."[13] Salvation is then equated with socialism, in explicit opposition to capitalism. Given the efforts of modernists like Rauschenbusch to associate salvation with socialism, combined with the evangelical resistance to their overall project, it is little surprise that theological conservatives drifted toward capitalism. Politics and economics muddied the waters of theology, but the central question remains the nature of salvation.

Francis Schaeffer balances cosmic redemption and individual salvation. He writes, "When Christ returns, judges, and restores, my personal salvation will, wonder upon wonder, be a part of a wonderful

---

[10.] Daniel L. Brunner, Jennifer L. Butler, and A. J. Swoboda, *Introducing an Evangelical Ecotheology: Foundations in Scripture, Theology, History, and Praxis* (Grand Rapids: Baker, 2014), 130–34.
[11.] Olson, *Story of Christian Theology*, 551 (see chap. 1, n. 28).
[12.] Rauschenbusch, *Theology for the Social Gospel*, 99 (see introduction, n. 23).
[13.] Rauschenbusch, 111.

total salvation of all that is now abnormal."[14] Schaeffer argues for cosmic redemption, just as is depicted in Col 1:20 and Rom 8:20–23, but unlike some like some theological liberals, he does not neglect personal salvation.[15] Instead, the redemption of individuals is placed within the context of cosmic redemption through the work of Christ. Schaeffer argues, "Christ's death will bring total restoration of creation. This is justification now—my guilt removed on the basis of Christ's death so that moral guilt no longer stands between me and God, but this personal salvation is not an isolated reality."[16]

Personal salvation means that individual righteousness is an important goal in life. God tells his people, "Be holy, because I am holy" (1 Pet 1:15–16). Substantial healing of systems and structures of society is also important for the Christian life. Schaeffer argues that Christians must actively resist the evil all around them in the world: "In this world a person can only be complacent if he or she is young enough, has money enough, is well enough, and at the same time lacks compassion for those about him. As soon as we face reality, the obscenity of the present situation strikes us in the face."[17] Thus, a faithful Christian must be interested in justice within society even as she seeks personal holiness.[18]

Social Justice

In recent years the term *social justice* has taken on a pejorative meaning among many evangelicals. That reputation is not entirely unwarranted, as in some cases the term is used to refer to something very similar to what Rauschenbusch was talking about with his Social Gospel. Social justice also sometimes comes with the assumption of perpetually concentrated government control over more of people's lives and

---

[14.] Schaeffer, "True Spirituality," 3:377.

[15.] For example, Matthew Fox, *The Coming of the Cosmic Christ* (San Francisco: Harper Collins, 1988), 151; Ernst Conradie, "The Salvation of the Earth from Anthropogenic Destruction," in *Worldviews* 14, no. 2/3 (2010):113; Rosemary Radford Ruether, *Introducing Redemption in Christian Feminism* (Sheffield: Sheffield Academic, 1998), 120.

[16.] Schaeffer, "True Spirituality," 3:376–77.

[17.] Schaeffer, "True Spirituality," 3:374.

[18.] Carson provides a helpful beginning point for research and discussion on the balance between social ethics and individual salvation: D. A. Carson, "Kingdom, Ethics, and Individual Salvation," *Themelios* 38, no. 2 (2013):197–201.

wealth. However, based on its roots in Aristotelian ethics and Catholic social teaching, the prominent capitalist thinker Michael Novak notes, "Social justice is not what most people think it is, a building up of state bureaucracies which are impersonal, inefficient, and expensive far beyond their own original forecasts."[19] In contrast, Novak works to retrieve the concept of social justice with several chapters of discussion on Catholic social teaching, but his most succinct summary is that "social justice is a virtue whose specific character is social in two ways: the skill in forming associations, and the aim of benefiting the human community, whether local, national, or international."[20] The concept Novak is tracing out might be best illustrated by God's command to the Israelites headed to exile in Babylon: "Pursue the well-being of the city I have deported you to. Pray to the LORD on its behalf, for when it thrives, you will thrive" (Jer 29:7).

Though Jeremiah's message was given to people who were citizens of the once-powerful nation of Israel, there is evidence that some of the same concepts carried through to new covenant believers. Paul exhorted the Romans, "Let everyone submit to the governing authorities, since there is no authority except from God, and the authorities that exist are instituted by God" (13:1). This approach was characteristic of the early church. As Bruce Winters argues, "All able-bodied members of the Christian community were to seek the welfare of others in their city, even though they might be treated as 'foreigners.'"[21] Concern for the well-being of the community was not limited to the nation of Israel in exile but was supposed to be extended through the lives of New Testament believers. Efforts to seek justice in the public square are not a product of modern theology in its various forms, but part of the DNA of Christianity.[22]

Therefore, this evidence that Christians have a duty both to pursue individual righteousness and the good of the city moves this argument toward the mission of the church. The next section examines how the

---

[19.] Michael Novak and Paul Adams, *Social Justice Isn't What You Think It Is* (New York: Encounter, 2015), 24.

[20.] Novak and Adams, 24–25.

[21.] Bruce W. Winters, *Seek the Welfare of the City: Christians as Benefactors and Citizens* (Grand Rapids: Eerdmans, 1994), 209.

[22.] See Tom Holland, *Dominion: How the Christian Revolution Remade the World* (New York: Basic Books, 2019).

local church should balance community activity with specific discipleship ministry as part of the mission of the church.

THE MISSION OF THE CHURCH

Kevin DeYoung and Greg Gilbert argue for a fairly narrow definition of the mission of the church when they write, "We believe the church is sent into the world as witness to Jesus by proclaiming the gospel and making disciples of all nations. This is our task. This is our unique and central calling."[23] They see evangelism and spiritual discipleship as the boundary of what can be called the mission of the church. While they affirm doing good works in the local community, especially poverty alleviation, they hold such activities to be distinct from the mission of the church. In a holistic sense, they argue, "As the church loves the world so loved by God, we will work to relieve suffering where we can, but especially eternal suffering."[24] There is tension in their definition, as they try to balance the function only the church can perform—evangelization of the lost—with the other activities many Christians feel called to perform—seeking the good of the city by pursuing substantial healing in both spiritual and physical dimensions. Their concern is not the performance of good deeds by individual Christians or local congregations, but that by expanding the stated mission of the church beyond verbal gospel proclamation (broadly understood), congregations risk missing the heart of the Great Commission, namely making disciples (Matt 28:18–20).

The concern DeYoung and Gilbert express is not without warrant. Our culture puts a premium on social justice, often to the detriment of orthodoxy, belief in truth, and other immaterial goods. As a result, there is pressure to neglect the hard task of evangelism in lieu of the more popular task of community service. Closely related to this argument is the ongoing debate over the nature of evangelicalism. Is evangelicalism primarily a doctrinal movement, driven by theology, or is it a social movement, focused on making cultural change? Douglas

---

[23.] Kevin DeYoung and Greg Gilbert, *What Is the Mission of the Church? Making Sense of Social Justice, Shalom, and the Great Commission* (Wheaton: Crossway, 2011), 26.

[24.] DeYoung and Gilbert, 27.

Strong argues against a doctrinal view of the movement, stating, "The long tradition of evangelicalism does not cohere well with rigid dogmatism or far right social views. By contrast, evangelicalism has been most effective when it has identified with the experiences of the poor and disenfranchised."[25] Strong never identifies what the measure of effectiveness is, other than to be more socially progressive. Making "progress" the goal of any movement results in its unmaking; if the substance of a movement is change, then it has no essence and cannot last as a movement.[26]

Within the progressive evangelical movement, a seismic shift is ongoing where the primary focus of such churches has become achieving some social ends rather than faithful worship and proclaiming the good news of salvation.[27] Being successful at achieving the wrong ends is bad news for an organization. For example, as Gilbert Meilaender writes, "The church risks irrelevance, in fact, when it makes central in its vocation God's preference for the poor and not his universal favor toward the poor in spirit."[28] Caution is well-warranted, then, not to allow non-spiritual ends to become ultimate over the spiritual purposes of the church. As the creation-care advocate Loren Wilkinson cautions, "We must be careful lest we simply use the gospel as a tool to bring about a program which we have decided on other grounds deserves our attention."[29] Other organizations can often better meet the social needs of our communities, while only the church is designated by God as the primary means of getting the gospel to the ends of the earth.

Missional Movement

Criticism of the expansion of the mission of the church is not directed merely at modernistic theological progressives, but also at the missional

25. Douglas M. Strong, "Conclusion to the Second Edition (2014)," in Donald W. Dayton, *Rediscovering an Evangelical Heritage: A Tradition and Trajectory of Integrating Piety and Justice* (Grand Rapids: Baker Academic, 2014), 197.

26. Chesterton, *Orthodoxy*, 104–6 (see introduction, n. 17).

27. For example, see Jim Wallis, *On God's Side: What Religion Forgets and Politics Hasn't Learned about Serving the Common Good* (Grand Rapids: Brazos, 2013), 3–24.

28. Meilaender, "To Throw Oneself into the Wave" in *The Preferential Option for the Poor*, ed. Richard John Neuhaus (Grand Rapids: Eerdmans, 1988), 74.

29. Wilkinson, *Earthkeeping in the Nineties: Stewardship of Creation* (Eugene, OR: Wipf and Stock, 2003), 345.

movement. As Christopher Wright explains it, the missional movement believes that "everything a Christian and a Christian church is, says and does should be missional in its conscious participation in the mission of God in God's world."[30] John Stott defines mission as "the global outreach of the global people of a global God."[31] This definition goes well beyond the ministry of the word as the prominent focus of the local church. As Wright eloquently states, "It is not so much the case that God has a mission for his church in the world but that God has a church for his mission in the world."[32] There is much to appreciate about the missional movement, especially as Wright has provided ample basis for a robust care for creation.[33] However, the missional movement's emphasis on everything as missions seems to risk losing the particular focus God has given his people on the teaching ministry of making disciples.

In his critique of various models of the missional church, Keller notes that some missional theologians seem to lose concern for individual salvation in the midst of corporate redemption. He writes, "Upon reflection [on the missional movement], I find that the individual and corporate aspects of salvation, mission, and Christian living are often pitted against one another, and the individual aspect nearly eliminated. These doctrinal shifts result in a very different way of understanding a local church's mission."[34] Instead, he continues, "It is best to think of the organized church's primary function as evangelizing and equipping people to be disciples and then sending the 'organic church'—Christians at work in the world—to engage culture, do justice, and restore shalom."[35] Keller maintains the broader focus on doing good through the congregation, but sees the institutional church in an equipping role, which drastically tightens its focus.

---

[30] Christopher J. H. Wright, *The Mission of God's People: A Biblical Theology of the Church's Mission* (Grand Rapids: Zondervan, 2010), 26.

[31] John Stott, *The Contemporary Christian: Applying God's Word to Today's World* (Leicester: IVP, 1992), 335.

[32] Wright, *The Mission of God*, 62 (chap. 3, n. 24).

[33] Wright, *The Mission of God's People*, 267–70.

[34] Timothy Keller, *Center Church: Doing Balanced, Gospel-Centered Ministry in Your City* (Grand Rapids: Zondervan, 2012), 268.

[35] Keller, 268.

Discipleship as Mission

There is another approach that does not explicitly limit the mission of the church. Differentiating between the gospel itself and the implications of the gospel seems to be more helpful than trying to put good works outside the mission of the church. Keller is helpful in making this distinction:

> I am convinced that belief in the gospel leads us to care for the poor and participate actively in our culture, as surely as Luther said true faith leads to good works. But just as faith and works must not be separated or confused, so the results of the gospel must never be separated from or confused with the gospel itself. I have often heard people preach this way: "The good news is that God *is* healing and *will* heal the world of all its hurts: therefore, the work of the gospel is to work for justice and peace in the world." The danger in this line of thought is not that the particulars are untrue (they are not) but that it mistakes effects for causes. It confuses what the gospel *is* with what the gospel *does*. When Paul speaks of the renewed material creation, he states that the new heavens and new earth are guaranteed to us because on the cross Jesus restored our relationship with God as his true sons and daughters.[36]

Keller's approach ensures that disciple-making—evangelism, catechism, spiritual formation, etc.—remains at the heart of the mission of the local church, but it seems to capture the heart of the Jerusalem council's affirmation of the gospel as Paul understood it, which was accompanied by the proviso: "They asked only that we would remember the poor, which I had made every effort to do" (Gal 2:10). The gospel is central, but the gospel demands that we do good works as a result of our conversion (cf. Eph 2:8–10).

Keller's understanding of the mission of the church relies on a transformational model of Christian cultural engagement. Keller ties his understanding to Abraham Kuyper's concept of sphere sovereignty,

---

[36.] Keller, 30.

which, in turn, is the foundation for much of what Francis Schaeffer thought and wrote from L'Abri. Schaeffer's thinking on these same questions led him to the idea of the church as a "pilot plant."

CHURCH AS PILOT PLANT

The term "pilot plant" is one that Schaeffer draws from the practice of creating a scaled-down proof of concept of an innovative idea. Schaeffer considered this sort of approach essential to demonstrating the value and integrity of the gospel. In his own words:

> When an industrial company is about to construct a big factory, they first of all make a pilot plant. This is to demonstrate that the full-scale plant will work. Now the church, I believe, ought to be a pilot plant in regard to the healing of man and himself, of man and man, and man and nature. Indeed, unless something like this happens, I do not believe the world will listen to what we have to say. For instance, in the area of nature, we ought to be exhibiting the very opposite of the situation I described earlier, where the pagans who had their wine stomps provided a beautiful setting for the Christians to look at, while the Christians provided something ugly for the pagans to see. That sort of situation should be reversed, or our words and our philosophy will, predictably, be ignored.
>
> So the Christian church ought to be this "pilot plant," through individual attitudes and the Christian community's attitude, to exhibit that in this present life man can exercise dominion over nature without being destructive.[37]

The most significant aspect of the "pilot plant" concept in Schaeffer's argument is that it is necessary for the credibility of the church's witness. When people's regular practice of life is inconsistent with their professed beliefs, the likelihood that others will be convinced by their arguments is drastically reduced. The obese physician may be entirely

---

[37.] Schaeffer, *Pollution and the Death of Man*, 5:48 (see chap. 2, n. 20).

correct that I need to exercise more and eat better, but if he does not value fitness sufficiently to achieve it, then why should I? Consistency is an important quality for those seeking to make a convincing case.

The Primacy of Faithful Practice

We must be clear, however, that our consistency is with the actual principles of Christianity, rather than cultural ideals people ascribe to Christianity. For example, many accuse orthodox Christians of inconsistency because they maintain a sexual ethics that is out of step with the culture's tune. They believe it to be unloving to describe some sexual behaviors as sin. This supposedly unloving behavior is then described as contrary to the Christian message.[38] Those who reduce the central message of Christianity down to "affirm others so they feel good" or "judge not" are much more likely to accuse faithful Christians of hypocrisy or inconsistency because they fundamentally misunderstand the center of Christianity.[39] Any criticism of the church must be measured against Scripture, rather than the standards of the world.

That being said, it is hard to reconcile the ecological thoughtlessness of many congregations with proper biblical stewardship. For example, in my experience, it is altogether too common to need a sweatshirt to feel comfortable in the sanctuary of a church in the summer. Similarly, many church building projects give little consideration to form, beauty, or ecological sustainability. When a design is implemented, sustainability measures are the most likely features to be cut if the project initially goes over budget. There are quantifiable, instrumental goods that overcome unmeasurable values. There are usually thoughtful reasons for the choices congregations make, but part of being a careful steward is thinking through the implications of our congregation's decisions beyond the budget and the apparent immediate impact on attendance or conversion numbers.

The point of Schaeffer's "pilot plant" idea is not that every congregation becomes an ecological think tank or installs solar panels at the

---

[38.] Daniel R. Heimbach, *True Sexual Morality: Recovering Biblical Standards for a Culture in Crisis* (Wheaton: Crossway, 2004), 33.

[39.] For example, Matthew Vines, *God and the Gay Christian: The Biblical Case in Support of Same-Sex Relationships* (New York: Convergent, 2014), 149–62.

expense of funding missions. Rather, it is that the community of faith, if it is shaped by the holistic message of Scripture, will reflect a love for creation because it was made by God. As Schaeffer notes,

> If I love the Lover, I love what the Lover has made. . . . But I must be clear that I am not loving the tree or whatever is standing in front of me for a pragmatic reason. It will have pragmatic *result,* the very pragmatic results that the men involved in ecology are looking for. But as a Christian I do not do it for the practical or pragmatic results; I do it because it is right and because God is the Maker. And then suddenly things drop into place.[40]

The church as "pilot plant," is not about being "green" for its own sake, but rather about asking what Scripture teaches about every aspect of life, applying it as best we can to the present context, and praying the result leads to greater glory of the one true God.

There is unavoidable tension in any attempt for a local church to be a "pilot plant." On the one hand, outcomes provide the most obvious evidence of a lively, consistent faith. As James argued, "Faith without works is useless" (Jas 2:20). On the other hand, when specific outcomes become identified as the only acceptable signs of faith, the free offer of the gospel is undermined (Eph 2:8–9). Goodhart's law states that "When a measure becomes a target, it ceases to be a good measure."[41] A focus on demonstrating our faith by our works can quickly become more central to our personal and corporate identity than the gospel. However, a failure to encourage works that result from faith can lead to a dull orthodoxy, which is a failure in discipleship. This takes the argument back to the mission of the church.

[40.] Schaeffer, *Pollution and the Death of Man*, 5:54. Emphasis original.

[41.] The actual phrasing Charles Goodhart used is "Any observed statistical regularity will tend to collapse once pressure is placed upon it for control purposes." *Monetary Theory and Practice: The UK Experience* (New York: Macmillan,1984), 96.

HOLISTIC DISCIPLESHIP

It is worth noting that although I have a somewhat broader under-standing of the mission of the church than DeYoung and Gilbert, there is not much distance between our desired practice. DeYoung and Gilbert, though they focus on verbal proclamation of the Word as the limit of the mission of the church, also affirm the legitimacy of social ministries. For example, they argue, "We believe that a local church could very well decide that adopting a local school and spending time and resources improving that school is actually a good way—though an indirect one—of furthering their mission of bearing witness to Jesus and making disciples."[42] The debate is over choosing activities that more or less relate to the verbal proclamation of the Word. They continue, "Generally speaking we would suggest that a local church should tend toward doing those activities and spending its resources on those projects that *more directly*, rather than *less directly* further its central mission."[43] The example they provide is a company holding a picnic for its employees to raise morale and improve teamwork.

I am strongly appreciative of the laser focus that DeYoung and Gilbert have on doctrine, truth, and the proclamation of the gospel. They are absolutely correct in their beliefs that (1) resources are limited, (2) the center of the mission of the local church is the gospel, and (3) Bible teaching is part of discipleship. A congregation that does not steward the gospel well is not fulfilling its calling in this world.

Discipleship as Practice

However, I would be very cautious of limiting discipleship to the verbal teaching ministry of the church. More than a decade of my working career has been spent in training men and women to operate military and commercial nuclear power plants. One of our repeated slogans is "Telling 'em ain't training 'em." This simply means there are many skills and attitudes that cannot be acquired without embodied application. Learning in a nuclear plant is both cognitive and practical. I

[42.] DeYoung and Gilbert, *What Is the Mission of the Church?*, 235.
[43.] DeYoung and Gilbert, 235. Emphasis original.

would argue that discipleship is similar. Practicing creation care as a local congregation can be part of the mission of the church if it is part of a holistic discipleship program—it helps shape believers into those who value creation properly, seek to steward it rightly, and demonstrate neighbor love by looking out for the interests of their community. As Rhyne Putman notes, "Our cultural practices and habits can have a greater effect on what we believe about the world than rigorously logical arguments."[44] Knowledge has both factual and experiential aspects.[45] Thus, being a pilot plant as Schaeffer describes is a form of discipleship. We can become better disciples as we demonstrate what being good disciples looks like.

Gilbert and DeYoung make good conversation partners because I largely agree with them theologically. All of us have the doctrinal richness of the gospel in mind when we consider the mission of the local church. The question, then, is not mainly about content, but about how that content should be applied and how wide or narrow the definition of the mission should be. The problem with the concept of the mission of the local church as outlined by DeYoung and Gilbert is that it undervalues the formative aspects of service as part of discipleship. While we certainly learn by hearing, we also learn by doing. In fact, there is significant evidence that when doing something is the preferred outcome, then participating in that activity directly is necessary for real learning to take place. Doing good works is part of the sanctification process, which is central to making disciples of the people who are doing the good works. As we focus on discipling our own congregations, we need to ensure we have structures that encourage experiential knowledge as well as factual knowledge.

Scripture is clear that good works are not necessary for salvation, but works are the proper outworking of salvation. Most famously, James said a Christian should be "a doer who works" (1:25) and that "faith, if it does not have works, is dead by itself" (2:17). Paul wrote to Titus, giving instructions for his theological and ecclesial reforms in Crete: "Let our people learn to devote themselves to good works for pressing needs, so that they will not be unfruitful" (Titus 3:14).

[44.] Putman, *The Method of Christian Theology*, 49 (see chap. 3, n. 15).

[45.] Andrew Davis, *An Infinite Journey: Growing toward Christlikeness* (Greenville, SC: Ambassador International, 2014), 83–125.

And, earlier, Paul noted that individuals are "created in Christ Jesus for good works, which God prepared ahead of time for us to do" (Eph 2:10). The proclamation of salvation by grace through faith has to remain primary, but it seems hard to imagine it totally eclipsing the practical discipleship of partnering as a church community to do specific good works in the community and support one another in those works. There is no easy resolution to this since the fallout of losing the verbal proclamation of the gospel is so obvious in our day and has such devastating consequences. And yet, the Christian calling is to a narrow road between extreme dangers: on one hand a cliff of inaction that drops to dead orthodoxy, on the other hand a miry swamp of activity that sees little value in truth.

The risk of focusing on practical ministry as a form of discipleship is that the rewards of such activities tend to be for the actions themselves, related to the response one gets from people for whatever is being done. It is altogether too easy for the motivation for service to the community to become praise and acceptance rather than a focus on application of the gospel. This is the phenomenon known as mission drift.

MISSION DRIFT

There is real danger in mission drift for local congregations who lack a clear mission. In this, local congregations are no different than any other organization. Imagine that a community has a real need for academic tutoring and after-school mentoring, so a congregation steps up to fill that need. That ministry can become the program that draws people to the congregation in an attractional, consumeristic culture. But the danger is that the good program can sap the church of resources and overtake more direct proclamation of the gospel. A good thing, which meets a real community need, can become a real distraction to the main focus of the ministry.

Making discipleship the mission of the church is a challenge in a culture that values quick, measurable results. Actual discipleship is impossible to measure because it takes a different form in every Christian, it is often very long term, and there are few empirical measures that capture the fruit of the Spirit. As a result, ministries have to count participation, giving, and baptisms as signs of growth. These are second-order metrics because the first-order metric is unmeasurable. However, culture shapes us to try to meet those goals we set, so the thing we can measure often becomes the actual goal. This is true of many churches. The stated mission may be to make disciples, but the real evaluation occurs against what can be measured, which creates perverse incentives. It can lead to mission drift.

The Proclivity to Drift

As Peter Greer and Chris Horst argue in *Mission Drift*, "Without careful attention, faith-based organizations will inevitably drift from their founding mission."[46] Their book walks through multiple cases of parachurch ministries that have left any vestiges of Christianity behind. They may accomplish a great deal for the common good but are often far afield from the vision of their founders. In every case, the practical impact of the organization was prioritized over core doctrinal beliefs. This is a greater threat to ministries that are not directly connected to churches, but it can be a threat to churches as well.

One approach to increasing environmental awareness within the local church is to make ecology, "green practices," and stewardship a focal point in the worship service. This is a dangerous thing too. The main purpose of the gathered body of Christ is to exalt him.[47] We can certainly exalt him by treating his good creation well. However, we always want to be mindful of the possibility that in seeking to love him by proper stewardship of creation, we do not draw people's attention away from the glory of God to the derived goodness of the world around us.

For example, one group of environmentalists recommends using elements for the Lord's Supper "that come from foreign lands by people who were paid equitably for their labor." The benefit, they argue, is that "this practice helps us reflect on the geographical, economic, and environmental implications of our food economy."[48] We may agree with

---

[46.] Peter Greer and Chris Horst, *Mission Drift: The Unspoken Crisis Facing Leaders, Charities, and Churches* (Bloomington, MN: Bethany House, 2014), 15.

[47.] Mark Dever, *The Church: The Gospel Made Visible* (Nashville: B&H, 2012), 76–77.

[48.] Brunner, Butler, and Swoboda, *Introducing an Evangelical Ecotheology*, 231.

these authors wholeheartedly that it is a good thing to think carefully about the ethics of our food, but when Christ initiated the Lord's Supper, his command was "Do this in remembrance of me" (Luke 22:19b). The focus while gathered around the communion table should be our crucified, resurrected, and reigning Savior. Our focus should not be environmental ethics or our own goodness for using properly sourced elements. By all means, use properly sourced elements, but do not distract the worshippers by making that the focus of the Lord's Supper.

Distracted Worship

The proponents of highlighting the sourcing of the elements of the Lord's Supper can argue that by doing so they will be improving awareness of environmental concerns, which is a form of discipleship toward a holistic stewardship. This is no doubt true, but it also serves to make the means of grace a focal point during a time when the grace that is being pointed to should be the main concern. Such efforts are also only impactful when they are novel, which can create a distraction. C. S. Lewis warns of novelty in a church service because it draws attention toward the elements of the service itself rather than pointing the worshipper to God. He writes:

> A good shoe is a shoe you don't notice. Good reading becomes possible when you need not consciously think about eyes, or light, or print, or spelling. The perfect church service would be one we were almost unaware of; our attention would have been on God.
>
> But every novelty prevents this. It fixes our attention on the service itself; and thinking about worship is a different thing from worshipping.[49]

Application of sound ecological practice within a congregation should never become a distraction from the God who is being worshipped. Putting solar panels on the roof can be a good ecological and economic decision for a congregation, but it should not become a distraction from the veneration of God. To paraphrase Jesus, "If

---

49. C. S. Lewis, *Letters to Malcolm* (San Francisco: HarperOne, 2017), 2.

ecological concern causes you to sin, take down the solar panels and throw them away." It should be possible to become a pilot plant for creation care without distracting from the proclamation of the gospel, though threading the needle is a challenge.

Christianity is a narrow road that demands both orthodoxy and orthopraxy. Our goal should not be to place a hedge around faithful obedience to prevent drift, but to focus on the end that we aspire to. When I was first driving in the snow in western New York, I learned to look where I wanted to go rather than at the thing I was seeking to avoid. It worked most of the time, though I still had to get myself out of the ditch more than once. We will instinctively steer a vehicle where we are looking, so if I was staring at the car in the ditch that I wanted to avoid, my hands would tend to move the car in that direction. More times than not, if I had any control at all, I was able to avoid problems by keeping my eyes riveted on the goal ahead. That is the secret to avoiding mission drift as well.

CONCLUSION

This chapter has argued that the church should be a pilot plant for substantial healing. The focus of a local congregation should always be the worship of God and the proclamation of the Word of God. However, we cannot neglect discipleship that leads people into a deeper understanding of what it means to be a Christian. This will include factual knowledge acquired through preaching, study, and one-on-one discipleship. It will also include experiential knowledge that must be acquired through practice. Ecology should never become the main focus of a local congregation, but sound ecological practices done for the love of the Creator are a part of a holistic discipleship and a proper element of the ministry of the contemporary local church.

KEY TERMS

Holistic Discipleship
Individualism

Mission Drift
Mission of the Church
Personal Ethics
Social Ethics
Social Justice

STUDY QUESTIONS

1. Why do personal ethics and gospel proclamation tend to be prominent concerns for theologically conservative evangelical Christians?
2. How do verbal proclamation of the gospel and holistic discipleship relate within the mission of the church?
3. What contributes to the tendency toward mission drift in Christian organizations?
4. How can ecological emphases within church services distract from worship activities?
5. What would it look like to be a "pilot plant" for the gospel in your local church?

CHAPTER 9

Conspiracies and Conflict

When I was a young submarine officer, one of the most challenging training exercises we had was to attempt to navigate the submarine out of the Thames River in Connecticut. We periodically practiced this task in a virtual reality simulator at the Groton submarine base. The hardest part was not actually navigating between buoys and shoals, but avoiding the dozens of watercraft that had been programmed to cross our travel path in the simulator. This was a real challenge. However, it did not take long for us to figure out the secret to gaming the exercise. If the officer of the deck stalled the boat at the mouth of the river and waited a couple of minutes, the vast majority of the simulated vessels would pass right in front of the sub, allowing for free and clear navigation to the intended destination. Avoidance was easier than dealing with the problem.

It would be much easier to simply to find a reason to deny there is any real problem with the environment than to deal with it.[1] Then we could either disengage from politics or put our political alliances on autopilot. However, being a faithful Christian requires a constant focus on the gospel and a repeated commitment to see the advance of the gospel truth and the fruit of gospel activity prosper in our lives and in the world around us.

This chapter wrestles with accusations that climate change is a conspiracy and evaluates some of the factors that have increased political conflict in our culture. Through all of this, the gospel is the thread that leads us on and helps us navigate the twin errors on either side.

CLIMATE CONSPIRACY?

After spending most of the book so far on a theology for creation care, I now have to venture into more controversial waters to discuss

---

[1.] Liederbach and Bible, *True North*, 24–27 (see chap. 5, n. 39).

climate change. For many readers, the first question may be whether concerns about climate change are anything more than a conspiracy.

In conservative political circles, the claim that climate change is a conspiracy is altogether too common.[2] James Inhofe (at the time a sitting US senator) published a book, *The Greatest Hoax: How the Global Warming Conspiracy Threatens Your Future*. The central claim of that volume is Inhofe's clear belief that "global warming is the greatest hoax ever perpetrated on the American people."[3] This is a bold statement that must have resonated with enough people in his state of Oklahoma to allow him to continue to sit as a US senator for at least a decade after publishing his book. But does climate change qualify as a conspiracy theory?

According to the conspiracy theory expert Joseph Uscinski, "A conspiracy involves a small group of powerful individuals acting in secret for their own benefit and against the common good."[4] Complicated or mysterious events are often the subject of conspiracy theories. "Conspiracy theory is an explanation of past, present, or future events or circumstances, as the primary cause, a conspiracy."[5] They are "inherently political," involve the "intentions and actions of powerful people," and they "contradict the proclamations of epistemological authorities, assuming such proclamations exist."[6] An epistemological authority is a distributed group of informed experts who evaluate claims on a particular topic and weigh in on their truthfulness.

We must be careful not to dismiss conspiracy theories as malarky without due consideration. Not everything labeled as a conspiracy theory is actually false. In fact, conspiracy theories tend to be *non-falsifiable*. That is, there is often no evidence that can disprove the claims.[7] Thus, Uscinski argues, "Because of their non-falsifiability, conspiracy theories should not be thought of as true or false, but rather as more

---

[2] Joseph E. Uscinski, ed., *Conspiracy Theories and the People Who Believe Them* (New York: Oxford University Press, 2019), 112–13.

[3] James M. Inhofe, *The Greatest Hoax: How the Global Warming Conspiracy Threatens Your Future* (Chicago: WND Books, 2012), 13.

[4] Uscinski, *Conspiracy Theories*, 22.

[5] Uscinski, 23.

[6] Uscinski, 23.

[7] Chesterton helpfully describes the conspiracist epistemology. Chesterton, *Orthodoxy*, 14–19 (see introduction, n. 17).

or less likely to be true."[8] This approach seems squishy at first glance, as if there is doubt about whether we can know truth. However, it is an accommodation to the limitedness of our current knowledge—we can't know everything for certain at this moment. Instead, we weigh the likelihood that something is or is not true and allow the clarity of time and further evidence to reveal reality from a more advantageous vantage point when the dust has settled.

There are two ways to fail with regard to conspiracy theories. The first is to dismiss any conspiracy theory as false and not worth considering. "Trust the experts." This seems reassuring; however, there are real conspiracies, like Watergate, the Tuskegee experiments, and the tobacco industry's misinformation campaign. All of those were once denied by epistemic authorities but have come to light as being true. The second way to fail with regard to conspiracy theories is to place too much weight on them. As some of the conspiracy theories surrounding the 2020 presidential election show, falling too deeply into the well of conspiracy theories can destroy someone's life.[9] This is true both in efforts to prove conspiracy theories and those dedicated to disproving them. "For the conspiracy theorist, the fact that we don't have good evidence of a conspiracy only shows that the conspirators are good at covering their tracks."[10]

Yet most real conspiracies tend to crumble fairly quickly, as anyone knows who has attempted to arrange a surprise party that required the involvement of a nontrivial number of people. If climate scientists had been bought off or silenced temporarily by nondisclosure agreements, eventually there would be significant leaks or a wide trail of surprisingly deceased climatologists and suppressed evidence. While there have been a few scandals along the way, the limited span of the evidence and the financial incentives of becoming a whistleblower seem to testify against climate change being a conspiracy.

In short, claims that climate change is a conspiracy theory are highly questionable. This does not mean that affirmation of climate change or any particular policies based on the theory is necessary, simply that

---

8. Uscinski, *Conspiracy Theories*, 27.

9. For example, see Bonnie Kristian, *Untrustworthy: The Knowledge Crisis Breaking Our Brains, Polluting Our Politics, and Corrupting Christian Community* (Grand Rapids: Brazos Press, 2022), 1–3.

10. Uscinski, *Conspiracy Theories*, 27.

it doesn't meet the definition of a conspiracy. Moreover, I believe that incorrectly claiming that climate change is a conspiracy is potentially damaging to the witness of individual Christians and the credibility of the gospel.

GOSPEL CREDIBILITY

Some huge claims lie at the heart of Christianity. The most significant one is that God became human, lived on the earth, died in our place on the cross, and physically rose from the dead three days later (1 Cor 15:3–4). This is such an important claim to Christianity that religious and political leaders of the day conspired to suppress it (Matt 28:11–15). The placement of the record of a conspiracy to undermine the story of the resurrection of Jesus immediately prior to the Great Commission (Matt 28:16–20) is not an accident. It communicates the reality that bad actors will try to undermine the hope-filled message of the gospel.

Sometimes conspiracies are real, but we undermine our own credibility when we get caught up in conspiracy thinking.[11] Uscinski defines conspiracy thinking as "an ideology or worldview in which the powerful actors that one doesn't like are orchestrating conspiracies."[12] A predisposition toward conspiracy thinking is somewhat natural. After all, it is less painful to say we lost a game because the referees were cheating for the other team than to admit the dropped pass, missed free throws, or careless penalties were the cause of defeat. Furthermore, a degree of dubious epistemology, with a side of conspiracy thinking, has been a regular part of the prophetic teaching among evangelicals and fundamentalists.

In *The Late Great Planet Earth,* Hal Lindsey writes that we should not seek answers from "philosophy, meditation, changing environment, science." He continues, "Please don't misunderstand me, all of these are good if used properly. However, if we are to be absolutely honest, if we are to use our intellectual integrity, let's give God a chance to

---

[11.] Kristian, *Untrustworthy,* 24–28.
[12.] Uscinski, *Conspiracy Theories,* 32.

present his views."[13] He then goes on to provide detailed explanations as to how the current events of 1970 line up with the prophecy of Scripture. There is a fair amount of winking and nudging that he's providing the links and missing information that "they" don't want you to know. Lindsey claims to be giving "God a chance to present his views," but he imposes so much on the text of Scripture that it distorts the content. In an attempt to bring premature clarity to the apocalyptic events in prophecy, Lindsey's approach did more to obscure truth than reveal it.[14] Given more than fifty years have elapsed since Lindsey's predictions and many of the events did not come to pass as he expected, it is little surprise his work is little discussed, apart from those critiquing evangelicalism. However, his sort of thinking and teaching shaped the imagination of a generation of evangelical and fundamentalist Christians, laying the groundwork for the vulnerability to conspiracy thinking that continues to influence our congregations.[15]

Scripture and Conspiracy Thinking

As Christians, we know there are real, supernatural persons seeking to do us harm (1 Pet 5:8). History also provides evidence of real conspiracies led by sinful humans. However, the existence of real conspiracies does not justify falling down the rabbit hole of a pattern of conspiracy thinking. Scripture provides a better approach.

The responses Peter commended to Satan's conspiratorial efforts are vitally important. First, humbling ourselves before God and "casting all your cares on him, because he cares about you" (1 Pet 5:7). Second, being sober-minded and alert (1 Pet 5:8). Third, resisting Satan with full knowledge that his opposition to Christianity is global (1 Pet 5:9). Fourth, answering the call to hope that God, "who called you to his eternal glory in Christ, will himself restore, establish, strengthen, and support you after you have suffered a little while" (1 Pet 5:10). The message to Christians facing the threat of a supernatural conspiracy

---

[13.] Hal Lindsey, *The Late Great Planet Earth* (Grand Rapids: Zondervan, 1970), 2.

[14.] Lindsey's interpretations have significantly impacted some segments of evangelical and fundamentalist interpretations of prophecy, which has, in some cases, seemed to push some readers to more sensationalist understandings of the text. See Amy Johnson Frykholm, *Rapture Culture: Left Behind in Evangelical America* (New York: Oxford University Press, 2004), 117–19.

[15.] Kristian, *Untrustworthy*, 77–93.

was to be hopeful in resistance, knowing that in the end God will make all things right.

The attitude described by Peter is a stark contrast to common responses to alleged conspiracies in recent years, which sometimes include death threats, violent protests, and overt hostility to the humans who are deemed to be on the other side of the conspiracy. Too often these have come from self-described Christians.[16] There is a better way for blood-bought children of the most high God. Peter's message about resisting conspiracies is much like Paul's call to put on the full armor of God because "our struggle is not against flesh and blood, but against the rulers, against the authorities, against the cosmic powers of this darkness, against evil, spiritual forces in the heavens" (Eph 6:12). Part of our ability to do this well rests in our seeing the value of the gospel above all other issues.

When we treat economic and political issues as ultimate things, it reveals that our hearts are set on this world rather than on our hope in the gospel.[17] None of this means that evangelism must be the only topic of conversation to come from our mouths, but it does mean that we should use our opportunities to discuss truth wisely. Being an active citizen is part of seeking the good of the city (Jer 29:7). Because politics tends to be contentious, we can find ourselves at odds with people over many different policies. But contending for a particular policy goal is different than the sort of alienating accusations that go along with conspiracy thinking.

Whether we agree with the apparent scientific consensus that humans are contributing to climate change, we have a limited number of opportunities to convince our neighbors of anything. We will have even fewer opportunities if we demonize those who disagree with us by accusing them of evil intentions, which is the heart of conspiracy thinking. As Christians, if we invest our relational capital in claiming political and social conspiracies, we may lose the opportunity to undermine the real Satanic conspiracy that blinds the minds of nonbelievers

---

16. For example, the man who raided the Washington, DC, pizzeria was a Christian who had become so convinced there was a child sex ring running out of the restaurant that he felt justified in picking up a rifle and charging into the eatery. Adrienne LaFrance, "The Prophecies of Q," *The Atlantic*, June 2020, accessed July 9, 2022 https://www.theatlantic.com/magazine/archive/2020/06/qanon-nothing-can-stop-what-is-coming/610567/.

17. Dietrich Bonhoeffer, *Ethics* (1955; repr., New York: Simon & Schuster, 1995), 125–42.

to the hope of the gospel (2 Cor 4:3–5). Perhaps more significantly, if we are wrong about what we belligerently claim is a conspiracy, then we may undermine our ability to unmask that more dangerous conspiracy that keeps the lost from finding salvation in Christ.

What we say is very important. How we say it is also very important. Christians must love our enemies (Matt 5:43–44). Even when discussion is made difficult by labels and terminology, Christians should be among the most gracious and generous of dialogue partners.[18] We should also be the most interested in truth as a good in and of itself.

PURSUING TRUTH

The goal of many debaters on the internet is to win an argument rather than to pursue truth. The common term for these bellicose keyboard warriors is "troll." Trolls are those individuals who "attempt to disrupt the [online] community in some way," usually by drawing others into discussions intended to waste time, create dissent within an online community, and cause emotional reactions that alienate community members and entice them to leave.[19] Research shows that trolls tend to demonstrate the "dark triad" of personality traits, which includes narcissism, Machiavellianism, and psychopathy. In some cases, this is combined with *schadenfreude*—pleasure gained from other people's discomfort—as part of the motivation to act on negative personality traits.[20] We don't need to delve into this research deeply to recognize that the traits described do not align with the fruit of the Spirit. These traits more closely align with the vices that Paul described as "the works of the flesh," about which he says "that those who practice such things will not inherit the kingdom of God" (Gal 5:19–21). In contrast, Christians should be committed to the pursuit of truth.

[18.] Ed Stetzer, *Christians in an Age of Outrage: How to Bring Our Best When the World Is at Its Worst* (Carol Stream, IL: Tyndale House, 2018), 195–254.

[19.] Ashlee Humphreys, *Social Media: Enduring Principles* (New York: Oxford University Press, 2016), 178.

[20.] Pamela Jo Brubaker et al., "The Power of Schadenfreude: Predicting Behaviors and Perceptions of Trolling Among Reddit Users," *Social Media + Society* (April–June 2021):1–13.

Honest Answers to Honest Questions

Francis Schaeffer taught that "Christianity is truth, and we must give honest answers to honest questions. Christianity is truth, truth that God has told us; and if it is truth, it can answer questions."[21] He also wrote, "Christianity is realistic because it says that if there is no truth, there is also no hope; and there can be no truth if there is no adequate base. It is prepared to face the consequences of being proved false and say with Paul: If you find the body of Christ, the discussion is finished; let us eat and drink, for tomorrow we die."[22] The point is that all truth is God's truth and our commitment should be to determining what is true rather than to winning arguments. This should be true not just in relation to "spiritual" truth, but to truth in all areas.

Thus, when we discuss important topics with other people, we should truly listen and seek to truly understand.[23] It might mean that if we are going to express an opinion on something, then we might have to do research beyond reading a handful of blogs that agree with our preferred conclusions. The message here is not to "trust the experts" but to recognize that if the slam dunk, meme-level arguments we picked up on social media were that powerful, it is unlikely that those deeply engaged in academic study of ecology and climate science would continue. (That is, unless the rude insults about their intelligence are true, which seems improbable.) Humility is in order.[24]

Many of the basic arguments against human-caused climate change are what Katharine Hayhoe calls "zombie arguments."[25] These arguments often sound convincing in a blog or with a few graphs with carefully scaled axes to illustrate, but there is usually a body of research that has caused those who study the topic deeply to shift away from these theories. Hayhoe is on target when she urges people talking about climate change to "have an answer [to these zombie arguments], but to keep it short. Acknowledge the objection, and provide a brief

---

[21.] Schaeffer, "Two Contents, Two Realities," 3:412 (see chap. 1, n. 14).

[22.] Schaeffer, "The God Who Is There," *The Complete Works of Francis A. Schaeffer* (Wheaton: Crossway, 1982), 1:45.

[23.] Alan Jacobs's book, *How to Think: A Survival Guide for a World at Odds* (New York: Crown, 2017), is helpful on this subject.

[24.] Kristian, *Untrustworthy*, 154–66.

[25.] Hayhoe, *Saving Us*, 38–39 (see introduction. n. 2).

response."[26] This is the same sort of approach we should take when dealing with arguments against Christianity, like those related to the immorality of the Crusades, questions about whether God can create a rock too big to lift, or whatever sophomoric defeater the internet offers. Just as we might get annoyed at disingenuous anti-Christian prodding, we should seek to avoid taking that approach with respect to other people's ideas.

At the same time, we need not fear being called a "science denier" if we end up at a different conclusion. The goal should be to listen honestly to determine why someone came to the conclusion they did, then carefully evaluate their position, and then come to our conclusions thoughtfully. In some cases, we may find that the reason many people oppose the theory of human-caused climate change (or any other environmental issue) is that they dislike the policy proposals other people conclude are the natural solution to what ails the environment. We also may come to the conclusion that we lack sufficient time or expertise to form a firm opinion, which should be an acceptable response, given the trajectory and cause of global climate shifts are extremely complex and much less significant than the eternal truths of the gospel.

CLIMATE CHANGE AND PASCAL'S WAGER

Based on what seems to be the preponderance of the evidence, I believe humans have contributed to an accelerated change in the climate by the increased use of fossil fuels over the past couple of centuries. I do not have proof in the sense of absolute empirical certainty, but when all the arguments for human contribution to a warming trend are added up, it seems like a reasonable explanation. At the same time, I am deeply concerned by those who attempt to use concerns about climate change as a "big idea" to reshape society in ways that undermine the well-being of the poor; devalue the unborn, the elderly, and the disabled; and consolidate power in ways that enable future abuses on a greater scale. I believe it is an important issue for which we need to take action, but upending society as some have proposed is unlikely

---

[26.] Hayhoe, 39.

to end well or result in the desired outcome. Change is needed, but revolution inevitably harms those whose cause it champions.

For those who tend to be more skeptical of climate change, it might help to take the approach similar to Pascal's famous wager. Pascal makes the argument that if someone lives like there is no God and is wrong, then the penalty is very high. However, to believe there is no God and act like there is one will bring the reward at a relatively low cost. Therefore, it makes sense to live as if God is real in hopes of avoiding damnation.[27] Obviously Pascal is assuming good works—or at least participation in Roman Catholic liturgy and avoiding gross sin—will lead to salvation. He is also assuming that the options are Roman Catholicism or unbelief. Though his argument may not be a particularly strong one as an apologetic for Christian faith, it is a good one for whether we seek to reduce our contribution to greenhouse gas emissions.

The key in applying the Pascal's wager approach is not to do things that would, in and of themselves, be overtly sinful. Notably, Paul Ehrlich makes Pascal's wager with regard to population control.[28] However, since his solutions include inhumane actions like killing unborn children, his use of the paradigm is different. It is not sufficient for someone to make an argument there is an emergency and insist that we violate our conscience to help ameliorate it. However, there is a difference between urging self-restraint in consumption patterns and calling for the death of innocent humans.

Self-Restraint

In most cases, what would actually be lost by living as if our CO_2 emissions were directly contributing to climate change? Assuming we set aside those actions that are forbidden by a holistic Christian ethics, like abortion, the answer is that very little would likely be lost.[29] We might travel to fewer vacation destinations or own fewer trinkets. We

---

[27] Blaise Pascal, *Pensées*, translated by A. J. Krailsheimer (New York: Penguin Classics, 1995), 121–25.

[28] Ehrlich, *Population Bomb*, 197–98 (see chap. 6, n. 27).

[29] Moo concludes his essay on New Testament eschatological implications for creation care with a call for self-restraint. Douglas Moo, "Nature in the New Creation," *JETS* 49, no. 3 (September 2006): 488.

might spend fewer hours ferrying our somewhat athletic children to competitions in distant cities. But some of these expenditures might be replaced by a deeper appreciation for our neighborhood, a greater love for our neighbors, and a healthier body due to more human-powered travel. On the other hand, if climate change is real and we all live like it's a lie, then the future will be objectively worse for our descendants, and we are participating in sin against the Creator of the universe. Everyone has some discretionary aspects of their lifestyle that could be eliminated without any real loss. And, indeed, self-restraint is a biblical virtue (cf. Gal 5:23).

What I envision for a lifestyle of self-restraint is not much different than what John Piper describes as a "wartime lifestyle" in his motivating book on spending your life for God's glory.[30] The greatest danger of wealth is that we will come to desire it, see as it as a worthy goal, and become those who "fall into temptation, a trap, and many foolish and harmful desires, which plunge people into ruin and destruction" (1 Tim 6:9). A helpful side effect of living a spare lifestyle for the cause of worldwide missions will be that our ecological footprint is also greatly reduced.

Self-restraint in the face of personal uncertainty about climate change is a simple choice, especially since (as will be discussed more in the final chapter) many actions that are good for the environment are also good stewardship in other ways. However, reasoning from voluntary personal actions to laws and regulations is more challenging, which often leads to conflict.

POLITICAL CONFLICT

Much of the conflict over climate change in the United States is really conflict over theories of governance. For a large portion of the population, politics has ceased to be a means to "adjudicate conflicts" and has, instead, become "an instrument for regulating conduct."[31] This

---

[30.] John Piper, *Don't Waste Your Life* (Wheaton: Crossway, 2003), 111–18. See also the helpful volume by David Platt, *Radical: Taking Back Your Faith from the American Dream* (Colorado Springs: Multnomah, 2010).

[31.] Roger Scruton, *How to Think Seriously about the Planet: The Case for an Environmental*

changes the character of the law, and it changes the way people make their case for the law. In many cases, environmentalists seek to bypass debate altogether, dismissing any resistance as based on ignorance, conspiracy, or selfishness. This is best accomplished by declaring an emergency, which helps explain the methods of communication of so many environmental issues.[32]

The Power of Emergencies

Thomas Malthus made his case that if measures were not taken to curb human population immediately, many people would starve.[33] For Paul Ehrlich, the main problem is "too many people," which will lead to a rise of "three of the four apocalyptic horsemen—war, pestilence, and famine." As a result, "it now seems inevitable that death through starvation will be at least one factor in the coming increase in the death rate."[34] Al Gore's predictions of sea-level rise and impending doom in *An Inconvenient Truth* were designed to frighten people into immediate action, especially political action in his favor.[35] Activist Naomi Klein argues that challenging capitalism, "through mass market counterpressure, is humanity's best shot at avoiding catastrophe."[36] This comes from her chapter titled "When Science Says that Political Revolution Is Our Only Hope."

There is a reason why this sort of alarm is frequently raised. As Scruton argues,

> Alarms turn problems into emergencies, and so bring the ordinary politics of compromise to a sudden stop. Faced with an emergency we prepare ourselves to obey orders, to follow leaders and to protect our backs. People who pursue a politics of

Conservatism (New York: Oxford University Press, 2012), 107.

[32] Ironically, some readers may be tempted to label my skepticism a conspiracy theory; however, the arguments for both method and ends have been published for everyone to read. It is not that the motives are nefarious, but that the consequence seems likely to differ from their declared goals.

[33] Thomas Malthus, *An Essay on the Principle of Population* (1798; repr., New York: Oxford University Press, 1999), 12–14.

[34] Ehrlich, *Population Bomb*, 69.

[35] Al Gore, *An Inconvenient Truth: The Crisis of Global Warming* (Emmaus, PA: Rodale, 2006), 184–209.

[36] Klein, *On Fire*, 113 (see introduction, n. 7).

top-down control therefore find emergencies extremely useful. This is surely one reason why alarms are so often sounded, and so quickly replaced.[37]

None of this means there is no cause for concern. As the fable goes, though the boy cried wolf falsely several times, there actually was a wolf in the end. However, it does tend to make one a bit more suspicious when the same people who have been seeking control of the levers of power seem to find all the solutions to the greatest problems always and only in their preferred approaches.

Convenient Fears

Instances of lumping unrelated political ideals, often leaning toward collectivism, into dealing with climate change abound. For example, Klein "denied change for longer than [she] care[s] to admit."[38] She later changed her mind because she encountered

> a vision in which we collectively use the crisis to leap some-where that seems, frankly, better than where we are now. . . . And through conversations with others in the growing climate justice movement, [she] began to see all kinds of ways that climate change could become a catalyzing force for positive change—how it could be the best argument progressives ever had to demand their vision is enforced.[39]

Therefore, it is little surprising to see that Klein advocates for the Green New Deal, which miraculously turns "supposedly unrelated demands for child care and free postsecondary education" into essentials because child care is "relatively low carbon and can be made even more so with smart planning."[40] Similarly, the ecophilosopher Whitney Bauman proposes that the proper solutions to the environmental crisis

---

[37.] Scruton, *How to Think Seriously about the Planet*, 39.
[38.] Naomi Klein, *This Changes Everything: Capitalism vs. the Climate* (New York: Simon & Schuster, 2014), 3.
[39.] Klein, *This Changes Everything*, 7.
[40.] Klein, *On Fire*, 268.

are free higher education, student loan bailouts, universal healthcare, and the promotion of leisure activities. These are political ideas that Bauman barely connects to their benefit to the environment, but that he seeks to justify as the substance of a "planetary ethic."[41] The earth has a fever and the prescription is whatever policies one happened to favor prior to the identification of the crisis.

Unfortunately for those seeking to use an emergency to justify their preferred policies, fear tends to be a poor motivator for long-term action. In fact, fear often creates resistance and apathy. Instead, as Hayhoe acknowledges, "Fear-based messaging can trigger awareness of our own mortality, invoking our finely tuned package of defenses against the notion of considering our own death—distraction, denial and rationalization."[42] As a result, Matt Frost concludes, "Climate politics has become the art of the impossible: a cycle of increasingly desperate exhortations to impractical action, presumably in hopes of inspiring at least some half-measures."[43] This sort of despair helps explain why many of those who profess deep concern for climate change are willing to reduce their climate advocacy to putting a bumper sticker on their SUV, which continues to idle at the same rate as they wait in the drive-thru line for their iced coffee in a cup made partially of recycled material. In order for a movement to inspire action, the members must believe that change is possible. Apart from real hope of change, environmentalism becomes a power struggle for who gets to manage the decline as we race toward extinction. Christians must have a better goal than the world offers.

A Better Goal

In his book *Rules for Radicals*, Saul Alinsky notes, "It is common for policy to be the product of power. You begin to build power for a particular program—then the program changes when some power has been built."[44] For some of the most vocal proponents of particular

---

41. Whitney Bauman, *Religion and Ecology: Developing a Planetary Ethic* (New York: Columbia University Press, 2014), 144–50.

42. Hayhoe, *Saving Us*, 69.

43. Matt Frost, "After Climate Despair," *The New Atlantis* 60 (Fall 2019): 4, https://www.the-newatlantis.com/publications/after-climate-despair.

44. Saul D. Alinsky, *Rules for Radicals: A Practical Primer for Realistic Radicals* (New York: Random

policies tied to environmentalism, Alinsky's wisdom appears to be generally accepted. The quest for power comes first, then policy is developed afterward. For example, Naomi Klein bluntly states, "We don't need to figure out every detail before we begin."[45] Emergency can be a pathway to power and implementation of sometimes unrelated goals. One response to this very Machiavellian approach is to mirror it, which has been the tactic of some bearing the banner of conservativism in contemporary United States. Such an approach, however, is off-limits for Christians, for whom "love, joy, peace, patience, kindness, goodness, faithfulness, gentleness, [and] self-control" (Gal 5:22–23) are traits that provide evidence of our ongoing sanctification.

The environment has been folded into the list of issues that have been consigned to the category of "culture wars." The conflict in culture is based on fundamental disagreements about the nature and sources of moral authority.[46] The conflict is real, but its description as a war has helped shape the response to it. Thus, the description itself has helped enable a shared hatred of the "other side." As Rod Dreher laments from a conservative perspective, "Our hatred of liberals is what holds us together, just as the liberals' hatred of us holds them together."[47] War has a way of callousing the heart of the warrior, which, for Christians, is another form of defeat.

As Bonhoeffer argues, "A world which has become evil succeeds in making the Christians become evil too. It is the same germ that disintegrates the world and that makes the Christians become radical."[48] Christians must remember that "our struggle is not against flesh and blood, but against the rulers, against the authorities, against the cosmic powers of this darkness, against evil, spiritual forces in the heavens" (Eph 6:12). Against such an enemy, Peter Kreeft argues, "The strongest weapon in the world is sanctity. Nothing can defeat it."[49] In a world

---

House, 1971), 106.

[45] Klein, *On Fire*, 39.

[46] James Davison Hunter, *Culture Wars: The Struggle to Define America* (New York: Basic Books, 1991), 42–43.

[47] Rod Dreher, *Crunchy Cons: The New Conservative Counterculture and Its Return to Roots* (New York: Three Rivers, 2006), 225.

[48] Bonhoeffer, *Ethics*, 129.

[49] Peter Kreeft, *How to Win the Culture War: A Christian Battle Plan for a Society in Crisis* (Downers Grove, IL: InterVarsity Press, 2002), 100.

in which anti-Christian bias is real and growing,[50] the appropriate response is not to fight fire with fire, but to pursue holiness.

The pursuit of holiness does not exempt us from being politically engaged. It just means we cannot use the same tactics as many of the most vocal advocates for and opponents of policies directly related to climate change. This, of course, makes sense, because the goal of a Christian environmental ethics is not the curbing of climate change but a holistic way of life built on the Word of God, with hope for God's creation in an age of futility, which will result in the reduction of the harmful effects of human activity among other things. Our goals matter immensely in the way we approach politics.

Avoiding Polarization

We must avoid polarization. Yet there are those, following Alinsky, who are actively attempting to create polarization. Alinsky writes, "Before men can act an issue must be polarized. Men will act when they are convinced that their cause is 100 per cent on the side of the angels and that the opposition are 100 per cent on the side of the devil. He knows that there can be no action until issues are polarized to this degree."[51] Though Alinsky claims the organizer must eschew ideology over pragmatic interests, what he depicts is intentional polarization for the sake of power.[52]

Polarization in the United States in all of politics is enabled by our national media. Arthur Brooks describes the problem aptly: "In the battle for public attention, elite opinion makers on both right and left increasingly describe our political disagreements as an apocalyptic struggle between good and evil, comparing the other side to animals and using metaphors of terrorism."[53] This can be seen in the dehumanizing rhetoric some environmentalists use toward people who have kids, calling them "breeders."[54] Conversely, when antienvironmentalists

---

[50.] George Yancey and David A. Williamson, *So Many Christians, So Few Lions: Is There Christianophobia in the United States?* (New York: Rowman and Littlefield, 2015), 15–28.

[51.] Alinsky, *Rules for Radicals*, 78.

[52.] Alinsky, 79–80.

[53.] Arthur C. Brooks, *Love Your Enemies: How Decent People Can Save America from the Culture of Contempt* (New York: HarperCollins, 2019), 29.

[54.] E.g., MacCormack, *Ahuman Manifesto*, 147 (see introduction, n. 16).

associate honest activism with the work of actual ecoterrorists, it tends to undermine the ability to relate to them as dialogue partners.[55]

Outrage is the currency that draws attention in our culture. Attention draws clicks, and clicks are cash. Thus, former Senator Ben Sasse argues, media and social media have a vested interest in keeping us clicking even if it is bad for everyone in the long run. He writes, "The [media] business model is entirely short term: They want to keep you right there, right now, clicking for as long as possible."[56] The shift of news media from a source of information to a source of entertainment has resulted in what Jeffrey Bilbro describes as the "macadamized mind," citing an earlier essay by Henry David Thoreau. One of the major effects of this fragmented uniformity is that "it warps our emotional sensibilities, directing them toward distant, spectacular events and making it more difficult to sympathize with and love our neighbors."[57]

In 1985, Neil Postman noted that the transition used in electronic media, "Now . . . this," "indicate[s] that what one has just heard or seen has no relevance to what one is about to hear or see, or possibly to anything one is ever likely to hear or see."[58] Thus, news of a drop in the stock market is immediately followed by a story about a mass shooting in a school in another state, which is then chased by news of rising climate change-induced floodwaters causing misery and famine in a distant nation that we will likely never visit. All of that is made further incoherent by ads for adult diapers and new electric cars before our attention is jolted back to a segment on who sexually assaulted whom, what political shenanigans are going on in Washington, and how a local high schooler is preparing for the coming recession. Bilbro notes, "By flooding us with information to which we can have no meaningful response, these technologies threaten to malform our affective sensibilities. The goal of a properly attentive life is right love

---

[55.] E.g., John Berlau, *Eco-Freaks: Environmentalism Is Hazardous to Your Health!* (Nashville: Thomas Nelson, 2006), 205–20.

[56.] Ben Sasse, *Them: Why We Hate Each Other—and How to Heal* (New York: St. Martin's, 2018), 110.

[57.] Jeffrey Bilbro, *Reading the Times: A Literary and Theological Inquiry into the News* (Downers Grove, IL: InterVarsity, 2021), 12.

[58.] Neil Postman, *Amusing Ourselves to Death: Public Discourse in the Age of Show Business* (New York: Penguin, 1985), 99.

and right action, and this goal is not served when we are caught up in distant dramas."[59] The natural response to the flood of competing signals we get and the overflow of problems is polarization. It seems futile to expect any change from the opposition; there is little hope apart from total conquest. We want to resolve things into a pattern of good guys and bad guys, where the answers are clearly absolutely right or absolutely wrong.

Polarization is cognitively satisfying because it resolves tension and ambiguity. It may be, as Alinsky argues, helpful in mobilizing action in the short term. It is, however, destructive to the sort of attitudes and dispositions that are necessary to make real improvements. Polarization leads to a whipsaw effect of opposite parties gaining and losing control, seeking to impose and destroy the signature achievements of the previous regime. It will ensure no real progress can be made for the environment. Paradoxically, changes that lead to behaviors compatible with the long-term health of the whole planet will likely come from an emphasis on love for home and a focus on local action.

Toward Localism

Many environmental problems are not local and are often multinational in scope. The tendency, then, is to seek to place control of the solutions at the highest level through international treaties. Hayhoe refers to this as attempting to hold a "global potluck," where nations bring their contributions to the table to attempt to bring down carbon emissions.[60] The climate activist Jeremy Rifkin argues the key is to encourage individuals to relinquish their local and national identities to "think like a species." He argues "humanity is moving toward a global, digitally interconnected world."[61] These arguments tend toward becoming global citizens, which is to say, citizens of nowhere.

It is easy to love humanity and hard to love specific humans. It is romantic to rhapsodize about small, rural villages with tight communities and limited energy use, but it is very hard to flourish in the

---

[59.] Bilbro, *Reading the Times*, 30.
[60.] Hayhoe, *Saving Us*, 151–53.
[61.] Rifkin, *The Green New Deal*, 220 (see introduction, n. 12).

lifestyle that community demands. Global citizenship sounds good in the abstract because it gives someone equal claim to the whole world. We must be more like J. R. R. Tolkien's hobbits who ventured into the wide world and took on many adventures for the sake of the Shire, which they loved because it was theirs.[62] The effectiveness of small hands turning the wheels of power is due to their love of a particular place. We need not head on a quest to Mount Doom to begin to make real change.

Real change for the sake of the environment must begin with individual action, and it will typically be local because love can only be properly demonstrated toward those with whom we have direct contact. As Augustine notes, "All people should be loved equally. But you cannot do good to all people equally, so you should take particular thought for those who, as if by lot, happen to be particularly close to you in terms of place, time, or any other circumstances."[63] And, surprisingly, this sentiment is shared by Naomi Klein, who recognizes, "Local is critical. . . . Local is showing us what the post-carbon economy looks and feels like."[64] Attitudes toward ecology are shaped by awareness of places that we know and love, not by abstract ideals.[65]

Roger Scruton describes this approach to environmentalism as developing *oikophilia*, which is a love of place.[66] This is a recurring theme through the work of Wendell Berry, whose concept of *membership* in a community leads to pursuing a lifestyle that leads to long-term ecological and relational health.[67] With our national and global politics highly polarized, localism has, in fact, been shown to be much less divisive and corrosive.[68] This is largely because it is much more difficult to deny the humanity and discard the opinion

[62] Matthew Dickerson and Jonathan Evans, *Ents, Elves, and Eriador: The Environmental Vision of J. R. R. Tolkien* (Lexington: University of Kentucky Press, 2006), 87–94.

[63] Augustine, *On Christian Teaching*, trans. R. P. H. Green (Oxford: Oxford University Press, 2008), 21.

[64] Klein, *On Fire*, 134.

[65] Hayhoe, *Saving Us*, 93–94.

[66] Scruton, *How to Think Seriously about the Planet*, 25–27.

[67] Jeffrey Bilbro, *Virtues of Renewal: Wendell Berry's Sustainable Forms* (Lexington: University of Kentucky Press, 2019), 135–50.

[68] Fallows and Fallows, *Our Towns*, 402 (see chap. 8, n. 7).

of someone you know personally and with whom you interact on a regular basis.

In this context, localism does not mean the scope of concern for all environmental problems is simply ecological degradation in one's own backyard. Rather, it recognizes that if electric cars are to be substituted for gasoline ones, there need to be charging stations located in neighborhoods regardless of economic status. It acknowledges that infrastructure that allows for bike commuting and walkability must be locally designed and implemented.[69] It is not enough to pass a law to make internal combustion engines illegal; unless there is real work done to create an alternative to an oil-powered lifestyle at a local level, then nothing will change. The good news is that change at the local level is effective and more likely to be sustained than instituting some sort of control from the top level of government.

CONCLUSION

As we have considered a range of issues in this chapter, the common theme has been the gospel. The world moves from futility at the fate of a cursed world to hope in a renewed creation through the message of the gospel. An emphasis on conspiracy thinking or political conflict undermines the gospel. This is an unthinkable risk for a faithful Christian. Having cleared some of the most common defeaters to engaging in practical action to care for creation, the following chapter offers suggestions for types of actions Christians can endorse within the sphere of politics, within the local church, and in their personal lives.

KEY TERMS

Conspiracy Theory
Conspiracy Thinking

[69.] E.g., Jeff Speck, *Walkable City: How Downtown Can Save America One Step at a Time* (New York: North Point, 2012), 51–63.

Gospel Credibility
Localism
Polarization

STUDY QUESTIONS

1. How does conspiracy thinking undermine gospel credibility?
2. How can listening well lead to opportunities for gospel witness?
3. In what ways could Pascal's wager apply to a Christian approach to climate change?
4. Why do constant emergencies tend to undermine responsible action?
5. What local efforts could improve the environment in your area?

CHAPTER 10

A Hopeful Exhortation

The news about the environment is nearly always bad. As stated in the last chapter, bad news draws clicks, and clicks result in ad revenue. The net result of the constant flood of bad news can be the sort of anger demonstrated by activists who block traffic, make angry speeches to world leaders, and walk out of school to show their indignation. Another common response is a sense of despair. People see the bad news about climate change and begin to assume that their good behavior won't really change anything major, so there is no point in trying. We are living in the prisoner's dilemma. There is a feeling of futility among many people who are deeply concerned about the environment, which can lead to apathy and behavior that simply makes things worse.

As Christians we are called to hope. Our hope is not that a technocratic society will make everything better through greater control from the Internet of Things.[1] Neither is it in the coming annihilation of creation wiping the slate clean. Our hope is in the substantial healing that God has promised for the elect and for all of his creation. We live out that hope by valuing creation and treating it well in anticipation of the coming restoration. As we live in the hope of the gospel, we also point others to that hope and demonstrate the integrity of the Christian worldview, which touches all aspects of life including ecology.

This chapter offers an exhortation to find faithful solutions to real environmental problems within the political spheres, in the local church, and as individuals. This is a call to hope in the face of perceived futility. It is a call to obedience to the gospel and to living a life consistent with our theology.

[1.] E.g, Rifkin, *The Green New Deal*, 85–92 (see introduction, n. 12).

POLITICAL SOLUTIONS

Critics of American-style democracy and free market economics often place the blame for environmental problems solely on capitalism. Even the more moderate Katharine Hayhoe expresses concern that "the free market has been elevated by many to the status of a doctrine."[2] More extreme critics like Naomi Klein see the root problem of the environment as the free market economy, which means that some form of socialism is the only answer she sees.[3] Klein does acknowledge some of the extreme environmental failures of centralized planning, but she makes the assumption that taking economic decisions out of the hands of market forces will work this time.[4] Regulation and market control, however, are often very unpopular with political conservatives.

Balanced Regulation

A significant part of the resistance of environmentalism by many conservatives has been on the basis of opposition to regulation. In 1960, Ronald Coase attempted to argue that regulation was unnecessary. Instead, he made the case that property rights and the ability to sue polluters would provide a means for those affected by pollution to recover damages from the polluter.[5] His argument has been part of anti-regulation arguments from conservatives in the past.[6] However, Scruton argues, "Coase's argument does not prove that regulation is unnecessary; only that it is unnecessary in certain special circumstances—where transaction costs are zero, and where the injured parties are identifiable."[7] This is not how most environmental problems work. As the constant pursuit of people with asbestosis and mesothelioma shows, it can sometimes be difficult to figure out who was actually

---

[2] Hayhoe, *Saving Us*, 145 (see introduction, n. 2).

[3] Klein, *This Changes Everything*, 64–119 (see chap. 9, n. 38).

[4] Klein, *On Fire*, 79–80 (see introduction, n. 7).

[5] Ronald Coase, "The Problem of Social Cost," *Journal of Law and Economics* 3 (October 1960): 1–44, https://www.law.uchicago.edu/files/file/coase-problem.pdf.

[6] For example, Iain Murray, *The Really Inconvenient Truths: Seven Environmental Catastrophes Liberals Don't Want You to Know about—Because They Helped Cause Them* (Washington, DC: Regnery, 2008), 203–33.

[7] Scruton, *How to Think Seriously about the Planet*, 156 (see chap. 9, n. 31).

harmed by pollution. In the United States, the only group clearly benefiting from many of the cases in our courts over earlier harms are the lawyers who are organizing the class action lawsuits.

Regulation is important, but it tends to work best when it incentivizes good behavior and punishes negative behavior. One of the critical flaws of the Endangered Species Act (ESA) is that it encourages owners of private property to "shoot, shovel, and shut up" when they find a species on their land so they are not denied the use of it.[8] The ESA contains punitive measures that prevent land owners from using their property when a listed species is discovered. Imagine how radically different the situation could be if those who discovered and protected endangered species were rewarded at approximately the fair market costs for finding and preserving at risk species by forgoing the use of those resources. First Peter 2:14 describes God's calling to governments as being "sent out by him to punish those who do what is evil and to praise those who do what is good." There is a place for positive and negative regulations, especially when they help increase the effect of nonmonetary values on the signals of the market.

Many proponents of regulation tend to identify the wrong targets as they craft their policy proposals. Their attention is often focused on corporations, rather than consumers who drive the market. As Milton and Rose Friedman note,

> In the case of pollution, the devil blamed is typically "business," the enterprises that produce goods and services. In fact, the people responsible for pollution are consumers, not producers. They create, as it were, a demand for pollution. People who use electricity are responsible for the smoke that comes out of the stacks of generating plants. . . . Ultimately, the cost of getting cleaner air, water, and all the rest must be borne by the consumer.[9]

Their proposed solution to the problem is "imposing effluent charges."[10] So, to be clear, Milton Friedman, one of the most signifi-

---

[8.] Iain Murray, *The Really Inconvenient Truths,* 235–72.

[9.] Friedman and Friedman, *Free to Choose: A Personal Statement* (New York: Houghton, Mifflin Harcourt, 1980), 215–16.

[10.] Friedman and Friedman, 215.

cant voices in the United States for free market economics during the twentieth century, was an advocate for a direct tax on pollution.

The Friedmans' proposed approach of directly taxing pollution ties well with Roger Scruton's understanding of good regulations. He argues that good environmental regulation "should be adjustable as circumstances change; and it should never confiscate the program from those who have the job of solving it, or prevent them from acquiring the resilience that will be needed in a real emergency."[11] Regulation should help resolve conflict, not be a means of establishing control. Regulation is necessary for a healthy environment, but it must be structured in a way to drive solutions (e.g., reduce pollution) rather than in a way that simply creates a permanent relationship between industries and governments. These relationships often lead to regulatory capture, where former (and future) industry members are embedded in the regulator and the purpose of regulation becomes to fend off competition rather than to solve the presenting problems.[12]

At some point it may sound like I'm talking out of both sides of my mouth. I'm simultaneously arguing for (good) environmental regulation and for more market input to help solve environmental problems. These things are not mutually exclusive. Regulation is a way of bringing noneconomic values into economic arguments. As the economist Charles Wilber argues, "An embedded moral code is essential for the day-to-day operation of any market economy."[13] One example where the free market has improved the state of the environment has been in the reintroduction of wolves to Yellowstone National Park. By enabling those who desire to see wolves reintroduced to compensate ranchers who suffer losses from wolves, the population of wolves has been growing and, while not entirely happy, the ranchers have been tolerant of the losses.[14] The final chapters of that story have not been

---

[11.] Scruton, *How to Think Seriously about the Planet*, 150.

[12.] See Stephanie Yates and Etienne Cardin-Trudeau, "Lobbying 'From Within': A New Perspective on the Revolving Door and Regulatory Capture," *Canadian Public Administration* 64, no. 2: 301–19.

[13.] Charles Wilber, "Contributions of Economic Theory to an Understanding of the Common Good in Catholic Social Thought," in *Empirical Foundations of the Common Good*, ed. Daniel Finn (New York: Oxford University Press, 2017), 126.

[14.] Terry Anderson, "Markets and the Environment: Friends or Foes?" Property and Environment Research Center, February 15, 2018, https://www.perc.org/2018/02/15/markets-and-the-environment-friends-or-foes/.

written, but there are hopeful signs that should cause people to try to create win-win outcomes using market systems rather than fighting for the particular environmental outcomes as if it must be a zero-sum game. The ability to gain from an interaction—or at least come close to breaking even—is important to reduce resistance from those who bear the costs of regulations. Poorly designed regulations simply mask other signals or create unhelpful ones, which can itself create further harms.

The good of the environment requires accurate market signals to be successful.[15] As bad as some critics of capitalism believe our current ecological crisis is, it is the highly regulated world of centralized planners that has created some of the worst environmental disasters. The Aral Sea is one of the worst human-caused ecological problems on earth, and it is the direct result of the actions of a centrally planned communist government. In China during the cultural revolution, Mao Zedong mobilized the people to destroy "pests" and ended up causing a famine that resulted in the death of approximately 30 million people.[16] These are historical realities that even advocates for the so-called Green New Deal have been forced to acknowledge.[17] Advocates for various forms of socialism are always quick to note that *their* socialism will be democratic with distributed control, but that is a promise that organizers tend to overpromise and under-deliver on.

The Problem of Control

In fact, there are frightening themes of extreme control among advocates for the Green New Deal. Naomi Klein calls for a culture-encompassing propaganda campaign for her cause.[18] She also notes that "any credible Green New Deal needs a concrete plan for ensuring that the salaries from all the good green jobs it creates aren't immediately poured

---

[15.] Christians must not rely *solely* on markets for morality. As the Friedmans noted previously, markets reflect the values of the consumers. On the other hand, Christian economists tend to recognize the need to go beyond the markets in pursuing the common good, as it is defined in Christian terms. E.g., Victor Claar and Robin Klay, *Economics in Christian Perspective* (Downers Grove: IVP Academic, 2007), 213–37.

[16.] E. Calvin Beisner, "Is Capitalism Bad for the Environment?," in Art Lindsley and Anne R. Bradley, *Counting the Cost: Christian Perspectives on Capitalism* (Abilene: Abilene Christian University Press, 2017), 306–12.

[17.] Klein, *On Fire*, 251.

[18.] Klein, 270–71.

into high-consumer lifestyles that inadvertently end up increasing emissions."[19] What Klein suggests is a totalizing control of spending, which could only be accomplished by rigorous techno-surveillance. This is similar to the sort of oversight another significant advocate of the Green New Deal proposes, where the government would be given power to monitor the daily lives of citizens to minimize their ecological footprint.[20] Sometimes it seems that people do not read the correct dystopian fiction or even recognize the problems of governmental abuse in current events.

Jeremy Rifkin, a Green New Deal advocate, was also instrumental in creating monitoring technologies in China, which have been used extensively to control the population.[21] Though Rifkin claims to support "distributed rather than centralized control"[22] and Klein also states she wants to avoid centralized control,[23] it is hard to believe that their promise of local empowerment will not end up as permanent top-down control. As Scruton wryly notes, "Control from the top down is never described as such; it is always presented as control from below, by the people, for whom the revolutionary elite is merely the 'vanguard,' anxious to capture power only in order to relinquish it to those who have the better claim."[24] There are times when the socialist George Orwell's satire of communism in *Animal Farm* seems altogether too prescient.

However, fear of bad regulation should not make us avoid regulation altogether. As the Friedmans write, "The preservation of the environment and the avoidance of undue pollution are real problems and they are problems concerning which the government has an important role to play."[25] There need to be laws that cause polluters to be punished and create "the incentives that will lead people to solve [problems] for themselves."[26] There is a lot of room for debate about what regulations

---

[19.] Klein, 264.

[20.] Rifkin, *The Green New Deal*, 38–45.

[21.] See Kai Strittmatter, *We Have Been Harmonized: Life in China's Surveillance State* (Exeter: Old Street, 2019).

[22.] Rifkin, *The Green New Deal*, 220.

[23.] Klein, *On Fire*, 251.

[24.] Scruton, *How to Think Seriously about the Planet*, 83.

[25.] Friedman and Friedman, *Free to Choose*, 214.

[26.] Scruton, *How to Think Seriously about the Planet*, 97.

look like, but the discussion needs to begin with an awareness of both the promise and limitations of government.

THE LOCAL CHURCH AS AN ECOLOGICAL COMMUNITY

As we saw in chapter 8, the mission of the church is to make disciples through the ministry of the Word. The church is to be a pilot plant for the substantial healing that we see in the world. This means that the local church should focus heavily on teaching people the cognitive content of Scripture and provide opportunities to live that content out in community. There are many applications of that idea. I will highlight several of the possibilities that relate more directly to creation care.

Consider Missions Carefully

The central plank of the mission of the church is to get the gospel to the ends of the earth. That means that Christians need to go to the ends of the earth to verbally proclaim the good news. In recent decades, short-term mission trips have become one way that local churches in the West seek to fill the Great Commission. This is sometimes an effective way to get the gospel out, but there are significant questions concerning whether these short-term mission trips are consistently effective.

In the seminal book *When Helping Hurts*, Steve Corbett and Brian Fikkert encourage reconsidering short-term missions because they are sometimes a waste of resources and can even harm the communities they are intended to help.[27] The concerns expressed in that volume are largely economic and social, but there are also ecological implications to short-term missions, especially those that have large groups of unskilled people travelling vast distances to essentially do a sort of humanitarian tourism. Even as we consider the warnings Fikkert and

---

[27.] Steve Corbett and Brian Fikkert, *When Helping Hurts: How to Alleviate Poverty without Hurting the Poor . . . and Yourself*, rev. ed. (Chicago: Moody, 2012).

Corbett offer, we should add to that the potential environmental costs of unnecessary travel.

The key, again, is thoughtfulness and due consideration. There are clear examples where short-term missions that require significant travel have a huge impact for the gospel that makes them an appropriate project.[28] Our goal should not be to establish hard-and-fast rules. The goal of a "wartime lifestyle" should be to recognize there is "a great and worthy cause for which to spend and be spent," but that cause is not our comfort, but the glory of God.[29] Stewardship that reflects that goal may lead to sharing resources.

Resource Sharing

I have a pressure washer sitting in my garage. It cost me about $300 several years ago. The cost was less than what I would have paid to have a contractor clean the vinyl siding on my ranch-style home. However, I've only used that tool a handful of times in the seven years I've owned it. I am confident there are others in my church that also own similar pressure washers and have likely used them about as rarely. There is little reason for each of us to own a pressure washer when it could be the sort of thing we share within our local congregation. Someone might own one, but there is little reason for many of us to own little-used tools.

Acts 4:32–35 is sometimes used as a defense of Christian socialism. There are reasons why I don't believe that argument to be compelling, which go well beyond the scope of the book.[30] However, those early Christians do provide a good example of sharing resources that we can implement when it comes to rarely used tools and other similar consumer goods. Rather than everyone in the congregation owning each one of the oddities necessary to go camping, wash a house, or perform some eccentric maintenance on a car or home, it makes more sense for

---

[28.] Richardson, president of the Pioneers mission organization, provides an example of a quilter using her skills on a short-term trip to help train women in an impoverished community so they could start a business and take the gospel to their neighbors. Steve Richardson, *Is the Commission Still Great? 8 Myths about Missions and What They Mean for the Church* (Chicago: Moody, 2022), 98–99.

[29.] Piper, *Don't Waste Your Life*, 114 (see chap. 9, n. 30).

[30.] See Craig L. Blomberg, *Christians in an Age of Wealth: A Biblical Theology of Stewardship* (Grand Rapids: Zondervan, 2013), 109–11.

the community of faith to share those reusable goods. By also sharing the labor accompanying such tasks, it may also enhance the sense of community, rather than each household existing as a consumeristic, self-contained island responsible for all its own well-being.

In our disrupted society, with many people living a great distance from their genetic families, often the local church functions as a support network, very similar to how a family functions. That is as it should be.[31] Christians can use that biblically inspired instinct, enhance the fellowship of the local congregation, and reduce their collective ecological impact by reducing the amount of consumer goods they buy and own through sharing.

Landscaping, Lighting, and Climate Control

I have visited churches in the South during the summer where I needed to have a sweatshirt on to avoid shivering. For those who have experienced the torpid heat of August in South Carolina, air conditioning is certainly a blessing. However, just as we think about controlling our home temperatures, we should consider the costs of excessive climate control for our church buildings. There needs to be balance between hospitality and conscientious resource use.

Similar thoughtfulness ought to go into our choices for landscaping and construction. Shifting to LED lighting saves a great deal of energy and is typically worth the expense in the long run. When new construction or remodeling is planned, there should be thought given to energy efficiency, climate-control zoning, and aesthetic appeal, both internal and external. In fact, one of Schaeffer's chief examples of non-Christians respecting nature better than Christians was in the aesthetics of two buildings across a valley from each other.[32] Churches may consider putting solar panels up. Solar isn't a panacea to all environmental problems, but it can be a good economic investment in the long term, and it produces very low carbon electricity for the life of the panels.

Similarly, the landscaping design should give due attention to the environment. In areas prone to drought, thought should be given to plants

---

[31.] Joseph H. Hellerman, *When the Church Was a Family: Recapturing Jesus' Vision for Authentic Christian Community* (Nashville: B&H Academic, 2009), 145–47.

[32.] Schaeffer, *Pollution and the Death of Man*, 5:24 (see chap. 2, n. 20).

that require little regular watering. Research should be done to avoid planting harmful invasive species. Moreover, churches should give thought to ways their landscaping can positively enhance the local ecosystem. My congregation gave me permission to plant an acre of wildflowers on an unused section of the property. With a little work and upfront cost, we have provided a resource for the local pollinators that helps to counter the traditional lawn that is often required per the building code.

The goal, of course, is not to distract the congregation from worship and discipleship through a new focus on being green. The purpose of these measures is to be a pilot plant and, thus, to try to point toward the sort of community we will be in the new heavens and new earth.

Teaching Them to Obey

Space does not permit a more exhaustive discussion of potential outlets for a congregation to be ecologically positive, but the brevity of this section should not undermine its significance. Remember that when Jesus gave the Great Commission, it included "teaching them to observe everything I have commanded you" (Matt 28:20). If an orthodox theology demands that we care for the environment, then a congregation's discipleship efforts will be lacking if they fail to engage church members in the process of creation care. Different congregations will have a different degree of emphasis on this piece of holistic discipleship, but those who will have to give an account (Heb 13:17) must pay attention to all of the topics, not just those that are politically or socially comfortable.

Additionally, as DeYoung and Gilbert point out, there are occasions when engaging in social action within the community can be an effective way to get the gospel out.[33] Congregations should latch on to those opportunities to be cobelligerents with organizations in the community where the projects align with our theology. We should also seek to live consistently with our theology as a way of validating the message of the gospel to the surrounding community. Christians should seek to live faithfully in our personal stewardship, and our congregational stewardship, as well as in our engagement in the political sphere.

[33.] DeYoung and Gilbert, *What Is the Mission of the Church?*, 227–29 (see chap. 8, n. 23).

LIVE THOUGHTFULLY

Many people believe that living a more environmentally friendly life-style is a difficult task that is incredibly expensive. I have found the opposite to be true.[34] There are certainly ways in which I can continue to improve my lifestyle to reduce my negative impact on the ecosystem around me, so I'm not making a claim to be a green saint. However, when I run my lifestyle through a carbon footprint calendar, I find that my five-person household is well below average for the developed world. This is largely a result of attempting to live more thoughtfully and see all of stewardship as one large project. Much of the impact of climate change is not due to overtly luxurious lifestyles, but "the most ordinary, mundane, good, and even necessary of human activities."[35] A hopeful life requires thought about daily activities.

We live in a fragmented world with a bunch of parallel tracks of responsibility running simultaneously. We may be trying to be a good parent, a productive worker, and an engaged church member. Mean-while we invest energy into trying to be more physically fit, saving some money for retirement, and growing intellectually and spiritually. When you add all of these identities and projects up as separate tracks of good living, you end up distracted and exhausted.

Every situation is different, and there are seasons where parallel tracks are unavoidable. However, many of us would benefit by taking some time to think about what "good" is, what we really enjoy, and what honors God. Then, we should work to build a life around that existence. Living a "greener" lifestyle is not just another task to add to our already overloaded to-do lists; it is really one aspect of a thoughtful life lived toward God.[36] The following suggestions are some ways that we can begin to think more carefully about who we are in Christ, about what matters, and about what represents the best form of stewardship.

---

34. For a case for frugality on the basis of environmental concern, see Emrys Westacott, *The Wisdom of Frugality: Why Less Is More—More or Less* (Princeton, NJ: Princeton University Press, 2016), 249–74.

35. Toly, *The Gardener's Dirty Hands*, 61 (see chap. 7, n. 51).

36. For a discussion of human finitude and the importance of accepting our own limits, see Kapic, *You're Only Human*, 3–16 (see chap. 6, n. 54).

Recapture the Wonder

One of the most tragic effects of the rise of scientific explanations for nature is that we have lost our sense of wonder. Alister McGrath laments this disenchantment of creation: "What once evoked a sense of awe from appreciative and respectful human beings has now been explained away, deconstructed and desacralized. It is as if a protective veil has been torn aside from the face of nature, inviting exploitation of what now lies exposed in all its vulnerability."[37] Though Christians may mentally acknowledge that "the heavens declare the glory of God" (Ps 19:1), we often treat creation as if it is nothing more than a resource for our disposal.

People talk about the environment like it is some foreign reality. To many people, the environment is rainforests on another continent or oceans we may have never seen. It's not uncommon for people to rhapsodize about the beauty of nature but never think twice about the flora and fauna in their own neighborhood. As we transition from office to car to home, we can sometimes forget that the environment is the physical world around us, and we should have a greater sense of wonder even at the familiar things.[38]

Wendell Berry argues that concern for creation comes from accepting the "preciousness of individual lives and places." He argues, "This does not come from science, but from our cultural and religious traditions." In fact, he goes on, it is vital for people to love their locality for the environment to flourish. He writes, "It is not quite imaginable that people will exert themselves greatly to defend creatures and places that they have dispassionately studied. It is altogether imaginable that they will greatly exert themselves to defend creatures and places that they have involved in their lives and invested their lives in."[39] This is an argument for love of place and love of the Creator who made this particular place in a particular way for his own glory. Creation points us toward God.

[37.] Alister McGrath, *The Reenchantment of Nature: The Denial of Religion and the Ecological Crisis* (New York: Doubleday, 2002), xi.

[38.] For a beautiful, accessible introduction to a sense of place and rootedness, see Andrew Peterson, *The God of the Garden: Thoughts on Creation, Culture, and the Kingdom* (Nashville: B&H, 2021).

[39.] Berry, *Life Is a Miracle*, 42–43 (see chap. 3, n. 40).

C. S. Lewis was certainly correct that modernity has pushed us toward the denial of the transcendent in creation because it teaches us "firstly, that all sentences containing a predicate of value are statements about the emotional state of the speaker, and secondly, that all such statements are unimportant."[40] This is the worldview that kills wonder in creation. As we discussed in chapter 5, creation has *inherent value*, which cannot be reduced to a mere emotional response to something we happen to prefer. The emotional response of wonder is real, but it points to the reality beyond the created order.

A primary task for Christians, therefore, is to return to a sense of reverent awe of nature—not for its own sake, but for the sake of the one who made it (cf. Rom 1:20). Wonder at creation should lead us to worship of God (e.g., Job 42:1–6). Wonder drove the writer of "How Great Thou Art" to "consider all the worlds [God's] hands have made" and respond with a soul belting out glorious praise. It is a beautiful song to sing with other Christians, loudly proclaiming God's goodness and the goodness of creation. A first step in living out a robustly Christian environmental ethics is to delight and wonder in what God has made for the glory of the God who made it.

Recapturing the wonder in creation is important for a full-throated creation care. It is also important for a spiritually healthy existence as a human. Mike Cosper describes the "enchanted" world that saw more than the instrumental value of creation:

In that world, men and women saw themselves as spiritual creations, vulnerable to blessings and curses, to angels and demons, and subject to the god or gods who made and oversaw the world. This enchanted world was part of a Cosmos, an orderly creation full of meaning. . . .

In disenchantment, we no longer live in a Cosmos; we live in a universe, a cold, hostile place whose existence is a big accident, where humanity is temporarily animated "stuff" that's ultimately meaningless and destined for the trash heap.[41]

[40.] Lewis, *Abolition of Man*, 4 (see chap. 6, n. 50).

[41.] Mike Cosper, *Recapturing the Wonder: Transcendent Faith in an Disenchanted World* (Downers Grove, IL: InterVarsity, 2017), 11.

Examples of encouragement to wonder at the glory of creation as it points to the Creator could be multiplied, but the point remains that when we delight in creation for the sake of the Creator, we will tend to treat it well for God's glory and in such a way that we point others toward him.

A Thoughtful Home

In my experience, I have been surprised to find that people often spend more time deciding on the destination of their next vacation than on the purchase of their next home. Given that the home is many times more expensive than the vacation and has the potential for future, ongoing costs, this should give us pause.

The real estate market is set up for fast decisions. Agents are paid a commission on the transaction, so the incentive is to get you into a house, make you love it, get you to make an offer, and move on to the next buyer. Offers and counteroffers include that unsettling phrase "time is of the essence." And anyone who has experienced the frustration of being outbid or having what seems to be the perfect home snapped up before they get to make a decision will know that often there isn't a lot of time to make a decision and think through the implications.

The whole process of home purchasing treats houses as if they are merely commodities and not homes. I am reminded of this tendency to see houses as purely financial investments when my homeowners association sends periodic emails celebrating the rise in prices in the neighborhood (which they attribute largely to their surveillance efforts rather than the general inflation in the market). This lends itself to perspectives on a home that neglect the function of the space in lieu of the raw square footage, the relative popularity of the colors and fittings, and the potential for resale.[42]

Houses may be good investments, but homes can be much more valuable. Rod Dreher describes much of suburbia as "sterile houses

---

[42.] Notably, as prices have lowered in the past few months, there have been no similar emails attributing that decline to their failures to regulate or even their overregulation, which has been cited by several families as a reason for relocating.

and neighborhoods."[43] He is not wrong, because the goal of most home builders is sameness and neutrality so as not to offend any taste. Another goal of most builders is to provide as much square footage for the lowest possible cost. Again, Dreher notes, "Americans have completely unrealistic ideas about how much space they need for their families."[44] Since 1973, the space per person in a US home has almost doubled, and the average new home is 1,000 square feet larger.[45]

This growth in home size has impact in at least three ways on the environment. First, the larger the home, the more energy it takes to heat, cool, and light it. Also, the more consumer goods it takes to furnish and fill it. All of this has a direct impact on the environment. Much of it is excessive. Second, since housing prices are often tied closely to square footage, this growth has a significant economic impact. This impact means that Americans often develop unhealthy patterns of work and spending. It sometimes drives families to have two wage earners, which sometimes increases miles driven, convenience foods purchased, and other activities that may unnecessarily impact the environment. Third, larger houses contribute to suburban sprawl, which requires new roads, more lights, longer commutes, and a continued growth of human impact on the environment.

There are many factors that go into home choices. However, modest homes that are close to work can be both economically and ecologically beneficial. We should be thoughtful about our home choices and also thoughtful about the way we use resources in and around our homes.

Emerald Green Lawns

The model suburban lawn is a beautiful carpet of rich, green grass cut to exactly the right height. It is well watered with municipal water that tastes slightly like the chlorine used to treat it. The perfect lawn is a homeowner's dream, enhances curb appeal, and for many of us is a trophy to be pursued.[46]

[43.] Dreher, *Crunchy Cons*, 101 (see chap. 9, n. 47).
[44.] Dreher, 122.
[45.] Mark Perry, "New US Homes Today Are 1,000 Square Feet Larger Than in 1973 and Living Space per Person Has Nearly Doubled," American Enterprise Ideas, June 5, 2016, https://www.aei.org/carpe-diem/new-us-homes-today-are-1000-square-feet-larger-than-in-1973-and-living-space-per-person-has-nearly-doubled/.
[46.] For an engaging discussion of the American infatuation with lawns, see Virginia Jenkins,

The problem is that maintaining the perfect lawn is often unhealthy for the environment.[47] Chemical fertilizers run off into storm drains and waterways. This can cause significant problems like the dead zone in the Gulf of Mexico, where phosphates and nitrogen cause algae blooms that consume the oxygen in the water, creating a space where many organisms cannot live.[48] Also, grass lawns are not friendly to pollinators, which rely on flowers as food sources even as they make the world a better place by enabling food production. The weedless suburban neighborhood with few, and often non-native, flowers is not a good place for many pollinators to survive.[49]

Many neighborhoods, like mine, have a homeowner association that frowns on anything that is different than normal. They might tolerate the occasional bare patch on the lawn, but certainly not replacement of the grass with a wildflower meadow. As part of our commitment to "live at peace with everyone," Christians should not want to overtly aggravate those around us by creating an eyesore. However, we do want to be part of pursuing more ecofriendly alternatives. Through requests and pushback on a few letters from the HOA, I have had luck in putting in some sizeable wildflower beds with bird feeders and pollinator houses. The result has been an uptick in sightings of birds and beneficial bugs as well as a general (but certainly not universal) appreciation of the blooms that start in the spring and last through the fall. Initial resistance has turned into appreciation at the variety, number, and beauty of the blooms in my wildflower beds. Those who live in less restrictive neighborhoods or in the country have even more opportunities.

A quick search on "wildflower meadow" or "pollinator garden" will provide many different resources that can help convert some empty land into a lovely paradise for pollinators. It's a small but important step toward having a positive impact on your local ecosystem in a very simple way.

The Lawn: A History of an American Obsession (Washington, DC: Smithsonian Institution, 1994).

[47.] See Paul Robbins, *Lawn People: How Grasses, Weeds, and Chemicals Make Us Who We Are* (Philadelphia: Temple University Press, 2007), 45–71.

[48.] Monica Bruckner, "The Gulf of Mexico Dead Zone," Microbial Life Educational Resources, accessed July 28, 2022, https://serc.carleton.edu/microbelife/topics/deadzone/index.html.

[49.] Abiya Saeed and Rebecca Krans, "Smart Lawns for Pollinators," Michigan State University Extension, January 2016, https://www.canr.msu.edu/uploads/files/Lawns_for_pollinators.pdf.

Resisting Consumerism

On Wednesday evenings, when my family walks through the neighborhood and adjoining park, we typically pass by the ninety-six-gallon trash bins rolled out to the street by our neighbors in preparation for pickup the next day. There is nothing remarkable about this, except that most of the bins are full to the point of overflowing nearly every week, even for houses that only have two to three people living in them.

There are some simple reasons for the overflow. First, there is often plenty of space in the bin, so families do not take the time to break down boxes to shrink the volume occupied by them. The garbage trucks have a compactor that takes care of this, so it is no concern. However, often the trash bins overflow because people are simply purchasing too much stuff. The bins are full of excessive packaging for unnecessary goods that are replacing discarded goods that were equally unnecessary.

The average American produces approximately five pounds of waste per day.[50] About a quarter of that is food waste, much of which is sent to landfills instead of being composted. There is a constant flow of consumer goods through our suburban neighborhoods that requires some form of pollution to produce, transport, and remove. J. Douma notes, "A 'cowboy economy' that follows the principle 'use something once and then pitch it' is unacceptable. The consumer mentality apparent in this kind of economy is incompatible with our stewardship, as it always has been."[51] Most of us buy without thinking and throw away without consideration. It is one way that we shape our identities and try to control the world around us.[52] That is a behavior we need to stop for the sake of our minds and souls as much as for the environment.

In a 1970 book, *The Harried Leisure Class*, Swedish economist Staffan Linder explains why rising levels of material prosperity and consumption have led to a perpetually more stressful life. He notes, "In the rich countries all slacks in the use of time have been eliminated, so far

---

[50.] "National Overview: Facts and Figures on Materials, Wastes and Recycling," US Environmental Protection Agency, accessed July 28, 2022, https://www.epa.gov/facts-and-figures-about-materials-waste-and-recycling/national-overview-facts-and-figures-materials.
[51.] Douma, *Environmental Stewardship*, 53 (see chap. 2, n. 17).
[52.] Bauman, *Liquid Modernity*, 80–90 (see chap. 4, n. 6).

as humanly possible. . . . This tyranny [of the clock] has developed, step by step, with our successful revolution against the dictatorship of material poverty."[53] One common solution to being harried is to acquire convenience products designed to save time. However, consumption of material goods often reduces our available time because our possessions require maintenance or replacement. So we have to earn a high income to purchase or repair goods that will continue to require us to earn a high income. Linder notes that this cycle creates an "increasingly hectic tempo of life," greater demands for maintenance of goods, neglect of the aged population, and less value assigned to "time devoted to the cultivation of mind and spirit and for the time spent of certain bodily pleasures."[54] One of those bodily pleasures that often gets displaced is that of eating well.

Choosing Your Food

To eat is one of the basic aspects of being alive. It is a reminder of our dependence upon God.[55] During the pandemic lockdown, one of the prominent complaints among US residents was supply chain issues. Grocery stores ran out of basic necessities like toilet paper and some food products, especially meat. This spotlighted the fragility of our supply system, which has been exacerbated by excessive corporate concentration in the name of efficiency, but it also impacted the options we have for creating menus. Even some staple items, like black beans, had intermittent availability in my local stores, thus requiring us to change some recipes and avoid others.

Most of the time, though, we do not have to think about what we are going to eat beyond deciding what flavor combinations we like or our prep time. We rarely have to consider where our food came from. Meat shows up in the refrigerator at the local supermarket under a cellophane wrapper, and we sometimes have a hard time imagining that it was once part of a 250-pound pig rolling in its own feces or a

---

[53.] Staffan B. Linder, *The Harried Leisure Class* (New York: Columbia University Press, 1970), 23.

[54.] Linder, 143–44.

[55.] Alexander Schmemann, *For the Life of the World* (Yonkers, NY: St. Vladimir's Seminary Press, 2018), 17–25.

grain-fattened steer that may have spent most of its life in a confined feed lot rather than in a pasture.

When Representative Alexandria Ocasio-Cortez first published her conceptual framework for a so-called Green New Deal, it contained references to the climate contributions of cow farts. That sophomoric language drew a great deal of scorn, but she's not entirely wrong to raise her concerns.[56] Many more cattle are raised for food than would otherwise naturally exist. Their flatulence contains methane, which is a greenhouse gas that more significantly contributes to climate change than carbon dioxide.[57] Additionally, the confinement-style operations of many feed lots can be ecologically harmful by concentrating animal waste as a pollutant, encouraging infections that require the excessive use of antibiotics, and putting animals in situations that are inconsistent with their normal habitat and are, in some cases, downright cruel.[58]

There are several movements that have clustered around greater thoughtfulness in eating.[59] The slow food movement has arisen as people seek to eat more deliberately, think about the source and preparation of their food, and almost liturgically delight in the process of eating.[60] This movement does not necessarily result in veganism or vegetarianism, but it does encourage a greater awareness. The farm-to-table movement is related. If slow food focuses on preparation, farm to table emphasizes where the food came from and how far away it is. Restaurants in this movement are concerned with the story of the food. The beef, chicken, and produce come from relatively local farms. While these foods are often more expensive, they can have a much smaller impact on the environment because the miles traveled tend to be less.

One potential question that naturally arises from Schaeffer's concept of substantial healing is whether it requires Christians to be vegetarians.

[56.] Timothy Cama, "Ocasio-Cortez Explains 'Farting Cows' Comment: 'We've Got to Address Factory Farming,'" *The Hill,* February 22, 2019, https://thehill.com/homenews/house/431119-ocasio-cortez-explains-farting-cows-comment-weve-got-to-address-factory/.

[57.] Hayhoe, *Saving Us*, 210.

[58.] Joel Salatin, *The Marvelous Pigness of Pigs: Respecting and Caring for All God's Creation* (New York: Faith Words, 2016), 20–21.

[59.] For a theological approach to food and eating, see Norman Wirzba, *Food and Faith: A Theology of Eating* (New York: Cambridge University Press, 2019).

[60.] Dreher, *Crunchy Cons*, 55–92.

After all, if death is no more in the new heavens and new earth (Rev 21:4) and if we are to treat creation in the way we anticipate it in new creation, then it seems like we would not kill animals for food. A few counterpoints help show why this is not necessary. First, in Genesis 9 when God established his covenant with creation, he specifically gave the animals as food for humans (v. 3). Thus, we are divinely authorized to eat meat even as we care for the animals that share in God's covenant with humans as part of creation (9:9–11).[61] Second, in Peter's vision of food being made clean after Christ's resurrection, the eating of meat was again authorized by God (Acts 10:9–13). Indeed, the range of potential meat options was broadened after the new covenant was inaugurated. Third, and most significantly, Jesus himself ate meat while on earth. There are clear examples of him eating fish (Luke 24:42–43), which requires the death of a living creature. Additionally, it is hard to imagine that he participated in the Passover celebration with his disciples without fulfilling the command in the Law to eat the Passover lamb in a particular fashion (Luke 22:10–13). So we are left with a question of prudence and conscience with respect to the consumption of meat (1 Corinthians 8).

Though we are permitted to eat meat, we may need to be more thoughtful about how much we eat. One approach to this question is the call to become "reducetarians," where meat is permitted and enjoyed but is a much smaller percentage of the normal diet.[62] If we take steps to be more thoughtful about where our meat comes from and how the animals are treated, this may be the necessary, logical outcome since more humane treatment of animals will tend to cost more. More thoughtful eating, whether in something like the slow food movement or by reducing our meat consumption, is a part of living a more thoughtful, quiet life.

Lead a Quiet Life

These suggestions are obviously just a few of the possible ways that we can live out creation care in our daily lives. The examples are

---

61. Ashford and Bartholomew, *The Doctrine of Creation*, 177–78 (see chap. 5, n. 37).
62. See Karen Swallow Prior, "Christianity's Complicated Relationship to Food," in *The Reducetarian Solution*, ed. Brian Kateman (New York: TarcherPerigree, 2017), 63–65.

representative and suggestive, not comprehensive. The overarching goal of being thoughtful about our lives is to follow Paul's exhortation to the church at Thessalonica: "Seek to lead a quiet life, to mind your own business, and to work with your own hands, as we commanded you, so that you may behave properly in the presence of outsiders and not be dependent on anyone" (1 Thess 4:11–12). A quiet life tends to be more ecologically sound and more spiritually healthy. Creation care is not intended to add one more duty to an already overfull task list, but to slow down, step back, and realign priorities in a way that allows us to be more human.

After an eighteen-month experiment living in a technologically limited anabaptist community, Eric Brende notes that *because of* the limited use of technology, "even in the busy season we had more time. . . . Things that technology had separated were reunited. The results were more than efficient; they were symphonic."[63] Being thoughtful resulted in a more humane existence, which helped point the conservative Roman Catholic family back toward a stronger sense of worship in all of life. A quiet life leads to greater spiritual depth.

Linder's most important point in *The Harried Leisure Class* is that idle time, the "time devoted to the cultivation of mind and spirit," does not require the consumption of material goods. In fact, that time is confounded by the consumption of material goods.[64] The quiet life is a life well-lived. This does not require us to live a monastic life of seclusion, but it does demand that we live radically different than the world around us.

Christians are to be "ready at any time to give a defense to anyone who asks you for a reason for the hope that is in you" (1 Pet 3:15). In the context, Peter was encouraging his readers to bear up under unjust persecution. However, there is a connection between Paul's concept of a quiet life and Peter's readiness to give a defense since one of the bases Paul provided for praying for authorities is "so that we may lead a tranquil and quiet life in all godliness and dignity" (1 Tim 2:2). If we live exactly as the world does, with the same materialistic goals and activities that lead to ecological damage, how is anyone ever to have

---

[63.] Eric Brende, *Better Off: Flipping the Switch on Technology* (New York: HarperCollins, 2004), 217.

[64.] Linder, *The Harried Leisure Class*, 14.

any reason to ask us about our hope? If we do not seek to live a quiet life, but join into the harried, consumeristic lifestyle of the prevailing culture, then we are telegraphing the fact that our hope is really no different than that of the world.[65] It may be that struggles with evangelism begin with a lack of a reason for someone to be interested in our message. It's up to us as individuals and members of local congregations to begin to change that reality.

CONCLUSION

Improvement of our present ecological concerns is possible. There is a place for effective regulation in incentivizing environmental improvement. One of the most significant changes needs to come through transformed attitudes of individuals throughout society.

Our present ecological problems have arisen because of thoughtless patterns of behavior. The solution is for us to consider more carefully our actions so that whether we eat or drink or run our air conditioning, we do it for the glory of God (Col 3:17). Individual patterns of behavior must then flow into corporate behaviors as we shape the culture and practices of our local congregations. Furthermore, as we engage in politics, we should do so in a way that takes into account all forms of stewardship, including the environment, as we pursue a more just society, even as we recognize that a perfect society is impossible on this side of the new heavens and new earth.

KEY TERMS

Decentralization
Reducetarianism
Regulation

[65.] Piper, *Don't Waste Your Life*, 107–29.

STUDY QUESTIONS

1. Where does regulation fit into stewardship of creation?
2. How can your local congregation take positive steps in creation care?
3. What role does awe at God's creation have in inspiring stewardship?
4. How does more thoughtful living contribute to environmental well-being?

Epilogue

Perhaps the greatest challenge in living out the Christian life is transitioning from merely knowing what to do to doing that which we know is right. Thus, James urged his ancient and modern readers, "Be doers of the word and not hearers only, deceiving yourselves" (Jas 1:22). It is at the point of application that Christians tend to stumble because gaining understanding is relatively easy, but putting our hands to the plow is much, much harder. The challenge for Christians in a globalized, consumeristic world is to determine what it means to not be conformed to this age of futility in our lifestyles, as well as our ideas. This book has been an attempt to work through Scripture to better understand how we can be transformed by the renewing of our minds in our stewardship of God's creation (Rom 12:2).

SUMMARY

We began by considering both the need for and dangers of creation care. To have a holistic gospel witness, Christians must care for creation in line with the patterns of Scripture. At the same time, we must be careful not to drift into patterns of thinking and behavior that claim the same goals but go about them with ungodly motives or through sinful means. Christianity is a long, narrow road of obedience with potential errors on either side.

Throughout history Christians have typically been no better and no worse than the surrounding culture in their treatment of the environment. Despite accusations that Christian theology is fatally anthropocentric or excessively dualistic, the orthodox faith is neither. Although the historical evidence shows there have been many Christians who have abused the environment, we have seen that this runs contrary to good Christian theology. Furthermore, though evangelicals in particular are often described as opposing the stewardship of God's creation, evidence suggests that on balance the attitudes of evangelical Christians have varied along with the culture.

The answer, therefore, is not to abandon orthodox Christian theology but to identify the key doctrines that constitute a theology for creation care and focus on exploring those. Ideas have consequences, as the saying goes, so firming up core doctrines for creation care is the heart of outlining an evangelical approach to creation care. The four topics of concern that appear most regularly in all approaches to creation care are the sources of moral authority, the value of creation, the place of humanity within creation, and the fate of the created order. These are the theological concepts we have explored to some extent in this volume.

For most of the history of Christianity, and particularly among Protestants since the Reformation, the moral authority of the Bible has been superior to any other data sources. At the same time, it is clear that *sola Scriptura* does not mean *nuda Scriptura*. General revelation has also historically provided information for making moral decisions, but the Bible has been the final guide for ethics and worship for orthodox Christians in the Protestant traditions. This means that evangelicals wrestling with creation care must take scientific data into account but always conform to the moral witness of Scripture.

Scripture testifies to the value of creation because it was made by God for his glory. This position stands in direct opposition to common treatments of God's creation as having primarily or solely instrumental worth. Isolating the instrumental value of creation tends toward abuse of creation. In reaction to abuses allowed by instrumentalizing creation's value, many environmentalists proposed treating nature as if it has intrinsic worth, that is, value because it exists and apart from its usefulness. Intrinsic worth can lead to worship of creation in some cases. In all cases, ascribing intrinsic value to creation makes moral decision-making challenging because if everything is intrinsically valuable, it becomes impossible to determine which object's value has priority. In contrast, inherent worth encourages valuing creation because of its relationship with and purpose according to the Creator. The inherent worth of creation aligns with the proper stewardship of creation by humans to glorify God.

The human relationship with the created order is necessarily at the heart of any discussion of creation care because the actor in the relationship is always a human. All of God's creation is inherently valuable, and he has given humanity a special place within creation. The purpose of humanity is to glorify God in creation. Christ, the perfect human, worked to push back the effects of creation's curse during his earthly ministry for the glory of God. We are called to imitate Christ's redemptive work. Our work of creation care anticipates the coming restoration of all creation.

At the end of history Christ will come to restore creation to its sinless perfection. God's plan of moving humanity from the garden of Eden to a garden city will be completed through his divine power. Though there is room for debate as to how this supernatural restoration will take place, it is clear that the end result will be a new heavens and new earth where humanity will dwell in God's presence for eternity. As we live in hope of the renovation of creation, which will be brought to completion by God's supernatural work, we seek to bring about substantial healing in the world today with the local church pursuing holistic discipleship, which includes training believers to care for creation.

The mission of the church is focused on the verbal proclamation of the good news, but it also includes teaching believers to live rightly within the world. The mission of the church avoids the modern myth of individual autonomy without falling into collectivism. The church should be what Schaeffer calls a "pilot plant," which is intended to provide a foretaste of what heaven will look like. This means that local churches will remain true to their mission by making the verbal proclamation of Scripture central while the practical demonstration of obedience to God's Word remains essential. The challenge is living out an ethics of creation care in a world that is fraught with discussions of conspiracies, conflict, and the need to find ways to cooperate without compromise.

Some evangelicals treat climate change as if it is an unadulterated conspiracy intended to take away freedom and lead believers into neo-pagan worship.[1] Conspiracy thinking is generally unhelpful for those trying to reach the lost for Christ. We must pursue truth wherever it leads us. Whether or not a believer finally accepts human-caused climate change as it is popularly described, there is a case for living as if it is true because many of the necessary responses are consistent with

---

[1.] Wanliss, *Resisting the Green Dragon* (see chap. 2, n. 10).

good stewardship undertaken for other reasons. At the same time, it is clear that climate change has been used by some as an emergency that negates the need for argument. Christians can avoid some of the worst elements of this power struggle by having God's glory as the central goal of all life and striving to work at a local level for the good of the environment. This approach will enable cooperation without total agreement, with the end goal of making real progress for the common good through creation care.

Although some Christians see most efforts at creation care as futile, there is hope for substantial healing through individual and cooperative efforts. The first step for a more hopeful outlook is for Christians to live thoughtfully by recapturing a sense of wonder at creation's goodness and choosing to live in reasonable homes, all while resisting consumerism. This is part of living a quiet life, as Paul advocated. Christians within the local church then live thoughtfully together as they think about the ecological costs of their ministries, consider environmental stewardship in their facility decisions, and pursue holistic discipleship. There are also broader political implications, as Christians can seek the good of their cities by advocating for just regulations that will tend to incentivize creation care without creating an undue burden on any party.

FURTHER EXHORTATION

I long for the day when the new heavens and new earth will be realized. Because of that hope, I see my daily efforts to bring a little healing into this world as part of my mission for God. When I plant wildflowers in my yard, it is so that the pollinators bring glory to God and my neighbors see the wonder of clusters of brilliant blooms that point toward a Creator. I see my solar panels as a wise financial investment that reduces my carbon footprint and enables me to divert more of my funds to reaching the unreached with the gospel. I see my consumer choices as an attempt, as best as I understand them today, to limit my impact on creation while delighting in the bounty God has provided us.

Living out care for creation does not require a dour lifestyle. It may not be possible to take every positive step toward a more environmentally friendly lifestyle right now, but it is important to take whatever reasonable steps are available. For example, my homeowner association requires a certain aesthetic, which requires I ensure my lawn is reasonably well kept and limits my landscaping choices so that I cannot do everything I might like for the sake of the environment. However, my family chose this home because it is close to work, close to church, close to our primary shopping needs, and adjoins a public park with a library where we can engage in recreation without burning gas. All of our choices have trade-offs, so we have to begin by doing the next right thing rather than worrying about what we cannot control. But we have to begin.

Small changes taken by many people can make a big difference. There is evidence that when people make the choice to get rooftop solar, even if primarily for its financial benefits, it encourages others to make similar choices.[2] I have been able to have a number of conversations about creation care and pollinators in particular since I planted wildflowers at my home and in an overgrown field at church. This has led people to express interest in planting wildflowers at their own homes. Change can take time, but the cumulative impact of small decisions can have a big impact in the long run. We demonstrate our hope in the redemption of all things by seeking to bring substantial healing to the world through our small choices every day. Discussions of this hope can turn into gospel conversations.

PRIMACY OF THE GOSPEL MESSAGE

Through all of our environmental efforts, we have to keep the main thing the main thing. Our attitudes toward creation and actions in caring for creation are important in a world evaluating the integrity of our Christian witness. However, we can never allow penultimate things to take the place of ultimate things. Substantial healing may point toward the new heavens and the new earth, but the reality of our hoped-for final redemption will remain unknown to our neighbors if we do not prioritize verbally sharing the gospel message.

Creation does indeed declare the glory of God, thus rendering

---

[2.] Hayhoe, *Saving Us*, 196–98 (see introduction, n. 2).

everyone in the world without excuse for their unbelief (Rom 1:18–23). That's where our duty to tell them the rest of the story comes in (Rom 10:14–17). Living as if we have hope is the best way to get people to ask us about our hope. But we have to be ready and willing to tell them about the reason for our hope; otherwise, all of our right living is futile. As creation moves from an age of futility to the realization of our hope, we should be helping others move from the futility of sin to hope of salvation through the gospel proclaimed.

CONCLUSION

This is where this volume ends. When you put this book down, there are a million choices to make about life and godliness. God has prepared many good works for you to do in this life (Eph 2:10). Some of them will include making wise choices about your impact on the created order. My prayer is that you will take the gospel with you as you go and seek to live a thoughtful life that glorifies God by taking into account the wonder and well-being of creation. As we seek to fulfill the Great Commission, creation care is part of living out the Great Commandment. It is also a way that we can authentically worship God by demonstrating that we rightly value all that he has made. May God's blessings follow you as you walk in his ways.

> *Now to him who is able to strengthen you according to my gospel and the proclamation about Jesus Christ, according to the revelation of the mystery kept silent for long ages but now revealed and made known through the prophetic Scriptures, according to the command of the eternal God to advance the obedience of faith among all the Gentiles—to the only wise God, through Jesus Christ—to him be the glory forever! Amen.*

(Rom 16:25–27)

Name & Subject Index

Scripture Index